SAT®
Math Prep

OVER 400 PRACTICE QUESTIONS + ONLINE

SAT® is a registered trademark of the College Board, which was not involved in the production of, and does not endorse, this product.

Editor-in-Chief
Alexandra Strelka, MA

Contributing Editors
Dr. Brandon Deason, MD; M. Dominic Eggert; Kathryn Sollenberger, MEd; Glen Stohr, JD

Special thanks to our faculty authors and reviewers
Michael Collins; John Evans; Jack Hayes; Jo L'Abbate; Bird Marathe; Melissa McLaughlin; Robert Reiss; Gail Rivers; Gordon Spector; Bonnie Wang; and Ethan Weber

Additional special thanks to
Matthew Callan; Paula L. Fleming, MA, MBA; Joanna Graham; Adam Grey; Rebecca Knauer; Michael Wolff; and the countless others who made this project possible

This publication is designed to provide accurate information in regard to the subject matter covered as of its publication date, with the understanding that knowledge and best practice constantly evolve. The publisher is not engaged in rendering medical, legal, accounting, or other professional service. If medical or legal advice or other expert assistance is required, the services of a competent professional should be sought. This publication is not intended for use in clinical practice or the delivery of medical care. To the fullest extent of the law, neither the publisher nor the editors assume any liability for any injury and/or damage to persons or property arising out of or related to any use of the material contained in this book.

© 2020 Kaplan, Inc.

Published by Kaplan Publishing, a division of Kaplan, Inc.
750 Third Avenue
New York, NY 10017

10 9 8 7 6 5 4 3 2 1

ISBN: 978-1-5062-3683-4

Kaplan Publishing print books are available at special quantity discounts to use for sales promotions, employee premiums, or educational purposes. For more information or to purchase books, please call the Simon & Schuster special sales department at 866-506-1949.

TABLE OF CONTENTS

How to Use This Book

This book will help you prepare for the two math sections of the SAT: the no-calculator section and the calculator section. Your combined raw score from both these sections is converted to a scaled score of between 200–800.

Start by becoming familiar with the structure of the two math sections. Then work your way through the chapters of this book and do as many of the practice sets as you have time for between now and test day. Be sure to review the explanations carefully. (Review them even for questions you got right, to make sure your calculations and reasoning are sound.) As your test date approaches, take the Math Practice Test found at the end of this book. Do this in a quiet environment and use the indicated timing guidelines. Again, be sure to review the explanations, found at the end of each chapter, to reinforce what you've learned.

If you're still looking for more practice questions once you've finished the question sets in this book, register your book at **kaptest.com/moreonline** to get even more practice.

The SAT Math Test

The SAT Math Test is broken down into a calculator section and a no-calculator section. Questions across the sections consist of multiple-choice questions and student-produced responses (Grid-ins).

	No-Calculator Section	Calculator Section	Total
Duration (minutes)	25	55	80
Multiple-Choice	15	30	45
Grid-in	5	8	13
Total Questions	20	38	58

The SAT Math Test is divided into four content areas: Heart of Algebra, Problem Solving and Data Analysis, Passport to Advanced Math, and Additional Topics in Math.

SAT Math Test Content Area Distribution	
Heart of Algebra (19 questions)	Analyzing and solving equations and systems of equations; creating expressions, equations, and inequalities to represent relationships between quantities and to solve problems; rearranging and interpreting formulas
Problem Solving and Data Analysis (17 questions)	Creating and analyzing relationships using ratios, proportions, percentages, and units; describing relationships shown graphically; summarizing qualitative and quantitative data
Passport to Advanced Math (16 questions)	Using function notation; creating, analyzing, and solving quadratic and higher-order equations; manipulating polynomials to solve problems
Additional Topics in Math (6 questions)	Making area and volume calculations in context; investigating lines, angles, triangles, and circles using theorems; working with trigonometric functions and complex numbers

A few math questions might look like something you'd expect to see on a science or history test. These "crossover" questions are designed to test your ability to use math in real-world scenarios. There are a total of 18 "crossover" questions that will contribute to subscores that span multiple tests. Nine of the questions will contribute to the Analysis in Science subscore, and 9 will contribute to the Analysis in History/Social Studies subscore.

Elimination and Guessing

Note that there is no penalty for guessing on the SAT, so it is in your best interest to answer every question. Ideally, taking a strategic guess means eliminating one or more choices and guessing from the rest to boost your chances of getting the question correct. However, if you are pressed for time, taking a guess on a potentially time-consuming question—even without eliminating any of the choices—can help you get to more questions and get more points out of a section.

A Note about Grid-Ins

You will see an occasional question without answer choices throughout the Math chapters of this book, starting in the next chapter. On the SAT, several of these Grid-in questions appear at the end of each Math section. Instead of bubbling in a letter, you'll enter your responses to these questions into a grid that looks like this:

If you are gridding a value that doesn't take up the whole grid, such as 50, you can enter it anywhere in the grid as long as the digits are consecutive; it doesn't matter which column you start in. Gridding mixed numbers and decimals requires some care. Anything to the left of the fraction bar will be read as the numerator of a fraction, so you must grid mixed numbers as improper fractions. For instance, say you want to grid the mixed fraction $5\frac{1}{2}$. If you enter 51/2 into the grid, your answer will be read as $\frac{51}{2}$. Instead, enter your response as 11/2, which will be read (correctly) as $\frac{11}{2}$. Alternatively, you could grid this answer as 5.5.

A repeating decimal can either be rounded or truncated, but it must be entered to as many decimal places as possible. This means it must fill the entire grid. For example, you can grid $\frac{1}{6}$ as .166 or .167, but not as .16 or .17.

Note that you cannot grid a minus sign or any value larger than 9,999, so if you get an answer to a Grid-in question that is negative or larger than 9,999, you've made a mistake and should check your work.

Prerequisite Skills and Calculator Use

Math Fundamentals

This book focuses on the skills that are tested on the SAT. It assumes a working knowledge of arithmetic, algebra, and geometry. Before you dive into the subsequent chapters where you'll try testlike questions, there are a number of concepts—ranging from basic arithmetic to geometry—that you should master. The following sections contain a brief review of these concepts.

Algebra and Arithmetic

Order of operations is one of the most fundamental of all arithmetic rules. A well-known mnemonic device for remembering this order is PEMDAS: Please Excuse My Dear Aunt Sally. This translates to Parentheses, Exponents, Multiplication/Division, Addition/Subtraction. Perform multiplication and division from left to right (even if it means division before multiplication) and treat addition and subtraction the same way:

$$(14 - 4 \div 2)^2 - 3 + (2 - 1)$$
$$= (14 - 2)^2 - 3 + (1)$$
$$= 12^2 - 3 + 1$$
$$= 144 - 3 + 1$$
$$= 141 + 1$$
$$= 142$$

Three basic properties of number (and variable) manipulation—commutative, associative, and distributive—will assist you with algebra on test day:

- **Commutative:** Numbers can swap places and still provide the same mathematical result. This is valid only for addition and multiplication:

$$a + b = b + a \rightarrow 3 + 4 = 4 + 3$$
$$a \times b = b \times a \rightarrow 3 \times 4 = 4 \times 3$$

  BUT: $3 - 4 \neq 4 - 3$ and $3 \div 4 \neq 4 \div 3$

- **Associative:** Different number groupings will provide the same mathematical result. This is valid only for addition and multiplication:

$$(a + b) + c = a + (b + c) \rightarrow (4 + 5) + 6 = 4 + (5 + 6)$$
$$(a \times b) \times c = a \times (b \times c) \rightarrow (4 \times 5) \times 6 = 4 \times (5 \times 6)$$

  BUT: $(4 - 5) - 6 \neq 4 - (5 - 6)$ and $(4 \div 5) \div 6 \neq 4 \div (5 \div 6)$

- **Distributive:** A number that is multiplied by the sum or difference of two other numbers can be rewritten as the first number multiplied by the two others individually. This does *not* work with division:

$$a(b + c) = ab + ac \rightarrow 6(x + 3) = 6x + 6(3)$$
$$a(b - c) = ab - ac \rightarrow 3(y - 2) = 3y + 3(-2)$$

  BUT: $12 \div (6 + 2) \neq 12 \div 6 + 12 \div 2$

Note: When subtracting an expression in parentheses, such as in $4 - (x + 3)$, distribute the negative sign outside the parentheses first: $4 + (-x - 3) \rightarrow 1 - x$.

Subtracting a positive number is the same as adding its negative. Likewise, subtracting a negative number is the same as adding its positive:

$$r - s = r + (-s) \rightarrow 22 - 15 = 7 \text{ and } 22 + (-15) = 7$$
$$r - (-s) = r + s \rightarrow 22 - (-15) = 37 \text{ and } 22 + 15 = 37$$

You should be comfortable manipulating both proper and improper fractions.

- To add and subtract fractions, first find a common denominator, then add the numerators together:

$$\frac{2}{3} + \frac{5}{4} \rightarrow \left(\frac{2}{3} \times \frac{4}{4}\right) + \left(\frac{5}{4} \times \frac{3}{3}\right) = \frac{8}{12} + \frac{15}{12} = \frac{23}{12}$$

- Multiplying fractions is straightforward: multiply the numerators together, then repeat for the denominators. Cancel when possible to simplify the answer:

$$\frac{5}{8} \times \frac{8}{3} = \frac{5}{\cancel{8}} \times \frac{\cancel{8}^{1}}{3} = \frac{5 \times 1}{1 \times 3} = \frac{5}{3}$$

- Dividing by a fraction is the same as multiplying by its reciprocal. Once you've rewritten a division problem as multiplication, follow the rules for fraction multiplication to simplify:

$$\frac{3}{4} \div \frac{3}{2} = \frac{\cancel{3}^{1}}{\cancel{4}_{2}} \times \frac{\cancel{2}^{1}}{\cancel{3}_{1}} = \frac{1 \times 1}{2 \times 1} = \frac{1}{2}$$

Absolute value means the distance a number is from 0 on a number line. Because absolute value is a distance, it is always positive or 0. Absolute value can *never* be negative:

$$|-17| = 17, |21| = 21, |0| = 0$$

Whatever you do to one side of an equation, you must do to the other. For instance, if you multiply one side by 3, you must multiply the other side by 3 as well.

The ability to solve straightforward, one-variable equations is critical on the SAT. For example:

$$\frac{4x}{5} - 2 = 10$$

$$\frac{4x}{5} = 12$$

$$\frac{5}{4} \times \frac{4x}{5} = 12 \times \frac{5}{4}$$

$$x = 15$$

Note: $\frac{4x}{5}$ is the same as $\frac{4}{5}x$. You could see either form on the SAT.

You will encounter **irrational numbers,** such as common radicals and π, on test day. You can carry an irrational number through your calculations as you would a variable (e.g., $4 \times \sqrt{2} = 4\sqrt{2}$). Only convert to a decimal when you have finished any intermediate steps and when the question asks you to provide an *approximate* value.

Mental Math

Even if you're a math whiz, you need to adjust your thought process in terms of the SAT to give yourself the biggest advantage you can. Knowing a few extra things will boost your speed on test day.

- Don't abuse your calculator by using it to determine something as simple as $15 \div 3$ (we've seen it many times). Besides, what if you're in the middle of the no-calculator section? Save time on test day by reviewing multiplication tables. At a bare minimum, work up through the 10s. If you know them through 12 or 15, that's even better!

- You can save a few seconds of number crunching by memorizing **perfect squares**. Knowing perfect squares through 10 is a good start; go for 15 or even 20 if you can.

- **Percent** means "out of a hundred." For example, $27\% = \frac{27}{100}$. You can write percents as decimals, for example, $27\% = 0.27$.

- The ability to recognize a few simple fractions masquerading in decimal or percent form will save you time on test day, as you won't have to turn to your calculator to convert them. Memorize the content of the following table.

Fraction	Decimal	Percent
$\frac{1}{10}$	0.1	10%
$\frac{1}{5}$	0.2	20%
$\frac{1}{4}$	0.25	25%
$\frac{1}{3}$	$0.333\overline{3}$	$33.3\overline{3}\%$
$\frac{1}{2}$	0.5	50%
$\frac{3}{4}$	0.75	75%

Tip: If you don't have the decimal (or percent) form of a multiple of one of the fractions shown in the table memorized, such as $\frac{2}{5}$, just take the fraction with the corresponding denominator ($\frac{1}{5}$ in this case), convert to a decimal (0.2), and multiply by the numerator of the desired fraction to get its decimal equivalent:

$$\frac{2}{5} = \frac{1}{5} \times 2 = 0.2 \times 2 = 0.4 = 40\%$$

Graphing

- Basic two-dimensional graphing is performed on a **coordinate plane**. There are two **axes**, *x* and *y*, that meet at a central point called the **origin**. Each axis has both positive and negative values that extend outward from the origin at evenly spaced intervals. The axes divide the space into four sections called **quadrants**, which are labeled I, II, III, and IV. Quadrant I is always the upper-right section and the rest follow counterclockwise, as shown below:

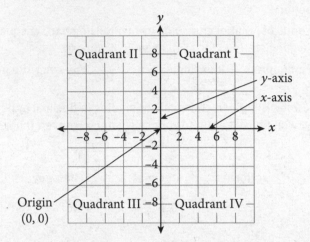

- To plot points on the coordinate plane, you need their coordinates. The **x-coordinate** is where the point falls along the *x*-axis, and the **y-coordinate** is where the point falls along the *y*-axis. The two coordinates together make an **ordered pair** written as (*x*, *y*). When writing ordered pairs, the *x*-coordinate is always listed first (think alphabetical order). Four points are plotted in the following figure as examples:

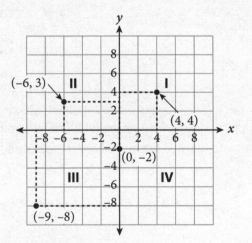

- When two points are vertically or horizontally aligned, calculating the distance between them is easy. For a horizontal distance, only the *x*-value changes; for a vertical distance, only the *y*-value changes. Take the positive difference of the *x*-coordinates (or *y*-coordinates) to determine the distance—that is, subtract the smaller number from the larger number so that the difference is positive. Two examples are presented here:

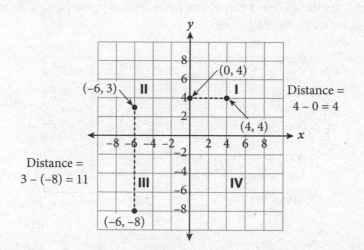

- Two-variable equations have an **independent variable** (input) and a **dependent variable** (output). The dependent variable (often *y*), depends on the independent variable (often *x*). For example, in the equation $y = 3x + 4$, *x* is the independent variable; any *y*-value depends on what you plug in for *x*. You can construct a table of values for the equation, which can then be plotted as shown below.

x	y
−3	−5
−2	−2
−1	1
0	4
1	7
2	10

→

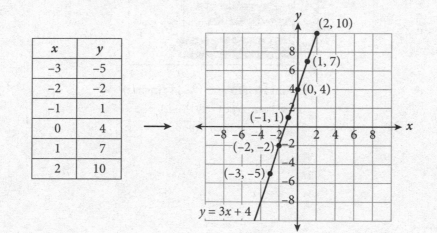

- You may be asked to infer relationships from graphs. In the first of the following graphs, the two variables are year and population. Clearly, the year does not depend on how many people live in the town; rather, the population increases over time and thus depends on the year. In the second graph, you can infer that plant height depends on the amount of rain; thus, rainfall is the independent variable. Note that the independent variable for the second graph is the vertical axis; this can happen with certain nonstandard graphs. On the standard coordinate plane, however, the independent variable is always plotted on the horizontal axis as shown below:

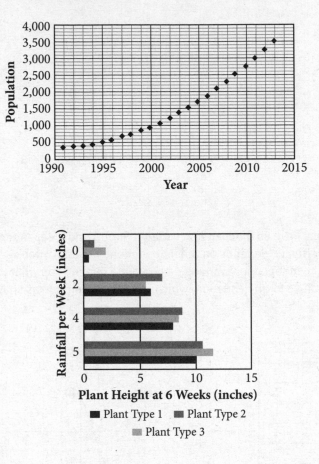

K

- When two straight lines are graphed simultaneously, one of three possible scenarios will occur:
  - The lines will not intersect at all (no solution).
  - The lines will intersect at one point (one solution).
  - The lines will lie on top of each other (infinitely many solutions).

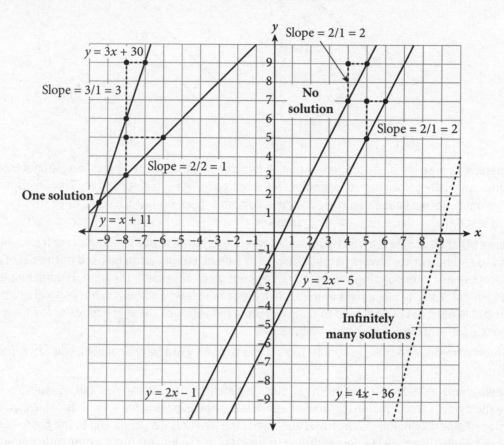

Geometry

- **Adjacent angles** can be added to find the measure of a larger angle. The following diagram demonstrates this:

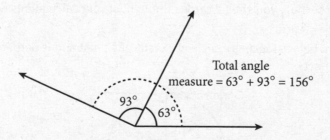

- Two angles that sum to 90° are called **complementary angles**. Two angles that sum to 180° are called **supplementary angles**.

- Two distinct lines in a plane will either intersect at one point or extend indefinitely without intersecting. If two lines intersect at a right angle (90°), they are **perpendicular** and are denoted with ⊥. If the lines never intersect, they are **parallel** and are denoted with ||:

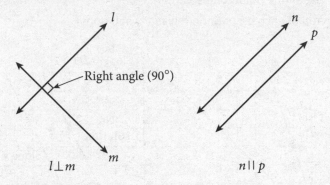

- **Perimeter** and **area** are basic properties that all two-dimensional shapes have. The perimeter of a polygon can easily be calculated by adding the lengths of all its sides. Area is the amount of two-dimensional space a shape occupies. The most common shapes for which you'll need these two properties on test day are triangles, parallelograms, and circles.

- The **area (A) of a triangle** is given by $A = \frac{1}{2}bh$, where b is the base of the triangle and h is its height. The base and height are always perpendicular. Any side of a triangle can be used as the base; just make sure you use its corresponding height (a line segment perpendicular to the base, terminating in the opposite vertex). You can use a right triangle's two legs as the base and height, but in non-right triangles, if the height is not given, you'll need to draw it in (from the vertex of the angle opposite the base down to the base itself at a right angle) and compute it.

- The **interior angles** of a triangle sum to 180°. If you know any two interior angles, you can calculate the third.

- **Parallelograms** are quadrilaterals with two pairs of parallel sides. Rectangles and squares are subsets of parallelograms. You can find the **area of a parallelogram** using $A = bh$. As with triangles, you can use any side of a parallelogram as the base, and again, the height is perpendicular to the base. For a rectangle or square, use the side perpendicular to the base as the height. For any other parallelogram, the height (or enough information to find it) will be given.

- A circle's perimeter is known as its **circumference (C)** and is found using $C = 2\pi r$, where r is the **radius** (distance from the center of the circle to its edge). The **area of a circle** is given by $A = \pi r^2$. The strange symbol is the lowercase Greek letter pi (π, pronounced "pie"), which is approximately 3.14. As mentioned in the algebra section, you should carry π throughout your calculations without rounding unless instructed otherwise.

- A **tangent line**, shown below, touches a circle at exactly one point and is perpendicular to a circle's radius at the point of contact:

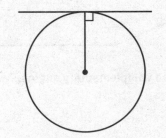

The presence of a right angle opens up the opportunity to draw otherwise hidden shapes, so pay special attention to tangents when they're mentioned.

- A shape is said to have **symmetry** when it can be split by a line (called an **axis of symmetry**) into two identical parts. Consider folding a shape along a line: if all sides and vertices align once the shape is folded in half, the shape is symmetrical about that line. Some shapes have no axis of symmetry, some have one, some have multiple axes, and still others can have infinite axes of symmetry (e.g., a circle):

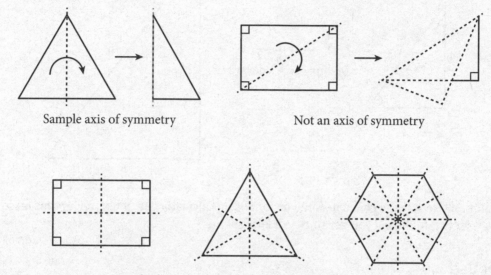

Sample axis of symmetry   Not an axis of symmetry

Sample shapes with corresponding axes of symmetry

- **Congruence** is simply a geometry term that means identical. Angles, lines, and shapes can be congruent. Congruence is indicated by using hash marks: everything with the same number of hash marks is congruent:

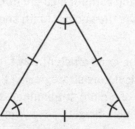

Equilateral triangle:
3 congruent sides,
3 congruent angles

Isosceles triangle:
2 congruent sides,
2 congruent angles

- **Similarity** between shapes indicates that they have identical angles and proportional sides. Think of taking a shape and stretching or shrinking each side by the same ratio. The resulting shape will have the same angles as the original. While the sides will not be identical, they will be proportional:

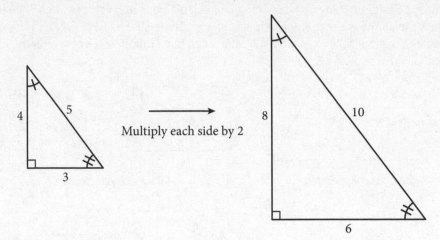

Multiply each side by 2

If you're comfortable with these concepts, read on for tips on calculator use. If not, review this lesson and remember to refer to it for help if you get stuck in a later chapter.

Calculator Use

Calculators and the SAT

Educators believe that calculators serve a role in solving Math questions, but they are sometimes concerned that students rely too heavily on calculators. They believe this dependence weakens students' overall ability to think mathematically. Therefore, the SAT has a policy on calculator use to promote the idea that students need to be able to analyze and solve math problems both with and without a calculator. The first Math section you see will require you to work without a calculator, while the second Math section will allow you to use one.

Many students never stop to ask whether using a calculator is the most efficient way to solve a problem. This chapter will show you how the strongest test takers use their calculators strategically; that is, they carefully evaluate when to use the calculator and when to skip it in favor of a more streamlined approach. As you will see, even though you can use a calculator, sometimes it's more beneficial to save your energy by approaching a question more strategically. Work smarter, not harder.

Which Calculator Should You Use?

The SAT allows four-function, scientific, and graphing calculators. No matter which calculator you choose, start practicing with it now. You don't want to waste valuable time on test day looking for the exponent button or figuring out how to correctly graph equations. Due to the wide range of mathematics topics you'll encounter on test day, **we recommend using a graphing calculator**, such as the TI-83/84. If you don't already own one, see if you can borrow one from your school's math department or a local library.

A graphing calculator's capabilities extend well beyond what you'll need for the test, so don't worry about memorizing every function. The next few pages will cover which calculator functions you'll want to know how to use for the SAT. If you're not already familiar with your graphing calculator, you'll want to get the user manual; you can find this on the Internet by searching for your calculator's model number. Identify the calculator functions necessary to answer various SAT Math questions, then write down the directions for each to make a handy study sheet.

When Should You Use a Calculator?

Some SAT question types are designed based on the idea that students will do some or all of the work using a calculator. As a master test taker, you want to know what to look for so you can identify when calculator use is advantageous. Questions involving statistics, determining roots of complicated quadratic equations, and other topics are generally designed with calculator use in mind.

Other questions aren't intentionally designed to involve calculator use. Solving some with a calculator can save you time and energy, but you'll waste both if you go for the calculator on others. You will have to decide which method is best when you encounter the following topics:

- Long division and other extensive calculations
- Graphing quadratics
- Simplifying radicals and calculating roots
- Plane and coordinate geometry

Practicing **long computations** by hand and with the calculator will not only boost your focus and mental math prowess, but it will also help you determine whether it's faster to do the work for a given question by hand or reach for the calculator on test day.

Graphing quadratic equations may be a big reason you got that fancy calculator in the first place; it makes answering these questions a snap! This is definitely an area where you need to have an in-depth knowledge of your calculator's functions. The key to making these questions easy with the calculator is being meticulous when entering the equation.

Another stressful area for many students is **radicals**, especially when the answer choices are written as decimals. Those two elements are big red flags that trigger a reach for the calculator. Beware: not all graphing calculators have a built-in radical simplification function, so consider familiarizing yourself with this process.

Geometry can be a gray area for students when it comes to calculator use. Consider working by hand when dealing with angles and lines, specifically when filling in information on complementary, supplementary, and congruent angles. You should be able to work fluidly through those questions without using your calculator.

If you choose to use **trigonometric functions** to get to the answer on triangle questions, make sure you have your calculator set to degrees or radians as required by the question.

To Use or Not to Use?

A calculator is a double-edged sword on the SAT: using one can be an asset for verifying work if you struggle when doing math by hand, but turning to it for the simplest computations will cost you time that you could devote to more complex questions. Practice solving questions with and without a calculator to get a sense of your personal style as well as your strengths and weaknesses. Think critically about when a calculator saves you time and when mental math is faster. Use the exercises in this book to practice your calculations so that by the time test day arrives, you'll be in the habit of using your calculator as effectively as possible!

PART ONE

SAT Math

CHAPTER 1

The Method for SAT Math Questions

SAT Math questions can seem more difficult than they actually are, especially when you are working under time pressure. The method we are about to describe will help you answer SAT questions, whether you are comfortable with the math content or not. This method is designed to give you the confidence you need to get the right answers on the SAT by helping you think through a question logically, one step at a time.

Here are the steps:

Method for SAT Math Questions	
Step 1	**State what the question is asking**
Step 2	**Examine the given information**
Step 3	**Choose your approach:**
	a. **Backsolve**
	b. **Pick numbers**
	c. **Do the traditional math**
	d. **Estimate**
	e. **Take a strategic guess**
Step 4	**Confirm that you answered the right question**

You can think of these steps as a series of questions to ask yourself: What do they want? What are they giving me to work with? How should I approach this? Did I answer the right question?

Take a look at the following question, and take a minute to think about how you would attack it if you saw it on test day. Then we'll describe how to work through it step-by-step.

Delores mixes two types of orange juice, one fortified and one unfortified, to drink with a meal. The fortified juice contains 250 milligrams of vitamin C per cup, and the unfortified juice contains 150 milligrams of vitamin C per cup. If one cup of Delores's mixture contains 210 milligrams of vitamin C, how much of the fortified orange juice is in one cup of the mixture?

A) $\frac{1}{4}$ cup

B) $\frac{2}{5}$ cup

C) $\frac{3}{5}$ cup

D) $\frac{3}{4}$ cup

Step 1. The question wants the amount of *fortified* orange juice in the mixture. That's what the answer choices represent.

Step 2. You're given the number of milligrams of vitamin C in both types of orange juice. The higher number, 250 per cup, is for the fortified juice. The lower number, 150 per cup, is for the unfortified juice. You're also given the number of milligrams of vitamin C in the mixture: 210 per cup. That's almost halfway between 150 and 250.

Step 3. Choose your approach. The test maker might be expecting you to set up a system of two equations to solve this question, but there are other ways to get to the answer that might be faster. For instance, you might choose to estimate: 210 is slightly closer to 250 than to 150, so slightly more than half of the mixture must be the fortified juice. The choice that's closest to "slightly more than half" is **(C)**. You might simply choose it and move on, especially if you were pressed for time.

Alternatively, you might use a technique called **Backsolving**, which means plugging in the answer choices to find the one that satisfies the requirements of the question. Starting with one of the middle choices, (B) or (C), is often a good idea for a reason that will become apparent in a moment. Say you started with (B). Two-fifths of a cup of fortified juice would contain $\frac{2}{5} \times 250 = 100$ milligrams of vitamin C. The mixture needs to be one cup, so that leaves $\frac{3}{5} \times 150 = 90$ milligrams of vitamin C that will come from the unfortified juice. That's a total of $100 + 90 = 190$ milligrams of vitamin C in one cup of the mixture. That's too small an amount; you need 210. This means you can eliminate not only (B) but also (A), since an even smaller amount of the fortified juice would result in an even lower amount of vitamin C.

You would check (C) next: $\frac{3}{5} \times 250 = 150$ milligrams of vitamin C from the fortified juice and $\frac{2}{5} \times 150 = 60$ milligrams of vitamin C from the unfortified juice. That's a total of $150 + 60 = 210$, the amount stated to be in the mixture. You can now confidently choose **(C)**.

Step 4. No matter how you chose to get to the answer, take a moment to make sure you answered the right question. The question asked for the amount of fortified orange juice. That's what you found. Note that (B) is a trap answer—it represents the amount of unfortified orange juice. Checking to make sure you're answering the right question will save you from making this type of speed mistake.

Another approach you can use in step 3 is called **Picking Numbers**. This strategy involves substituting concrete numbers for unknowns presented in the question. Here's an example of that strategy:

> At a picnic, x pitchers of iced tea are made by adding y packets of iced tea mix to cold water. If $y = 3x + 2$, how many more packets of iced tea mix are needed to make each additional pitcher of iced tea?
>
> A) 0
>
> B) 1
>
> C) 2
>
> D) 3

Step 1. The question asks for the number of additional packets of mix needed to make each additional pitcher of iced tea. Think of it as the number of packets for one more pitcher.

Step 2. You're given an algebraic expression describing the relationship of pitchers, x, to packets, y: $y = 3x + 2$.

Step 3. Pick a number for x to determine how many packets of mix will be needed, and then pick another number for x to see how the number of packets changes.

Say $x = 1$. Then $y = 3(1) + 2 = 5$, so there are 5 packets of mix needed to make one pitcher of iced tea. Now try $x = 2$: $y = 3(2) + 2 = 8$. For one additional pitcher, the packets needed increased from 5 to 8, which is a change of 3. Therefore, **(D)** is correct.

Step 4. Confirm that you answered the right question. You found the additional number of packets needed for each additional pitcher, so you can confidently move on.

Take your time on the practice set below. Think through the steps as you attempt each question so that relying on them becomes second nature.

Math Method Practice Set

DIRECTIONS: Keep a calculator handy as you work through this practice set, but reserve it for those questions that have a calculator icon next to them—and even on those questions, use it only if you really need it. Questions without the icon are intended to be done without a calculator, to help you prepare for the no-calculator section of the SAT.

---

1. The state fair sells food coupons for \$2 each and ride coupons for \$3 each. If Marlon wants to buy at least 15 coupons and spend no more than \$40, what is the largest number of ride coupons he can buy?

   A) 9

   B) 10

   C) 11

   D) 12

$$\frac{x}{x-4} = \frac{3x}{6}$$

4. Which of the following represents all the possible values of x that satisfy the equation above?

   A) -6 and 0

   B) -6 and 2

   C) 2 and 3

   D) 6 and 0

2. Lourdes is hiking up a mountain trail that starts at an elevation of 225 feet. If, as Lourdes hikes, she increases her elevation at a constant rate of 83 feet per minute, which of the following equations gives Lourdes's elevation e, in feet, m minutes after she starts hiking up the mountain?

   A) $e = 83m + 225$

   B) $e = 83m + \frac{225}{60}$

   C) $e = 225m + 83$

   D) $e = 225m + \frac{83}{60}$

$$\frac{2}{3x-1} + 4$$

5. Which of the following is equivalent to the expression above for $x > \frac{1}{3}$?

   A) $\frac{4x+3}{3x-1}$

   B) $\frac{8x+3}{3x-1}$

   C) $\frac{12x-2}{3x-1}$

   D) $\frac{12x+2}{3x-1}$

3. If $\frac{7}{a} = 35$, what is the value of a?

   A) 225

   B) 50

   C) 5

   D) 0.2

6. What is the set of all solutions to the equation $\sqrt{x+18} = -2x$?

   A) $\{-2, -6\}$

   B) $\{-2\}$

   C) $\{3\}$

   D) There are no solutions to the given equation.

7. Physicists use both joules and calories as units to measure energy, and 1 dietary calorie contains 4.184 kilojoules. Celine studies physics and runs track. Her track coach recommends that all track athletes consume 4,000 dietary calories per day. Approximately how many kilojoules per day should Celine consume if she follows her coach's advice?

A)　　0.25

B)　　25

C)　4,180

D)　16,700

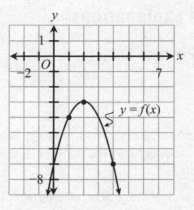

8. The graph of the function f in the xy-plane above is a parabola. Which of the following defines f?

A)　$-x^2 + 4x - 7$

B)　$-(x + 2)^2 - 3$

C)　$(x - 2)^2 - 5$

D)　$x^2 + 4x - 7$

Answers and Explanations

Math Method Practice Set

1.   B

Difficulty: Medium

Strategic Advice: Backsolving is a sound strategy here. Because this question asks for a maximum value, start with the largest choice.

Getting to the Answer: Test the choices, starting with (D). If Marlon buys 12 ride coupons, he needs to buy 3 food coupons to make his minimum total of 15 coupons. Check the money: $12 \times \$3 = \$36$ for rides and $3 \times \$2 = \$6$ for food. $\$36 + \$6 = \$42$. (D) is too large, so eliminate it.

Test (C): If Marlon buys 11 ride coupons, he needs to buy 4 food coupons to make his minimum total of 15 coupons. Check the money: $11 \times \$3 = \$33$ for rides and $4 \times \$2 = \$8$ for food. $\$33 + \$8 = \$41$. (C) is still too large; eliminate.

Test (B): If Marlon buys 10 ride coupons, he needs to buy 5 food coupons to make his minimum total of 15 coupons. Check the money: $10 \times \$3 = \$30$ for rides and $5 \times \$2 = \$10$ for food. $\$30 + \$10 = \$40$. **(B)** is correct.

Alternatively, if you noticed that you were only $1 off after testing (C), and that the difference in the price of the coupons was $1, you could have chosen **(B)** and been confident you were correct.

2.   A

Difficulty: Easy

Strategic Advice: If word problems like this one give you trouble, Picking Numbers is a good strategy to try.

Getting to the Answer: Pick a small, permissible number for m, the number of minutes Lourdes has hiked. Since Lourdes moves 83 feet up the mountain every minute, 10 minutes is a good choice for m, and Lourdes moved $83 \times 10 = 830$ feet up in that time. Add her starting elevation of 225, and Lourdes's final elevation is $225 + 830 = 1,055$.

If you recognized that (A) represents the same mathematical operations, choose it. If not, substitute 10 for m in each choice, and eliminate those that don't result in 1,055. Eliminate (B) and (D) without testing, since these choices have fractions. (A) yields 1,055, and (C) yields 2,333, so **(A)** is correct.

3.   D

Difficulty: Easy

Strategic Advice: If you like algebra, use it. If not, backsolve.

Getting to the Answer: Test the values for a in the choices, starting with either (B) or (C). For (B), $\frac{7}{50}$ is less than 1. This choice yields an answer that is too small, so the correct answer will also be a smaller number since it is the denominator of the fraction, and a smaller denominator will make the value of the fraction larger. Eliminate (B) and (A). Testing (C), $\frac{7}{5}$ is a little larger than 1, so this choice is also too large. **(D)** is the only choice remaining, so it is the correct answer.

4.   D

Difficulty: Medium

Strategic Advice: Testing a value that appears in two or more choices will allow you to eliminate two choices at once.

Getting to the Answer: Scan the choices and test any values that repeat first. So for this question, start with -6, 2, or 0. Since the calculations will be quickest with 0, substitute 0 for x in the equation to see if the equation is true:

$$\frac{0}{0-4} = \frac{3(0)}{6}$$
$$0 = 0$$

It is, so the correct answer must include 0. Eliminate (B) and (C). Now, test -6 or 6. Positive numbers are usually easier to work with, so use 6:

$$\frac{6}{6-4} = \frac{3(6)}{6}$$
$$\frac{6}{2} = \frac{18}{6}$$
$$3 = 3$$

6 also makes the equation true, so **(D)** is correct.

5. C

Difficulty: Hard

Strategic Advice: Picking numbers is a quick way to get to the correct answer.

Getting to the Answer: Since the expression must be true for every $x > 0$, pick an easy positive number; $x = 1$ is a good choice because the expression becomes $\frac{2}{3(1) - 1} + 4 = 1 + 4 = 5$. Now, substitute 1 for x in each of the choices and eliminate any choice that does not equal 5. (A) yields $\frac{7}{2}$; eliminate. (B) yields $\frac{11}{2}$; eliminate. (C) yields $\frac{10}{2} = 5$. Keep this choice for now. When you pick numbers, you must check every choice, so test (D). (D) yields $\frac{14}{2} = 7$; eliminate. **(C)** is correct.

6. B

Difficulty: Medium

Strategic Advice: If you like algebra, square both sides of the equation. If you don't, backsolve.

Getting to the Answer: Substitute values from the choices into the equation. Start with -2 because it appears in two choices. Does $\sqrt{-2 + 18} = -2(-2)$? Yes, $\sqrt{16} = 4$, so -2 must be in the solution set. Eliminate (C) and (D). Now, test -6. Does $\sqrt{-6 + 18} = -2(-6)$? No, $\sqrt{12} \neq 12$. Eliminate (A), so **(B)** is correct.

7. D

Difficulty: Easy

Strategic Advice: Just because you *can* use your calculator doesn't mean you *should*! Estimation enables you to answer this question as fast as you can read it.

Getting to the Answer: "Approximately" and the big spread among the choices indicate that this question can be answered by estimation. 1 calorie $\approx$ 4 kilojoules. You want the equivalent of 4,000 calories, so multiply both sides by 4,000 to get 4,000 calories $\approx$ 16,000 kilojoules. **(D)** is closest to this value.

8. A

Difficulty: Hard

Strategic Advice: If a question asks you to match a graph to an equation, pick points on the graph and test them in the equations in the choices.

Getting to the Answer: You're going to learn the different forms of the equation for a parabola in chapter 10, but you can answer this tough question quickly by picking numbers from the given points. The function $y = f(x)$ means that when you replace the value in the equation with x, the equation will yield the value of y, so start with $(1, -4)$. This point is a good choice because multiplying by 1 will be an easy calculation. Replace x in each choice with 1 and eliminate any choice that does not equal -4. Testing (A): $-(1)^2 + 4(1) - 7 = -4$. Keep this choice, but continue to test the remaining choices. Testing (B): $-(1 + 2)^2 - 3 = -(3)^2 - 3 = -12$. Eliminate. Testing (C): $(1 - 2)^2 - 5 = (-1)^2 - 5 = -4$. Keep this choice. Testing (D): $1^2 + 4(1) - 7 = 5 - 7 = -2$. Eliminate.

Choose one of the other points to determine if (A) or (C) is the correct choice. If you use $(2, -3)$, testing (A): $-(2)^2 + 4(2) - 7 = -3$. Keep this choice. Testing (C): $(2 - 2)^2 - 5 = (0)^2 - 5 = -5$. Eliminate. **(A)** is correct.

CHAPTER 2

Linear Equations

Solving Linear Equations

An equation is a statement in algebra that says two expressions are equivalent. A *linear equation* is one in which the highest power on any variable is 1. To isolate a variable in a linear equation, use inverse operations to "undo" whatever is being done to the variable, remembering to do the same thing to both sides to keep them equal. For example, in the equation $\frac{x}{8} = 5$, x is being divided by 8. The inverse operation of division is multiplication, so multiply both sides of the equation by 8 to find that $x = 40$.

It usually makes sense to proceed in this order:

1. Eliminate any fractions
2. Collect and combine like terms
3. Divide to leave the desired variable by itself

For example, here's how you would isolate x in the equation $\frac{1}{3}(x + 11) = \frac{1}{2}(4x - 6)$:

$$\left(\frac{6}{1}\right)\frac{1}{3}(x + 11) = \left(\frac{6}{1}\right)\frac{1}{2}(4x - 6)$$
$$2(x + 11) = 3(4x - 6)$$
$$2x + 22 = 12x - 18$$
$$40 = 10x$$
$$4 = x$$

Modeling Real-World Scenarios

Linear equations and linear graphs can be used to model relationships and changes, such as those concerning time, temperature, or population. When a linear equation is presented in the context of a "real-world" word problem, it's up to you to extract and solve an equation. When you're answering these questions, you'll need to translate from English into math. The following table shows some of the most common phrases and mathematical equivalents you're likely to see on the SAT.

Word Problems Translation Table	
English	**Math**
equals, is, equivalent to, was, will be, has, costs, adds up to the same as, as much as	=
times, of, multiplied by, product of, twice, double, by	×
divided by, per, out of, each, ratio	÷
plus, added to, and, sum, combined, total, increased by	+
minus, subtracted from, smaller than, less than, fewer, decreased by, difference between	−
a number, how much, how many, what	x, n, etc.

Working with Linear Graphs

Working with linear equations algebraically is only half the battle. The SAT will also expect you to work with graphs of linear equations. Here are some important facts to remember about graphs of linear equations:

- When a linear equation is written in slope-intercept form, $y = mx + b$, the variable m gives the slope of the line, and b represents the point at which the line intersects the y-axis.

- In a real-world scenario, slope represents a unit rate, and the y-intercept represents a starting amount.

- The rate of change (slope) for a linear relationship is constant (does not vary).

- Slope is given by the formula $m = \dfrac{y_2 - y_1}{x_2 - x_1}$, where (x_1, y_1) and (x_2, y_2) are coordinates of points on the line. To help you remember the slope formula, think "rise over run."

- A line with a positive slope runs up and to the right ("uphill"), and a line with a negative slope runs down and to the right ("downhill").

- A horizontal line has a slope of 0 (because it does not rise or fall from left to right).

- A vertical line has an undefined slope.

- Parallel lines have the same slope.

- Perpendicular lines have negative reciprocal slopes (for example, 3 and $-\frac{1}{3}$).

To choose a graph that matches a given equation (or vice versa), find the slope of the line and its y-intercept. You can also use this strategy to write the equation of a line given a context, but you may need to translate two data points into ordered pairs before you can find the slope.

Solving Equations Drill

Solve each of the following equations for x.

1. $2x + 3 = 7 + x$

2. $-2x + 4 = 5x - 10$

3. $(4x + 5) - (-2x + 11) = x + 4$

4. $\frac{1}{2}x + 1 = 3x - 4$

5. $\frac{3}{4}x + \frac{1}{3}x = x + 1$

6. $2kx + 3 = x - 1$

7. $12x + 16 = 8x + 20y + 12z$

8. $3x + 2y - 4 = 7x + 8z + 2$

9. $y(x + 4) = 2x + 7$

10. $(x - 3)(x + 4) = (x - 2)(x + 5)$

Translation Drill

Translate from English to math.

1. The number of robins is 4 less than 3 times the number of bluebirds.

2. After a 15 percent decrease in the original purchase price, a certain stock is worth $92 per share.

3. Average speed if the total distance traveled in two and one-half hours is D miles.

4. The product of x and y is equivalent to their sum increased by 5.

5. Jose's age in 5 years will be 1 year more than double what Beatrice's age was 2 years ago.

6. If 2 more blue chips are added to a pile, the ratio of blue to red chips will be 3:1.

7. The total of the ages of Rachel's siblings if she has one sibling that is 3 years younger and three siblings that are 2, 4, and 5 years older.

8. If the number of dimes in a piggy bank is decreased by 2, then 3 out of every 5 coins in the piggy bank will be dimes.

9. The product of x decreased by y and one-third the sum of x and half of y.

10. If the value of Martine's assets increased by $10,000, then the combined assets of Martine and Angela would be twice what Martine's assets would be if they were increased by half.

Slope-Intercept Form Drill

Write the equation for the line that passes through each set of points.

1. $(5, 5), (4, 3)$

2. $(-7, 3), (-5, 1)$

3. $(-3, 4.5), (3, 4.5)$

4. $(-5, -4), (8, -3)$

5. $\left(-\frac{1}{2}, 7\frac{1}{2}\right), \left(3\frac{1}{4}, 0\right)$

Linear Equations Practice Set

> **DIRECTIONS:** Keep a calculator handy as you work through this practice set, but reserve it for those questions that have a calculator icon next to them—and even on those questions, use it only if you really need it. Questions without the icon are intended to be done without a calculator, to help you prepare for the no-calculator section of the SAT.

1. If $a = \frac{1}{3}b$ and $b = 24$, what is the value of $7a + 8$?

   A)   5

   B)   29

   C)   56

   D)   64

2. If $4x + 5$ is 4 less than 10, what is the value of $2x$?

   A) $\frac{1}{4}$

   B) $\frac{1}{2}$

   C)   4

   D)   8

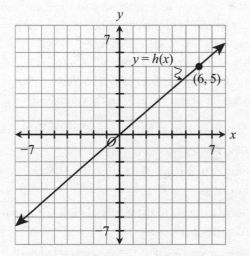

3. In the xy-plane above, a point (not shown) with coordinates (a, b) lies on the graph of the linear function h. If a and b are positive integers, what is the ratio of a to b?

   A)   2:3

   B)   3:2

   C)   5:6

   D)   6:5

$$\frac{3}{4}(8x + 12) + 5 = 8x + 12$$

4. Based on the equation above, what is the value of $5x + 1$?

5. A line that passes through the origin in the xy-plane has a slope of $\frac{7}{3}$. Which of the following is a point on the line?

   A) $(-14, -6)$

   B) $(-6, -14)$

   C) $(-6, 14)$

   D) $(14, 6)$

6. Sara is waiting in line to ride the amusement park's newest roller coaster. The number of people in front of her can be represented by the equation $P = 34 - 2m$, where P is the number of people in front of her and m is the number of minutes Sara has waited in line. What is the meaning of the value 34 in this equation?

    A) Sara will reach the front of the line within 34 minutes.

    B) Sara started with 34 people in front of her.

    C) Sara moves up in the line at a rate of 34 people per hour.

    D) Sara moves up in the line at a rate of 34 people per minute.

7. If $|d - 9| + 5 = 11$, what is a possible value of d?

8. A line passes through the origin and points $(-4, c)$ and $(c, -9)$. What is one possible value of c?

    A) 4

    B) 6

    C) 9

    D) 12

$$w = 240 + 1.2d$$

9. The weight of a flask containing a solution can be modeled by the equation above, where w is the weight in grams and d is the number of drops of solution that are in the flask. What is d when w is 300?

    A) 50

    B) 120

    C) 276

    D) 600

10. For some value b, which of the following expressions is equal to -2?

    A) $|b - 2| - 2$

    B) $|b - 2| + 2$

    C) $|b + 2| - 1$

    D) $|2 - b| + 1$

11. Sunjay is traveling to a national park. The number of miles he needs to travel can be represented by the equation $M = 172 - 57h$, where M is the the number of miles to the national park and h is the number of hours Sunjay has to travel. What is the meaning of the value 57 in this equation?

    A) Sunjay started at a distance 57 miles from the national park.

    B) Sunjay will reach the national park in 57 hours.

    C) Sunjay travels to the national park at a rate of 57 miles per hour.

    D) Sunjay has traveled 172 miles in 57 hours.

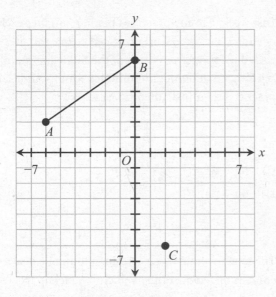

14. Julius has budgeted $150 per month for electricity. Last month his electricity bill was $190 based on a rate of $0.12 per kilowatt hour. Which of the equations below represents the number of kilowatt hours, k, by which Julius needs to reduce his electricity usage this month in order to meet his budget?

A) $\dfrac{k}{0.12} = 40$

B) $\dfrac{k}{12} = 40$

C) $0.12k = 40$

D) $0.12k = 150$

12. What is the equation of the line connecting the midpoint of line segment AB with point C in the figure above?

A) $y = -2x - 2$

B) $y = -2x + 5$

C) $y = \dfrac{2}{3}x + 6$

D) $y = 2x - 2$

15. The line with the equation $\dfrac{2}{3}x - \dfrac{7}{8}y = 2$ is graphed in the xy-plane. What is the x-coordinate of the x-intercept of the line?

13. Line $y = mx + 5$ passes through point (a, b), where $a \neq 0$ and $b \neq 0$. If m is a constant, what is the slope of the line in terms of a and b ?

A) $\dfrac{b-5}{a}$

B) $\dfrac{a-5}{b}$

C) $\dfrac{5-b}{a}$

D) $\dfrac{5-a}{b}$

16. A factory produces parts on two eight-hour shifts per day. Each shift produces the parts at a different, but constant, rate. The number of parts produced by each shift are added to obtain a cumulative total for the day. If the cumulative number of parts produced by the end of two hours of the second shift was 320 and the cumulative number produced by the end of five hours of the second shift was 440, how many parts per hour did the first shift produce?

    A) 30

    B) 40

    C) 70

    D) 240

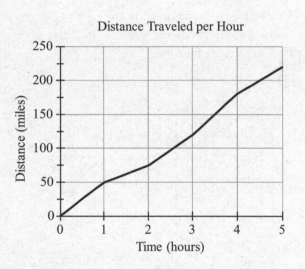

Distance Traveled per Hour

17. In the graph above, what is the speed, to the nearest 5 miles per hour, between 1 and 2 hours?

18. Last week, Kimmy practiced piano p minutes each day for 5 days, and Carl practiced cello c minutes each day for 6 days. Which of the following represents the total number of minutes Kimmy and Carl practiced their instruments last week?

    A) $11pc$

    B) $30pc$

    C) $5p + 6c$

    D) $6p + 5c$

19. The total inventory of a certain automobile dealer consists of $\frac{1}{3}$ sport utility vehicles, $\frac{1}{4}$ pickup trucks, $\frac{1}{5}$ sedans, and 26 vehicles that are not one of these three types. How many vehicles are in the dealer's inventory?

    A) 50

    B) 80

    C) 120

    D) 160

20. The number of members that joined the Spanish club between 2000 and 2010 is twice the number of members who joined between 1990 and 2000. If 17 members joined the Spanish club between 1990 and 2000 and m members joined between 2000 and 2010, which of the following equations is true?

    A) $17m = 2$

    B) $2m = 17$

    C) $m + 2 = 17$

    D) $\frac{m}{2} = 17$

Answers and Explanations

Solving Equations Drill

1. $2x + 3 - x = 7 + x - x$
$x + 3 = 7$
$x = 4$

2. $-2x + 4 + 2x + 10 = 5x - 10 + 2x + 10$
$14 = 7x$
$2 = x$

3. $4x + 5 + 2x - 11 = x + 4$
$6x - 6 = x + 4$
$6x - x - 6 + 6 = x - x + 4 + 6$
$5x = 10$
$x = 2$

4. $2\left(\frac{1}{2}x + 1\right) = 2(3x - 4)$
$x + 2 = 6x - 8$
$x - x + 2 + 8 = 6x - x - 8 + 8$
$10 = 5x$
$2 = x$

5. $\frac{3}{3}\left(\frac{3}{4}x\right) + \frac{4}{4}\left(\frac{1}{3}x\right) = x + 1$
$\frac{9}{12}x + \frac{4}{12}x = x + 1$
$\frac{13}{12}x = x + 1$
$\frac{13}{12}x - \frac{12}{12}x = x - x + 1$
$\frac{1}{12}x = 1$
$x = 12$

6. $2kx + 3 - x - 3 = x - 1 - x - 3$
$2kx - x = -4$
$x(2k - 1) = -4$
$x = \frac{-4}{2k - 1}$

7. $\frac{12x + 16}{4} = \frac{8x + 20y + 12z}{4}$
$3x + 4 = 2x + 5y + 3z$
$3x - 2x + 4 - 4 = 2x + 5y + 3z - 2x - 4$
$x = 5y + 3z - 4$

8. $3x + 2y - 4 - 3x - 8z - 2 = 7x + 8z + 2$
$\qquad\qquad\qquad\qquad -3x - 8z - 2$
$2y - 8z - 6 = 4x$
$\frac{2y - 8z - 6}{4} = \frac{4x}{4}$
$\frac{y - 4z - 3}{2} = x$

9. $xy + 4y = 2x + 7$
$xy + 4y - 2x - 4y = 2x + 7 - 2x - 4y$
$xy - 2x = 7 - 4y$
$x(y - 2) = 7 - 4y$
$x = \frac{7 - 4y}{y - 2}$

10. $x(x + 4) - 3(x + 4) = x(x + 5) - 2(x + 5)$
$x^2 + 4x - 3x - 12 = x^2 + 5x - 2x - 10$
$x^2 + x - 12 = x^2 + 3x - 10$
$x - 12 - x + 10 = 3x - 10 - x + 10$
$-2 = 2x$
$-1 = x$

Translation Drill

1. $R = 3B - 4$
2. $\$92 = (1.00 - 0.15)P = 0.85P$
3. $S = \frac{D}{2.5}$
4. $xy = x + y + 5$
5. $J + 5 = 2(B - 2) + 1$
6. $\frac{B + 2}{R} = \frac{3}{1}$
7. $(R - 3) + (R + 2) + (R + 4) + (R + 5)$
8. $D - 2 = \frac{3}{5}C$
9. $(x - y)\left(\frac{1}{3}\left(x + \frac{1}{2}y\right)\right)$
10. $(M + 10{,}000) + A = 2\left(M + \frac{1}{2}M\right)$

Slope-Intercept Form Drill

1. $m = \left(\frac{3-5}{4-5}\right) = \frac{-2}{-1} = 2$

$5 = 2(5) + b$

$b = -5$

$y = 2x - 5$

2. $m = \frac{1-3}{-5-(-7)} = \frac{-2}{2} = -1$

$3 = -1(-7) + b$

$b = -4$

$y = -x - 4$

3. $m = \frac{4.5 - 4.5}{3 - (-3)} = \frac{0}{6} = 0$

$4.5 = 0(-3) + b$

$b = 4.5$

$y = 4.5$

4. $m = \frac{-3 - (-4)}{8 - (-5)} = \frac{1}{13}$

$-3 = \frac{1}{13}(8) + b$

$b = -3\frac{8}{13}$

$y = \frac{1}{13}x - 3\frac{8}{13}$

5. $m = \frac{0 - 7\frac{1}{2}}{3\frac{1}{4} - \left(-\frac{1}{2}\right)} = \frac{-\frac{15}{2}}{3\frac{3}{4}} = \frac{-\frac{30}{4}}{\frac{15}{4}} = -2$

$0 = -2\left(3\frac{1}{4}\right) + b$

$b = 6\frac{1}{2}$

$y = -2x + 6\frac{1}{2}$

Linear Equations Practice Set

1. D

Difficulty: Easy

Strategic Advice: Substitute the given value for b to solve for a, and then plug that value into the second equation.

Getting to the Answer: Start with $a = \frac{1}{3}(24) = 8$. Plug this value into the second equation: $7(8) + 8 = 56 + 8 = 64$. Choice **(D)** is correct.

2. B

Difficulty: Easy

Strategic Advice: Translate the wording into an equation and solve for $2x$.

Getting to the Answer: The phrase "4 less than 10" means $10 - 4$, or 6. So $4x + 5 = 6$. Simplifying, $4x = 1$, and $\frac{4x}{2} = 2x = \frac{1}{2}$. Choice **(B)** is correct.

3. D

Difficulty: Hard

Strategic Advice: Because the line passes through the point (0, 0), the ratio of y:x, where x and y are the coordinates of any point on the line, will be the slope. Keep in mind that the question asks for the ratio of x:y, so your final answer will be the reciprocal of the slope.

Getting to the Answer: Using the point (6, 5), the slope is 5:6, but this is the trap choice (C) since the question asks for the ratio of a:b rather than b:a. Therefore, **(D)**, 6:5 is correct.

4. 6

Difficulty: Medium

Strategic Advice: Look for any patterns in the given equation that may help you efficiently solve the equation.

Getting to the Answer: Notice that the term $8x + 12$ appears on both sides of the equation, so rewrite the equation as $5 = \frac{4}{4}(8x + 12) - \frac{3}{4}(8x + 12)$. So $5 = \frac{1}{4}(8x + 12)$. Thus, $5 = 2x + 3$, so $2x = 2$, and $x = 1$. The value of $5x + 1$ is $5(1) + 1 = $ **6**.

5. B

Difficulty: Medium

Strategic Advice: Set up an equation in $y = mx + b$ format, then plug the values in the choices into that equation.

Getting to the Answer: Since the line passes through the origin, the y-intercept is 0, and the equation is simply $y = \frac{7}{3}x$. For **(B)**, $-14 = \frac{7}{3}(-6) = 7(-2) = -14$. There's no need to go any further.

6. B

Difficulty: Easy

Strategic Advice: Describe what the parts of the given equation mean in terms of the wording of the stem, then evaluate the choices.

Getting to the Answer: The equation is in $y = mx + b$ format, so the number of people in front of Sara is 34 when $m = 0$, and the number of people in front of Sara decreases at the rate of 2 people per minute. Only **(B)** is a correct interpretation.

7. 3 or 15

Difficulty: Easy

Strategic Advice: Isolate the term inside the absolute value signs. This can be either positive or negative values of the same magnitude. Since this is a Grid-in question, you only need to solve for one or the other.

Getting to the Answer: Start with $|d - 9| = 11 - 5 = 6$. One solution is $d - 9 = 6$, so $d = $ **15**. (If $d - 9 = -6$, then $d = $ **3**.)

8. B

Difficulty: Hard

Strategic Advice: Since the line passes through the origin, the equation for the line is $y = mx$. Write two equations for the slope using the given points and solve for c.

Getting to the Answer: Using the first point, the slope of the line is $\frac{c - 0}{-4 - 0} = -\frac{c}{4}$. Using the second point, the slope is $\frac{-9 - 0}{c - 0} = -\frac{9}{c}$. Since the slope is constant, set these two expressions equal to each other and solve for c: $-\frac{c}{4} = -\frac{9}{c}$. So, $c^2 = 36$, and $c = \pm 6$. Only **(B)** matches.

9. A

Difficulty: Easy

Strategic Advice: Plug the given value for w into the equation and solve for d.

Getting to the Answer: Start with $300 = 240 + 1.2d$. Solve to find that $60 = 1.2d$, and $d = 50$. Choice **(A)** is correct.

10. A

Difficulty: Medium

Strategic Advice: Regardless of the value of b, the absolute value term must be greater than or equal to 0. Evaluate the choices accordingly.

Getting to the Answer: For (A), if $b - 2 = 0$, then the expression equals -2. **(A)** is correct.

11. C

Difficulty: Medium

Strategic Advice: Relating the wording to the equation, 172 is the starting distance to the park. This is reduced by 57 miles for each hour of travel.

Getting to the Answer: (A) is incorrect per the analysis. (B) is incorrect because h is the number of hours, not 57 (which is an absurd value as well). The analysis shows that 57 is the number of miles traveled each hour, so **(C)** is correct.

12. A

Difficulty: Hard

Strategic Advice: Determine the coordinates of the points. Find the midpoint of AB using x- and y-value averages, then determine the equation connecting that midpoint to point C expressed in slope-intercept form.

Getting to the Answer: Point A is $(-6, 2)$, point B is $(0, 6)$, and point C is $(2, -6)$. The x-value of the midpoint of AB is $\frac{-6 + 0}{2} = -3$, and the y-value is $\frac{2 + 6}{2} = 4$. The slope of the line passing through this point, $(-3, 4)$, and point C is $\frac{-6 - 4}{2 - (-3)} = \frac{-10}{5} = -2$. The only choices with $-2x$ are (A) and (B). You could solve for the y-intercept, but a quick glance at the figure enables you to see that **(A)** is correct.

13. A

Difficulty: Hard

Strategic Advice: Plug the values a and b into $y = mx + 5$ and solve for m.

Getting to the Answer: The equation becomes $b = ma + 5$, so $ma = b - 5$. Divide both sides by a to get $m = \dfrac{b-5}{a}$, which is **(A)**.

14. C

Difficulty: Easy

Strategic Advice: Use the units to help convert the wording into an equation.

Getting to the Answer: The unit given in the stem is 0.12 dollars per kilowatt hour, so when multiplied by kilowatt hours, the units work out to dollars:

$$\frac{\$0.12}{1 \text{ kilowatt hour}} \times k \text{ kilowatt hours} = 0.12k \text{ dollars}.$$

The amount by which Julius wants to reduce his electric bill is $40. So, delete the units and set this equal to 40 to get $0.12k = 40$. Choice **(C)** is correct.

15. 3

Difficulty: Medium

Strategic Advice: At the x-intercept of the line, $y = 0$.

Getting to the Answer: To find the x-intercept, replace y in the equation with 0, and solve for x:

$$\frac{2}{3}x - \frac{7}{8}y = 2$$
$$\frac{2}{3}x - \frac{7}{8}(0) = 2$$
$$\frac{2}{3}x = 2$$
$$x = 2\left(\frac{3}{2}\right)$$
$$x = 3$$

The correct answer is **3**.

16. A

Difficulty: Hard

Strategic Advice: The cumulative number of parts produced at the start of the second shift is the number produced in 8 hours by the first shift. Find the slope of the production for the second shift, then the initial amount, using the form of an equation $y = mx + b$. The amount at the beginning of the second shift will be the amount produced by the first shift. Use that value to determine the rate of production for the first shift.

Getting to the Answer: The slope (production per hour) of the second shift is $\dfrac{440 - 320}{5 - 2} = \dfrac{120}{3} = 40$. Plug in the values from the end of the second hour to get the y-intercept for the second shift: $320 = 2(40) + b$, so $b = 320 - 80 = 240$. This is the cumulative total number of parts after the first shift. Since the first shift is 8 hours long, the production rate is $\dfrac{240 \text{ parts}}{8 \text{ hrs}} = 30 \dfrac{\text{parts}}{\text{hr}}$. Choice **(A)** is correct.

17. 25

Difficulty: Medium

Strategic Advice: Since the y-axis is miles and the x-axis is hours, the slope of the line will be speed in miles per hour.

Getting to the Answer: The y-value at 2 hours is about 75, and the y-value at 1 hour is 50. Thus, the slope between these points is $\dfrac{75 - 50}{2 - 1} = \mathbf{25}$.

18. C

Difficulty: Easy

Strategic Advice: Translate the wording into an equation and evaluate the choices.

Getting to the Answer: The question asks for the total practice minutes for both students. For Kimmy, that is $5p$, and for Carl, that is $6c$. The total will be the sum of the two terms. Since the terms have different variables, they cannot be combined, so **(C)** is correct.

19. C

Difficulty: Medium

Strategic Advice: Take advantage of the fact that the total inventory must be divisible by 3, 4, and 5; otherwise, there would be fractional cars and trucks.

Getting to the Answer: Since $3 \times 4 \times 5 = 60$, the total inventory must be evenly divisible by 60. Only **(C)** meets that requirement. For the record, if you chose to set up and solve an equation to arrive at the answer, the correct starting equation would be as follows (t is the total number of vehicles): $\frac{1}{3}t + \frac{1}{4}t + \frac{1}{5}t + 26 = t$. This simplifies to $20t + 15t + 12t + 1{,}560 = 60t$, so $1{,}560 = 13t$, and $t = 120$.

20. D

Difficulty: Easy

Strategic Advice: Translate the wording into an equation and isolate m.

Getting to the Answer: Since twice as many members joined between 2000 and 2010 as the 17 who joined between 1990 and 2000, $m = 2 \times 17 = 34$. Divide both sides by 2 to get $\frac{m}{2} = \frac{34}{2} = 17$, which is **(D)**.

CHAPTER 3

Systems of Linear Equations

What Is a System of Equations?

A system of equations is a set of two or more equations that usually contains multiple variables. In general, when you are given a situation involving n variables, you need a system of n equations to arrive at fixed values for these variables. Thus, if you have two variables, you need two equations. Three variables would require three equations, and so on.

To solve a two-variable system of equations, the equations that make up the system must be independent. *Independent equations* are equations for which no algebraic manipulations can transform one of the equations into the other.

Consider the equation $4x + 2y = 8$. You could use properties of equality to rewrite this equation in a number of different ways. For example, you could multiply both sides by 2, resulting in the equation $8x + 4y = 16$. But note that this new equation has the same core variables and relationships as the original one. These two equations are called **dependent equations**. Two dependent equations cannot be used to solve for two variables because they really represent the same equation, just written in different forms. If you attempt to solve a system of dependent equations, you will end up with the same thing on both sides of the equal sign (e.g., $16 = 16$), which is always true and indicates that the system has infinitely many solutions.

At other times, you'll encounter equations that are fundamentally incompatible with each other. For example, given the two equations $4x + 2y = 8$ and $4x + 2y = 9$, it should be obvious that there are no values for x and y that will satisfy both equations at the same time. Doing so would violate fundamental laws of math. In this case, the system of equations has no solution.

Solving Systems of Equations

The two main methods for solving a system of linear equations are substitution and combination (sometimes referred to as elimination or elimination by addition).

Substitution is the most straightforward method for solving systems and can be applied in every situation. However, the process can get messy if none of the variables in either of the equations has a coefficient of 1. To use substitution, solve the simpler of the two equations for one variable and then substitute the result into the other equation.

Combination involves adding or subtracting the two equations, or a multiple of one or both equations, to eliminate one of the variables. You're left with one equation and one variable, which can be solved using inverse operations.

Caution: Although most students prefer substitution, questions on the SAT that involve systems of equations are often designed to be quickly solved using combination. To really boost your score on test day, be sure to practice both these techniques.

Graphing Systems of Equations

Knowing how many solutions a system of equations has tells you how graphing the equations on the same coordinate plane should look. Conversely, knowing what the graph of a system of equations looks like tells you how many solutions the system has.

Recall that the solution(s) to a system of equations is the point or points where the graphs of the equations intersect. The table below summarizes three possible scenarios:

If your system has . . .	. . . then it will graph as:	Reasoning
no solution	two parallel lines	Parallel lines never intersect.
one solution	two lines intersecting at a single point	Two straight lines have only one intersection.
infinitely many solutions	a single line (one line directly on top of the other)	One equation is a manipulation of the other—the graphs are the same line.

Systems of Linear Equations Drill

Solve each system of equations for both variables.

1. $a - 3b = 1$
    $3a + 2b = 25$

2. $3a + b = 14$
    $5a + 2b = 25$

3. $3a + 3b = -9$
    $7a - 11b = 15$

4. $2a = -3b$
    $7a + 4b = 13$

5. $4a + 5b + 11 = -3a + 2b - 23$
    $14a - 12b + 5 = 3(3a - 3b - 15)$

Systems of Linear Equations Practice Set

DIRECTIONS: Keep a calculator handy as you work through this practice set, but reserve it for those questions that have a calculator icon next to them—and even on those questions, use it only if you really need it. Questions without the icon are intended to be done without a calculator, to help you prepare for the no-calculator section of the SAT.

$$-2x + 9y = 25$$
$$3x + 6y = 21$$

1. Which of the following ordered pairs (x, y) is a solution to the system of equations above?

    A) $(-3, -1)$

    B) $(-1, -3)$

    C) $(1, 3)$

    D) $(3, 1)$

$$5x - 2y = -12$$
$$2x + 3y = -1$$

2. If (x, y) is a solution to the system of equations above, what is the value of $x + y$?

    A) -3

    B) -1

    C) 1

    D) 3

3. Two lines that are graphed on the xy-plane intersect at the point (a, b). The first line has a slope of $-\frac{1}{2}$ and passes through the point $(-2, 2)$. The second line passes through the points $(-1, -1)$ and $(1, 3)$. What is the value of ab?

4. A nursery sells fertilizer in 25-pound and 100-pound bags. If Juliet bought 13 bags of fertilizer for her landscaping business that contained 775 pounds of fertilizer, how many 100-pound bags did she buy?

    A) 5

    B) 6

    C) 7

    D) 8

$$x - y = -2$$
$$\frac{1}{3}(5x + 3y) = 4$$

5. The solution to the system of equations above is (x, y). What is the value of x ?

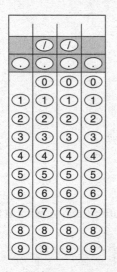

6. Line l has a slope of $\frac{1}{2}$ and an x-axis intercept of -4. Line m is perpendicular to line l. The two lines intersect on the y-axis. Which of the following is the equation of line m ?

A) $y = -\frac{1}{2}x + 2$

B) $y = \frac{1}{2}x + 4$

C) $y = -2x + 2$

D) $y = -2x + 4$

$$14x - ay = -\frac{9}{2}$$
$$\frac{7}{2}x - y = -\frac{1}{4}$$

7. If a is a constant for the given system of equations above, for what value of a will the system of equations have no solution?

A) -7

B) 2

C) 4

D) 14

8. If the equations $4x - y = 6$ and $ay = 6x - 9$ in the xy-plane have infinitely many solutions, what is the value of a ?

9. Due to train schedules, it takes Yvette longer to return from work to her home in the evening than it takes for her to get from home to work in the morning. If Yvette's average total daily commuting time was 1 hour 12 minutes and her average morning commuting time was 8 minutes less than her evening average, what was her average commuting time returning home?

A) 32 minutes

B) 36 minutes

C) 40 minutes

D) 42 minutes

10. A pet supplies store maintains an inventory of a certain brand of dog food in 15-pound and 30-pound bags. The store pays $0.60 per pound for the 15-pound bags and $0.50 per pound for the 30-pound bags. The store's current inventory of this product is 32 bags of this dog food for which it paid $408. Which of the following systems of equations can be used to determine the number of 15-pound bags, s, and the number of 30-pound bags, b ?

A) $s + b = 32$
$9s + 15b = 408$

B) $s + b = 32$
$15s + 30b = 408$

C) $s + b = 45$
$9s + 15b = 408$

D) $s + b = 408$
$15s + 30b = 32$

$$y = b + 5$$
$$y = mx^2$$

11. For which of the following values of m and b does the system of equations above have exactly two real solutions?

A) $m = -1, b = -6$

B) $m = -1, b = 10$

C) $m = 2, b = -10$

D) $m = 2, b = -6$

$$2x + y = 25$$
$$x + 2y = 20$$

12. Based on the system of equations above, what is the value of $4x + 4y$?

13. The 8 soup cans in Carlos's pantry contain either 8 or 12 ounces each. Carlos has 4 ounces more soup in 8-ounce cans than in 12-ounce cans. How many 12-ounce cans of soup are in his pantry?

    A) 2

    B) 3

    C) 4

    D) 5

$$y = a\left(\frac{x}{2} + b\right)$$
$$y = 3x + 14$$

14. The lines for the two equations above are parallel and separated by a vertical distance of 2 when graphed in the xy-plane. Which of the following could be the value of b?

    A) 2

    B) 3

    C) 4

    D) 6

$$ax - by = 5$$
$$3x - 4y = 15$$

15. The system of equations above has infinitely many solutions. What is the value of $\frac{a}{b}$?

    A) $-\frac{4}{3}$

    B) $-\frac{3}{4}$

    C) $\frac{3}{4}$

    D) $\frac{4}{3}$

Answers and Explanations

Systems of Linear Equations Drill

1.
$$a = 1 + 3b$$
$$3(1 + 3b) + 2b = 25$$
$$3 + 9b + 2b = 25$$
$$11b = 22$$
$$b = 2$$
$$a = 1 + 3(2) = 1 + 6 = 7$$

2.
$$2(3a + b) = 2(14)$$
$$6a + 2b = 28$$
$$-(5a + 2b = 25)$$
$$\overline{ a = 3}$$
$$5(3) + 2b = 25$$
$$2b = 25 - 15 = 10$$
$$b = 5$$

3.
$$\frac{3a + 3b}{3} = \frac{-9}{3}$$
$$a + b = -3$$
$$a = -3 - b$$
$$7(-3 - b) - 11b = 15$$
$$-21 - 7b - 11b = 15$$
$$-18b = 36$$
$$b = -2$$
$$a = (-3) - (-2) = -1$$

4.
$$2a + 3b = 0$$
$$7(2a + 3b) = 7(0)$$
$$14a + 21b = 0$$
$$2(7a + 4b) = 2(13)$$
$$14a + 8b = 26$$
$$-(14a + 21b = 0)$$
$$\overline{ -13b = 26}$$
$$b = -2$$
$$2a = -3(-2) = 6$$
$$a = 3$$

5.
$$4a + 5b + 11 + 3a - 2b - 11 = -3a + 2b - 23$$
$$+ 3a - 2b - 11$$
$$7a + 3b = -34$$
$$14a - 12b + 5 = 3(3a - 3b - 15)$$
$$14a - 12b + 5 - 9a + 9b - 5 = 9a - 9b - 45 - 9a$$
$$+ 9b - 5$$
$$5a - 3b = -50$$
$$+ (7a + 3b = -34)$$
$$\overline{ 12a = -84}$$
$$a = -7$$
$$5(-7) - 3b = -50$$
$$-3b = -15$$
$$b = 5$$

Systems of Linear Equations Practice Set

1.   C

Difficulty: Medium

Strategic Advice: The ordered pair will be the x- and y-values that satisfy the system of equations, so use substitution or combination to solve for x and y.

Getting to the Answer: Since substitution might create some awkward coefficients, use combination to solve. Multiply the first equation by 3 and the second by 2 to get x-coefficients of -6 and 6, then add the equations:

$$3(-2x + 9y) = 3(25) \rightarrow -6x + 27y = 75$$
$$\underline{2(3x + 6y) = 2(21) \rightarrow +(6x + 12y = 42)}$$
$$39y = 117$$
$$y = 3$$

You don't need to solve for x since only **(C)** has the correct y-coordinate.

Alternatively, you could backsolve by plugging the values from the choices into one of the equations.

2.   B

Difficulty: Medium

Strategic Advice: Examine the coefficients of x and y to see if there is an easy way to solve for $x + y$ directly. If not, use substitution or combination to solve for x and y, then add the results.

Getting to the Answer: The coefficients are such that solving directly for $x + y$ is cumbersome. Since substitution might create some awkward coefficients, use combination to solve. You can multiply the first equation by 3 and the second by 2 and add the equations to eliminate y:

$$3(5x - 2y) = 3(-12) \rightarrow 15x - 6y = -36$$
$$\underline{2(2x + 3y) = 2(-1) \rightarrow +(4x + 6y = -2)}$$
$$19x = -38$$
$$x = -2$$

Now plug this value for x into one of the equations: $2(-2) + 3y = -1$, so $3y = 3$, and $y = 1$. Thus, $x + y = -2 + 1 = -1$. Choice **(B)** is correct.

3.   0

Difficulty: Hard

Strategic Advice: Determine the equations for both lines, and set them equal to each other to find the coordinates of the intersection.

Getting to the Answer: The equation for the first line is $y = -\frac{1}{2}x + b$. Plugging in the known point results in $2 = -\frac{1}{2}(-2) + b$. So $2 = 1 + b$, and $b = 1$. For the second line, the slope is $\frac{3 - (-1)}{1 - (-1)} = \frac{4}{2} = 2$. Plug in a known point to get $-1 = 2(-1) + b$, so $b = 1$. Set the equations for the two lines equal to each other: $-\frac{1}{2}x + 1 = 2x + 1$, which only works if $x = 0$. Since this value of x is a, the product ab must be **0**.

4.   B

Difficulty: Medium

Strategic Advice: Set up one equation for the number of bags and one for weight, then solve the system for the number of 100-pound bags.

Getting to the Answer: Using x for the number of 25-pound bags and y for the number of 100-pound bags, write the equations $x + y = 13$ and $25x + 100y = 775$. Since you are solving for y, substitute $x = 13 - y$ into the second equation to get $25(13 - y) + 100y = 775$. This simplifies to $325 - 25y + 100y = 775$, which further simplifies to $75y = 450$, so $y = 6$. Choice **(B)** is correct.

5.   3/4 or .75

Difficulty: Medium

Strategic Advice: Solve for x using substitution since the first equation is simple.

Getting to the Answer: Using the first equation, $y = x + 2$. So, $\frac{1}{3}(5x + 3(x + 2)) = 4$, which means that $5x + 3x + 6 = 3(4)$. Thus, $8x + 6 = 12$, $8x = 6$, and $x = \frac{6}{8} = \frac{3}{4} = \mathbf{0.75}$.

6.   C

Difficulty: Hard

Strategic Advice: Recall that the slopes of perpendicular lines are negative reciprocals. Use the x-axis intercept for line l to determine its equation. That equation will enable you to determine the point where the two lines intersect, so you can use that and the slope to find the equation for line m.

Getting to the Answer: The equation for line l with the coordinates of the x-intercept plugged in is $0 = \frac{1}{2}(-4) + b$, so $b = 2$. Since the lines intersect on the y-axis, this constant is the y-intercept and it applies to both equations. The slope of line m is $-\frac{1}{\frac{1}{2}} = -2$, so the equation for line m is $y = -2x + 2$. Choice **(C)** is correct.

7.   C

Difficulty: Hard

Strategic Advice: Two lines that are parallel when graphed in the xy-plane have no intersection and, therefore, no solutions. The slopes of the two lines are equal, but the intercepts are different. Restate the equations in $y = mx + b$ format and set the slopes equal.

Getting to the Answer: The first equation can be restated as $ay = 14x + \frac{9}{2}$. Dividing by a yields $y = \frac{14}{a}x + \frac{9}{2a}$. The second equation can be rearranged to $y = \frac{7}{2}x + \frac{1}{4}$. Set the two slopes equal: $\frac{14}{a} = \frac{7}{2}$. Cross-multiply to get $7a = 28$, so $a = 4$. (You don't need to check the intercepts since 4 is the only value for a that makes the slopes the same.) Choice **(C)** is correct.

8.   3/2 or 1.5

Difficulty: Medium

Strategic Advice: Since the two equations are equivalent, their coefficients and constants must be the same multiple of each other.

Getting to the Answer: Restate the first equation as $y = 4x - 6$. Note that $6x$ is 1.5 times $4x$ and 9 is 1.5 times 6, so ay must be 1.5 times y. Therefore, a must be **1.5**.

9.   C

Difficulty: Medium

Strategic Advice: Set up equations to solve for the evening commuting time.

Getting to the Answer: Let e represent Yvette's evening commuting time and m her morning commuting time. The evening time is 8 minutes greater than her morning commute time, so $e = m + 8$. The total of the two is 1 hour and 12 minutes, which is $60 + 12 = 72$ minutes; so $e + m = 72$. Rearrange the first equation to get $m = e - 8$. Set up the equation $e + (e - 8) = 72$. This simplifies to $2e = 80$, or $e = 40$. Choice **(C)** is correct.

10.   A

Difficulty: Hard

Strategic Advice: Convert cost per pound to cost per bag. Then set up two equations, one for cost and one for the number of bags.

Getting to the Answer: The total cost of a 15-pound bag is $\$0.60 \times 15 = \$9$, and the total cost of a 30-pound bag is $\$0.50 \times 30 = \$15$. Thus, you can write an equation for cost as $9s + 15b = 408$. The equation for the number of bags is $s + b = 32$. Choice **(A)** is correct.

11.   A

Difficulty: Hard

Strategic Advice: The first equation is a horizontal line and the second is a parabola. In order to have two solutions, the line must cross the parabola twice. Plug the values from the choices into the equations to see which pair of values has two solutions.

Getting to the Answer: For (A), $y = b + 5 = -6 + 5 = -1$. Plug this and $m = -1$ into the second equation: $-1 = -1(x^2)$, so $x^2 = 1$. This means that $x = \pm 1$. This represents two solutions, so **(A)** is correct.

12. 60

Difficulty: Medium

Strategic Advice: Be prepared to use substitution or combination to solve for x and y, but be alert for the possibility that you may be able to save time by solving directly for $x + y$.

Getting to the Answer: Add the two equations:

$$\begin{array}{r} 2x + y = 25 \\ x + 2y = 20 \\ \hline 3x + 3y = 45 \end{array}$$

Divide both sides by 3 to see that $x + y = 15$, then multiply by 4 to get $4x + 4y = \mathbf{60}$. Alternatively, you could have multiplied by $\frac{4}{3}$ to get the result directly.

13. B

Difficulty: Medium

Strategic Advice: Set up two equations, one for ounces and one for the number of cans, and solve using substitution or combination.

Getting to the Answer: Designate the number of 8-ounce cans as e and the number of 12-ounce cans as t. So $e + t = 8$ and $8e - 12t = 4$. Since the question asks for the number of 12-ounce cans, substitute $e = 8 - t$ into the second equation to get $8(8 - t) - 12t = 4$. Thus, $64 - 20t = 4$, which means that $60 = 20t$ and that $t = 3$. Choice **(B)** is correct.

14. A

Difficulty: Hard

Strategic Advice: Parallel lines share the same slope but have a different y-intercept. Since the separation of the two lines is 2, the constant term for the first equation must be 12 or 16. Use these properties to solve for a and then b.

Getting to the Answer: When the factor a is distributed, the first equation is $y = a\left(\frac{x}{2}\right) + ab$. Since the slopes of the two lines must be equal, $\frac{a}{2} = 3$. So, $a = 6$. The constant in the first equation becomes $6b$, which must be 14 ± 2. If $6b = 12$, then $b = 2$, which is one of the choices. If $6b = 16$, then $b = 2\frac{2}{3}$, which is not among the choices. Choice **(A)** is correct.

15. C

Difficulty: Hard

Strategic Advice: When a system has infinitely many solutions, the equations are the same line in the xy-plane. Make the equations look alike to get values for a and b.

Getting to the Answer: Multiply the first equation by 3 to get $3ax - 3by = 15$. The x- and y-coefficients of this equation and the second equation must be the same, so $3a = 3$ and $-3b = -4$. It follows that $a = 1$ and $b = \frac{4}{3}$. Therefore, $\frac{a}{b} = \frac{1}{\frac{4}{3}} = 1 \times \frac{3}{4} = \frac{3}{4}$. Choice **(C)** is correct.

CHAPTER 4

Inequalities

Solving Inequalities

Working with inequalities is similar to working with equations, but with a few key differences:

- The language used to describe inequalities tends to be more complex than the language used to describe equations. You "solve" an equation for x, but with an inequality, you might be asked to "describe all possible values of x" or provide an answer that "includes the entire set of solutions for x." This difference in wording exists because an equation describes a specific value of a variable, whereas an inequality describes a **range of values**.

- Instead of an equal sign, you'll see a sign denoting either "greater/less than" ($>$ and $<$) or "greater/less than or equal to" ($\geq$ and $\leq$). The open end of the inequality symbol should always point toward the greater quantity.

- When solving an inequality that involves multiplying or dividing by a negative number, the inequality symbol must be reversed. For example, if given $-4x < 12$, you must reverse the symbol when dividing by -4, which will yield $x > -3$ (NOT $x < -3$).

Compound Inequalities

Sometimes you'll see a variable expression wedged between two quantities. This is called a compound inequality. For example, $-5 < 2x + 1 < 11$ is a compound inequality. You solve it the same way (using inverse operations), keeping in mind that whatever you do to one piece, you must do to all three pieces. And, of course, if you multiply or divide by a negative number, you must reverse both inequality symbols.

Graphing Inequalities

Inequalities can be presented graphically in one or two dimensions. In one dimension, inequalities are graphed on a number line with a shaded region. For example, $x > 1$ is graphed like this:

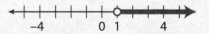

Notice the open dot at 1, which indicates that 1 is not a solution to the inequality. This is called a strict inequality. By contrast, the graph of $x \leq 0$ looks like this:

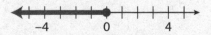

Notice the solid dot at 0, which indicates that 0 should be included in the solution set for the inequality.

K   37

In two dimensions, things get a bit more complicated. While linear equations graph as simple lines, inequalities graph as lines called **boundary lines** with shaded regions known as **half planes**. Solid lines indicate inequalities that have $\leq$ or $\geq$ because the values on the line itself are included in the solution set. Dashed lines involve strict inequalities that have $>$ or $<$ because, in these cases, the values on the line itself are not included in the solution set. The shaded region (and the line if it is solid) represents all points that make up the solution set for the inequality. For example, the graph below represents the solution set to the inequality $y < \frac{1}{4}x - 3$:

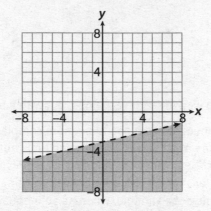

If you're not sure whether to shade above or below a boundary line, plug a pair of coordinates into the inequality. If the coordinates satisfy the inequality, then the region in which that point lies should be shaded. If the coordinates violate the inequality, then that region should not be shaded. An easy point to use when testing inequalities is the origin, $(0, 0)$. In the example above, $0 \not< -3$, so the half plane that contains $(0, 0)$ should not be shaded (which it isn't).

Solving Systems of Inequalities

Multiple inequalities can be combined to create a system of inequalities. Systems of inequalities can also be represented graphically with multiple boundary lines and multiple shaded regions. Follow the same rules for graphing single inequalities, but keep in mind that the solution set to the system is the region where the shaded half planes overlap. Shading in different directions (e.g., parallel lines slanted up for one inequality and down for the other) makes the overlap easier to see. Just as with single inequalities, you can pick coordinates to plug into a system of inequalities to determine which side of the boundary lines should be shaded.

Inequalities Drill

Solve for x.

1. $\dfrac{1}{2}x - 3 > 2$

2. $3x + 5 \leq 2x + 9$

3. $-2x - 7 < 3x + 13$

4. $6 < -2x + 4 < 10$

5. $\dfrac{1}{5} \leq \dfrac{1}{4}x \leq \dfrac{3}{10}$

Inequalities Practice Set

> **DIRECTIONS:** Keep a calculator handy as you work through this practice set, but reserve it for those questions that have a calculator icon next to them—and even on those questions, use it only if you really need it. Questions without the icon are intended to be done without a calculator, to help you prepare for the no-calculator section of the SAT.

$$3b - 4 \geq 8 - 9b$$

1. For the inequality above, which of the following is NOT a solution?

   A) -1

   B) 1

   C) 5

   D) 11

2. Which of the following inequalities is equivalent to $5b > 20 + 10a$?

   A) $2a - b < -4$

   B) $b - 2a > 4$

   C) $2a - b > 4$

   D) $b - 2a > -4$

3. If $5r + 7 \leq 2r - 5$, what is the greatest possible value of $2r + 3$?

   A) -5

   B) -4

   C) 7

   D) 11

4. When the stadium, which has seating capacity up to 70,000, opened to the public two hours before the game, there were 35,215 spectators at the stadium. Each minute after, the number of spectators increased by 230. If t represents the time, in minutes, after the stadium opened, which of the following inequalities represents the range of minutes when the stadium is at or above capacity?

   A) $70,000 - 230 \leq t$

   B) $70,000 \leq 230t$

   C) $70,000 - 230t \geq 35,215$

   D) $35,215 + 230t \geq 70,000$

$$y \leq -x + 5$$
$$y \geq 2x - 4$$

5. If a point with coordinates (p, q) is a solution to the given system of inequalities, what is the maximum possible value of p?

   A) 2

   B) 3

   C) 5

   D) 6

6. Malikah is assembling the gear she requires to lead a youth group on a camping trip. She needs to rent some tents and buy some meals-ready-to-eat (MREs). She cannot spend more than $350. Malikah knows that she will need at least 8 tents, which cost $15 each to rent, and 40 MREs, which are priced at $5 each. She knows that she will need at least 5 MREs per tent. Which of the following systems of inequalities represents the limitations above if t is the number of tents and m is the number of MREs?

A) $15t + 5m \leq 350$
   $m \geq 5t$
   $t \geq 8$
   $m \leq 40$

B) $15t + 5m \leq 350$
   $m \geq 8t$
   $t \geq 8$
   $m \geq 40$

C) $15t + 5m \geq 350$
   $m \geq 5t$
   $t \geq 8$
   $m \geq 40$

D) $15t + 5m \leq 350$
   $m \geq 5t$
   $t \geq 8$
   $m \geq 40$

7. Yamen predicts that the winning team of a tournament will score p points. To win a contest, his prediction must be within 3 points of the actual score. If the actual score is a, then which of the following inequalities represents the relationship between p and a required to win the contest?

A) $|a - p| \leq 3$
B) $|a - p| \geq 3$
C) $|a + p| \leq 3$
D) $|a + p| \geq 3$

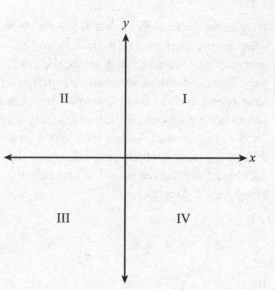

8. If the system of inequalities $y \leq -\dfrac{3}{2}x + 2$ and $y < 3x - 1$ is graphed in the xy-plane above, which of the following quadrants contain possible solutions to the system?

A) I and II only
B) I, III, and IV only
C) II, III, and IV only
D) III and IV only

9. Joaquin receives a commission of $35 for every desktop computer system that he sells and $25 for every laptop computer. His goals for the month were to sell more than 60 computers and to earn at least $1,600 in commissions. Joaquin exceeded his commission goal, but fell short of reaching his goal for the number of computers sold. Which of the following systems of inequalities describes the number of desktop computers, d, and laptop computers, p, that Joaquin sold?

   A) $d + p \leq 59$
          $35d + 25p > 1{,}600$

   B) $d + p \leq 60$
          $25d + 35p > 1{,}600$

   C) $d + p \leq 60$
          $35d + 25p > 1{,}600$

   D) $d + p < 60$
          $35d + 25p \geq 1{,}600$

$$y \geq -3x + 4$$
$$y \geq 2x - 6$$

10. If a point with coordinates (p, q) is a solution to the given system of inequalities, what is the minimum possible value of q?

   A) -4
   B) -2
   C) 0
   D) 2

$$y > -x - p$$
$$y < x - q$$

11. If $(0, 0)$ is a solution to the given system of inequalities, which of the following relationships must be true?

   A) $q < p$
   B) $q > p$
   C) $|q| > |p|$
   D) $p = -q$

12. Maria's cellular phone company charges $30 per month plus $3 for every gigabyte or portion thereof for data usage. If Maria does not want to spend more than $50 this month, what is the maximum data, in gigabytes, she can use?

   A) $4\dfrac{1}{3}$

   B) 6

   C) $6\dfrac{2}{3}$

   D) 7

Answers and Explanations

Inequalities Drill

1. $\frac{1}{2}x - 3 + 3 > 2 + 3$

   $\frac{1}{2}x > 5$

   $x > 10$

2. $3x + 5 - 2x - 5 \leq 2x + 9 - 2x - 5$

   $x \leq 4$

3. $-2x - 7 - 3x + 7 < 3x + 13 - 3x + 7$

   $-5x < 20$

   $x > -4$

4. $6 - 4 < -2x + 4 - 4 < 10 - 4$

   $2 < -2x < 6$

   $-1 > x > -3$

5. $4\left(\frac{1}{5}\right) \leq 4\left(\frac{1}{4}x\right) \leq 4\left(\frac{3}{10}\right)$

   $\frac{4}{5} \leq x \leq \frac{12}{10}$

   $\frac{4}{5} \leq x \leq \frac{6}{5}$

Inequalities Practice Set

1. A

Difficulty: Easy

Strategic Advice: Manipulate the given inequality to find a range for b.

Getting to the Answer: Add $9b$ and 4 to both sides: $3b - 4 + 9b + 4 \geq 8 - 9b + 9b + 4$. This simplifies to $12b \geq 12$, so $b \geq 1$. The only choice that is not within this range is **(A)**, -1.

2. A

Difficulty: Medium

Strategic Advice: Notice that the choices have the variables on the left and the constant on the right. Rearrange the given inequality to conform to that format.

Getting to the Answer: Start by subtracting $10a$ from both sides to get $-10a + 5b > 20$. Divide all terms by 5 to yield $-2a + b > 4$. The coefficients are the same as those for (A), but the signs are reversed. Multiply both sides by -1 and flip the inequality sign: $2a - b < -4$. Choice **(A)** is correct.

3. A

Difficulty: Medium

Strategic Advice: Solve the inequality for r, then plug that value into $2r + 3$.

Getting to the Answer: Isolate r in the given inequality $5r + 7 - 2r - 7 \leq 2r - 5 - 2r - 7$, to get $3r \leq -12$. Thus, $r \leq -4$. Plugging the maximum value of -4 into $2r + 3$ yields $2(-4) + 3 = -5$. Choice **(A)** is correct.

4. D

Difficulty: Easy

Strategic Advice: When modeling real-life situations with a linear function or inequality, the starting point is the y-intercept and the slope is the rate of change.

Getting to the Answer: There were 35,215 spectators at $t = 0$, so that is the constant, b. The number of spectators increases at a rate of 230 per minute, or $230t$, so the number of spectators at time t minutes is $35,215 + 230t$. The question asks for the range of minutes when the stadium is at or above capacity, so write the inequality $35,215 + 230t \geq 70,000$. Choice **(D)** is an exact match.

5. B

Difficulty: Medium

Strategic Advice: Since p is the x-coordinate, combine the inequalities and determine the maximum value of x.

Getting to the Answer: Combining the two inequalities results in $2x - 4 \leq y \leq -x + 5$. Since it's not necessary to know the value of y, drop the middle term and solve for x. Add x to both sides to get $3x - 4 \leq 5$. Add 4 to both sides to get $3x \leq 9$, so $x \leq 3$. Either (A) 2 or (B) 3 is an allowable value, but the question asks for the maximum, so **(B)** is correct.

6.   D

Difficulty: Medium

Strategic Advice: Translate each of the statements in the stem into inequalities and compare the results to the choices.

Getting to the Answer: "At least" means greater than or equal to. There must be at least 40 MREs, so $m \geq 40$; eliminate (A). Moreover, the number of MREs must be greater than or equal to five times the number of tents, so $m \geq 5t$; eliminate (B). Finally, "not more than" means less than or equal to, so the amount spent must be ≤ 350. Eliminate (C). Choice **(D)** is correct.

7.   A

Difficulty: Easy

Strategic Advice: Translate the wording in the stem to an inequality.

Getting to the Answer: The positive difference between Yamen's prediction, p, and the actual score, a, is simply $|a - p|$. (You could also write it as $|p - a|$.) This must be less than or equal to 3, so **(A)** is correct.

8.   B

Difficulty: Hard

Strategic Advice: Sketch a graph of the solution, and identify which quadrants are within that space.

Getting to the Answer:

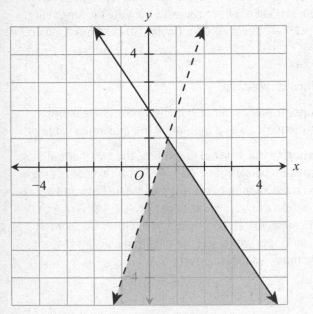

Only quadrant II does not appear within the shaded area, so **(B)** is correct.

9.   C

Difficulty: Medium

Strategic Advice: Translate the wording in the stem to a system of inequalities.

Getting to the Answer: One inequality is Joaquin's sales by type of computer. Since the goal was to sell more than 60, any total less than or equal to 60 would not meet the goal. So this inequality is $d + p \leq 60$. Because Joaquin exceeded his target commission, that inequality is $35d + 25p > 1,600$. Choice **(C)** is correct.

10.   B

Difficulty: Hard

Strategic Advice: Since q is the y-coordinate, the question is actually asking for the minimum value of y. This question can be most efficiently answered by sketching a graph of the two inequalities. Draw the lines as if the inequalities were equations, then shade the area above both lines.

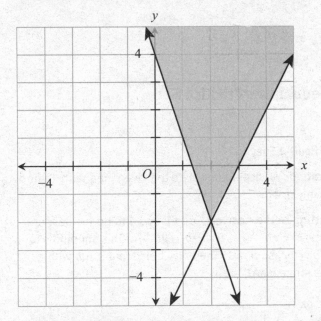

Getting to the Answer: The least value of y in the shaded area is -2, so **(B)** is correct.

11. A

Difficulty: Medium

Strategic Advice: Substitute 0 for x and y in the inequalities, then determine the relationship between p and q.

Getting to the Answer: The first inequality becomes $0 > -p$, and the second becomes $0 < -q$. Combine these to get $-p < 0 < -q$. Multiply this by -1 and flip the inequality signs: $p > 0 > q$. Thus, q is less than p, so **(A)** is correct.

12. B

Difficulty: Medium

Strategic Advice: Translate the wording into an inequality, and solve. Alternatively, you could backsolve starting with (D) and work upward until the choice results in a cost less than or equal to $50.

Getting to the Answer: There is a fixed charge of $30 plus a variable charge of $3 per gigabyte. When answering the question, keep in mind that any portion of a gigabyte will lead to a $3 charge. With that in mind, the inequality, using g for gigabytes, is $30 + 3g \leq 50$. Solving for g, $3g \leq 20$. So, $g \leq \frac{20}{3}$, which is $6\frac{2}{3}$. Since any portion of a gigabyte results in a $3 charge, this must be rounded *down* to 6. Choice **(B)** is correct.

CHAPTER 5

Rates, Proportions, and Percents

Rates, Measurement, and Unit Conversions

You're likely already familiar with all kinds of rates—kilometers per hour, meters per second, and even miles per gallon are all considered rates.

Many rate questions can be solved using some form of the *DiRT equation*: Distance = rate × time. If you have two of the three components of the equation, you can easily find the third.

Units of measurement are important when answering rate questions (as well as questions that require a unit conversion). The **factor-label method** is a simple yet powerful way to keep calculations organized and to ensure that you arrive at an answer that has the required units.

For example, suppose you need to find the number of cups in 2 gallons. To use the factor-label method, start by identifying the initial unit (gallons), and then identify the desired unit (cups). The next step is to piece together a path of relationships (conversion factors) that will convert gallons into cups, canceling units as you go:

$$2 \text{ gallons} \times \frac{4 \text{ quarts}}{1 \text{ gallon}} \times \frac{2 \text{ pints}}{1 \text{ quart}} \times \frac{2 \text{ cups}}{1 \text{ pint}} = (2 \times 4 \times 2 \times 2) \text{ cups} = 32 \text{ cups}$$

Don't worry if you don't know all the measurement conversions—these will be provided within the context of the question.

Ratios and Proportions

A **ratio** is a relationship that compares the relative size of two amounts. You might see ratios written with a colon, 2:5, as a fraction, $\frac{2}{5}$, or using words, 2 to 5. A ratio can compare a part to a part or a part to a whole. For example, suppose you make a fruit salad using 6 oranges, 3 apples, and 2 pears. The ratio of apples to pears is 3:2. The ratio of apples to all the fruit is 3:11.

Proportions are simply two ratios set equal to each other. They are an efficient way to solve certain problems, but you must exercise caution when setting them up. Watching the units of each piece of the proportion is critical. Writing the proportion in words first is a good way to avoid careless errors. To solve a proportion, cross-multiply and then solve for the unknown quantity. You can also use cross-multiplication to verify that two ratios are proportional. For example $\frac{a}{b} = \frac{c}{d}$ if and only if $ad = bc$.

Percents

A **percent** is a type of proportion that means "per 100." Here are some useful percent formulas to learn before test day:

- Percent $\times$ whole = part
- Percent $= \dfrac{part}{whole} \times 100\%$
- Percent change $= \dfrac{amount\ of\ change}{initial\ amount} \times 100\%$

When doing calculations involving percents, it is generally most useful to write them as a decimal. For example, $30\% = 0.30$.

 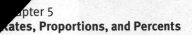

Proportions Drill

Solve for the given variable.

1. The ratio of x to y is 5:2. If $y = 12$, then $x =$

2. $\frac{x}{\frac{1}{2}} = \frac{\frac{1}{3}}{y}$. If $y = \frac{1}{24}$, then $x =$

3. If a jar contains nickels, dimes, and quarters in the ratio of 2:5:7, what is the ratio of nickels to the total number of coins?

4. If the ratio of ingredient x in a mixture to the total mixture is 3:10 and the ratio of ingredient y to the total mixture is 1:2, what is the ratio of x to y?

5. If $\frac{x-1}{y-2} = \frac{3}{5}$ and $y = x + 3$, what is the value of x?

Unit Conversion Drill

Solve for x.

1. If there are 36 inches in a yard, then 216 inches are how many yards?

2. If there are 28.35 grams in an ounce, then how many grams are in 3 ounces?

3. If there are 2 pints in a quart and 4 quarts in a gallon, how many gallons are equivalent to 120 pints?

4. If there are 16 ounces in a pound and 2.2 pounds in a kilogram, how many ounces are in 3 kilograms?

5. If there are 60 seconds in a minute, 60 minutes in an hour, and 5,280 feet in a mile, how many feet per second are equivalent to 40 miles per hour?

Percents Drill

1. 40 is what percent of 500 ?

2. What is 62.5 percent of 224 ?

3. A price reduction from $150 to $120 is what percent change?

4. A 20 percent increase in output from 45 units/hour results in an output of how many units/hour?

5. The price of an item is reduced by 20 percent, then further reduced by 15 percent. What is the total percent reduction in price?

Rates, Proportions, and Percents Practice Set

DIRECTIONS: Keep a calculator handy as you work through this practice set, but reserve it for those questions that have a calculator icon next to them—and even on those questions, use it only if you really need it. Questions without the icon are intended to be done without a calculator, to help you prepare for the no-calculator section of the SAT.

1. The sum of three numbers is 576. One of the numbers, n, is 25 percent more than the sum of the other two numbers. What is the value of n?

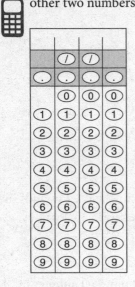

2. If p pounds and 10 ounces is equal to 90 ounces, what is the value of p? (Note: 1 pound = 16 ounces.)

   A) 5
   B) 6
   C) 9
   D) 15

3. Sandra scored approximately 12 percent lower than Simpson scored on the exam. Simpson scored 89. Which of the following is approximately equal to Sandra's exam score?

   A) 69
   B) 78
   C) 91
   D) 100

4. A beard-second is equal to 5 nanometers, and 1,000 nanometers is equal to 1 micrometer. How many beard-seconds are in 16 micrometers?

   A)   0.08
   B)   12.5
   C)   312.5
   D)   3,200

5. Charlene can assemble at least 2 cabinets per hour and at most 4 cabinets per hour. What is the minimum number of hours it would take Charlene to assemble 12 cabinets?

   A) 2
   B) 3
   C) 4
   D) 6

6. Kuam's annual salary is $57,390. If he worked 30 hours each week last year, which is the closest to the average amount he earned, in dollars per hour? (Note: 1 year = 52 weeks.)

   A) $22
   B) $28
   C) $37
   D) $40

7. A baker uses 57 percent of the revenue from sales to pay for ingredients. The remainder of the revenue is the baker's profit. For every loaf of bread sold, the baker earns $4. If 33 loaves were sold in one day, what is the profit earned from that day's sales?

   A) $43.56

   B) $56.76

   C) $62.04

   D) $75.24

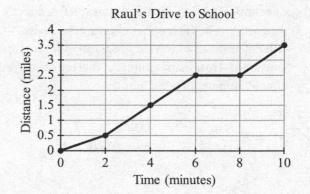

Raul's Drive to School

Number of First-Year Students Admitted

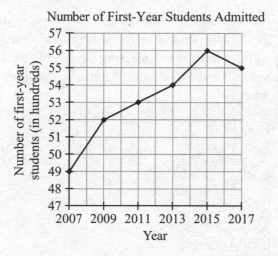

8. Based on the given graph, the number of first-year students admitted to the university in 2017 is what proportion, rounded to the nearest hundredth, of the total number of first-year students admitted in 2013 and 2015?

   A) 0.48

   B) 0.50

   C) 0.51

   D) 0.55

9. The graph shows the time it took Raul to drive to school. Based on the graph, what is Raul's average speed for the entire trip in miles per hour?

$$0.20a + 0.50b = 0.38(a + b)$$

10. A food company mixes a gallons of a 20 percent vinegar solution with b gallons of a 50 percent vinegar solution in order to create a 38 percent vinegar solution. The equation above represents this situation. If the company uses 1,000 gallons of the 50 percent vinegar solution, approximately how many gallons of the 20 percent vinegar solution will it need to use?

   A) 433

   B) 667

   C) 967

   D) 1,033

11. The number of gallons of fuel consumed is directly proportional to the number of minutes traveled. After 30 minutes of traveling, 0.6 gallons of fuel are consumed. How many gallons of fuel are consumed after 90 minutes of traveling?

    A) 0.2

    B) 0.8

    C) 1.0

    D) 1.8

12. A furlong is equal to 660 yards or 40 rods. How many yards are in 12 rods?

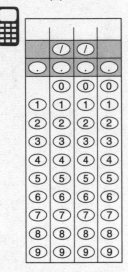

13. Michelle is replenishing inventory for her jewelry store. She has 12 necklaces and 18 bracelets in stock. She has ordered an additional 22 necklaces. How many more bracelets does she need to order so that $\frac{3}{5}$ of the total necklaces and bracelets in stock will be bracelets?

    A) 18

    B) 24

    C) 27

    D) 33

14. One solution that comprises a quarter of a mixture of two solutions contains 40 percent chemical A. If the total mixture contains 16 percent chemical A, what percentage chemical A does the second solution that makes up the mixture contain?

    A)   8

    B)   10

    C)   12

    D)   14

15. If a certain runner can average 12 miles per hour for distances up to a mile, how long, in seconds, will it take her to complete one lap of a 440 yard track? (Note: 1 mile = 5,280 feet, and 1 yard = 3 feet.)

16. Yogurt A contains 490 milligrams of potassium per cup, and Yogurt B contains 625 milligrams of potassium per cup. Hideo decides to mix Yogurt A and Yogurt B for breakfast. One cup of Hideo's mixture contains 517 milligrams of potassium. What fraction of his mixture is made up of Yogurt B?

    A) $\frac{1}{6}$

    B) $\frac{1}{5}$

    C) $\frac{1}{4}$

    D) $\frac{1}{3}$

17. Qing Qing assembles jigsaw puzzles as a hobby. She completes the same fraction of a puzzle each time she works on her hobby. When she is able to do this four times each week, she can complete 16 puzzles in 12 weeks. How many more times per week would Qing Qing have to work on her hobby in order to complete 10 puzzles in 5 weeks, assuming that her puzzle completion rate per session remains constant?

   A) 1

   B) 2

   C) 4

   D) 6

18. In the United States, there are 100,000 car wash facilities, and an estimated 8 million cars go through a car wash a day. If a car wash facility is open 8 hours in a day and washes cars at the rate of the daily national average, which is the closest to the number of cars washed per hour at that facility?

   A) 8

   B) 10

   C) 64

   D) 80

19. One fluid ounce of a mixture consists of 3 parts ingredient A, 7 parts ingredient B, and 6 parts water. How many ounces of ingredient B are contained in 2 gallons of the mixture? (Note: 1 gallon = 128 ounces.)

20. Last week, approximately 23 percent of museum visitors under 30 years old purchased a museum membership, and 52 percent of the visitors who are at least 30 years old purchased a museum membership. If there were 436 visitors under 30 years old and 102 visitors who are at least 30 years old, which of the following is closest to the total number of visitors at the museum last week who purchased a membership?

   A) 153

   B) 182

   C) 250

   D) 404

Answers and Explanations

Proportions Drill

1. $\frac{5}{2} = \frac{x}{12}$

   $2x = 60$

   $x = 30$

2. Substitute the given fraction for y and cross-multiply to solve:

   $\frac{x}{\frac{1}{2}} = \frac{\frac{1}{3}}{\frac{1}{24}}; \frac{x}{24} = \frac{1}{6}; 6x = 24; x = 4$

3. $\frac{2}{2+5+7} = \frac{2}{14} = \frac{1}{7}$, which is equivalent to 1:7.

4. 1:2 is the same as 5:10, so $\frac{x}{y} = \frac{\frac{3}{10}}{\frac{5}{10}} = \frac{3}{5}$, or 3:5.

5. $\frac{x-1}{x+3-2} = \frac{x-1}{x+1} = \frac{3}{5}$. Cross-multiply to find that $3x + 3 = 5x - 5$. So $8 = 2x$, and $x = 4$.

Unit Conversion Drill

1. $\frac{1\ \text{yd}}{36\ \text{in}} \times 216\ \text{in} = 6\ \text{yd}$

2. $\frac{28.35\ \text{g}}{1\ \text{oz}} \times 3\ \text{oz} = 85.05\ \text{g}$

3. $120\ \text{pt} \times \frac{1\ \text{qt}}{2\ \text{pt}} \times \frac{1\ \text{gal}}{4\ \text{qt}} = 15\ \text{gal}$

4. $3\ \text{kg} \times \frac{2.2\ \text{lb}}{1\ \text{kg}} \times \frac{16\ \text{oz}}{1\ \text{lb}} = 105.6\ \text{oz}$

5. $\frac{1\ \text{min}}{60\ \text{sec}} \times \frac{1\ \text{hr}}{60\ \text{min}} \times \frac{5{,}280\ \text{ft}}{1\ \text{mi}} \times \frac{40\ \text{mi}}{1\ \text{hr}} \approx 58.7\frac{\text{ft}}{\text{sec}}$

Percents Drill

1. $\frac{40}{500} \times 100\% = 8\%$

2. $0.625 \times 224 = 140$

3. $\frac{150-120}{150} \times 100\% = \frac{30}{150} \times 100\% = 20\%$

4. $\left(1 + \frac{20}{100}\right)(45) = (1.2)45 = 54$

5. Assume a price of 100. The first decrease results in $(1.00 - 0.20)100 = 80$, and the second results in $(1.00 - 0.15)80 = 68$. The total discount is $100 - 68 = 32$, and $\frac{32}{100} \times 100\% = 32\%$.

Ratios, Proportions, and Percents Practice Set

1. 320

Difficulty: Medium

Strategic Advice: Translate the words into an equation and solve for n.

Getting to the Answer: Since the total of the three numbers is 576, the sum of the two numbers other than n is $576 - n$. Thus, $n = 1.25(576 - n)$, and $n = 720 - 1.25n$. Combine like terms to get $2.25n = 720$, which means that $n = \mathbf{320}$.

2. A

Difficulty: Easy

Strategic Advice: Translate from English into math and solve for p.

Getting to the Answer: Since a pound is 16 ounces, $16p + 10 = 90$. So $16p = 80$, and $p = 5$. Choice **(A)** is correct.

3. B

Difficulty: Easy

Strategic Advice: The key word "approximately" means that you can use estimation to solve the question quickly.

Getting to the Answer: Round Simpson's score to 90 and the difference to 10%, in which case Sandra's score would be $90 - 0.1(90) = 90 - 9 = 81$. Only **(B)** is close to this value.

4. D

Difficulty: Medium

Strategic Advice: Use the units given to set up a conversion so that both units are stated in terms of nanometers.

Getting to the Answer: The conversion equation is

$16 \text{ micrometers} \times \dfrac{1,000 \text{ nanometers}}{\text{micrometer}} =$

$x \text{ beard seconds} \times \dfrac{5 \text{ nanometers}}{\text{beard second}}$.

What's left after all the cancelation is $16,000 = 5x$, so $x = 3,200$. Choice **(D)** is correct.

5. B

Difficulty: Easy

Strategic Advice: Since the question asks for the least time to assemble the cabinets, use Charlene's fastest rate to calculate this value.

Getting to the Answer: At the fastest rate, $t = 12 \text{ cabinets} \times \dfrac{1 \text{ hr}}{4 \text{ cabinets}} = 3 \text{ hr}$. Choice **(B)** is correct.

6. C

Difficulty: Medium

Strategic Advice: Use the units given to set up a conversion from annual to hourly pay.

Getting to the Answer: Set up the equation $x = \dfrac{\$57,390}{\text{year}} \times \dfrac{1 \text{ year}}{52 \text{ weeks}} \times \dfrac{1 \text{ week}}{30 \text{ hours}} \approx 36.8 \dfrac{\$}{\text{hr}}$.

Choice **(C)** is closest to this value.

7. B

Difficulty: Easy

Strategic Advice: Calculate the day's sales, then multiply by the percentage that is actually profit.

Getting to the Answer: Selling 33 loaves at $4 each brings in $132 for the day's sales. The profit is $100\% - 57\% = 43\%$ of those sales. Multiply by 43% to find the amount of the day's sales that is profit: $\$132 \times 0.43 = \$56.76$. Choice **(B)** is correct.

8. B

Difficulty: Medium

Strategic Advice: From the graph, determine the number of first-year students admitted in 2017 and the sum of the number of first-year students admitted in 2013 and 2015. Then divide the number of first-year students admitted in 2017 by the total number of first-year students admitted in 2013 and 2015 to calculate the proportion.

Getting to the Answer: According to the graph, the number of first-year students admitted in 2017 is 55 hundred, and the total number of first-year students admitted in 2013 and 2015 is $54 + 56 = 110$ hundred. Thus, the number of first-year students admitted in 2017 is $\dfrac{55}{110} = 0.50$ of the total number of first-year students admitted in 2013 and 2015. Choice **(B)** is correct.

9. 21

Difficulty: Medium

Strategic Advice: Use the formula Average speed $= \dfrac{\text{total distance}}{\text{total time}}$. Then, convert to miles per hour.

Getting to the Answer: According to the graph, the total distance Raul travelled is 3.5 miles, and the total time it took Raul to drive to school is 10 minutes. Thus, Raul's average speed $= \dfrac{3.5}{10} = 0.3$ miles per minute. Multiply by $\dfrac{60 \text{ minutes}}{1 \text{ hour}}$ to get Raul's average speed in miles per hour: $0.35 \dfrac{\text{miles}}{\text{minute}} \times \dfrac{60 \text{ minutes}}{1 \text{ hour}} = \mathbf{21} \dfrac{\text{miles}}{\text{hour}}$.

10. B

Difficulty: Medium

Strategic Advice: Use the given equation and the provided value to find a.

Getting to the Answer: Plug the given value of 1,000 for b into the equation and then solve for a:

$$0.20a + 0.50(1,000) = 0.38(a + 1,000)$$
$$0.20a + 500 = 0.38a + 380$$
$$120 = 0.18a$$
$$\frac{120}{0.18} = a$$
$$666.\overline{6} = a$$

Choice **(B)** is correct.

11. D

Difficulty: Easy

Strategic Advice: Set up a proportion based on the information in the stem.

Getting to the Answer: The proportion is $\frac{0.6}{30} = \frac{x}{90}$, so $54 = 30x$, and $x = 1.8$. Alternatively, if you noticed that 90 minutes is 3 times 30 minutes, you could have simply multiplied 0.6 by 3 to get 1.8. Choice **(D)** is correct.

12. 198

Difficulty: Medium

Strategic Advice: Set up a proportion using the given conversion ratios to calculate the number of yards.

Getting to the Answer: The proportion is $\frac{12}{y} = \frac{40}{660}$, so $40y = 7{,}920$, and $y = $ **198**.

13. D

Difficulty: Hard

Strategic Advice: Since the target inventory is a part-to-whole ratio, this can be solved by setting up a proportion.

Getting to the Answer: The proportion to end up with the desired ratio, using b for the number of bracelets to order, is $\frac{3}{5} = \frac{18+b}{12+18+22+b}$, so $\frac{3}{5} = \frac{18+b}{52+b}$. Cross-multiply to get $3(52) + 3b = 5(18) + 5b$, which simplifies to $66 = 2b$, so $b = 33$. Choice **(D)** is correct.

14. A

Difficulty: Medium

Strategic Advice: This is an averages question that features fractions of an unknown quantity. The average of the final mixture will be the sum of the products of the proportion of each solution times the concentration of each.

Getting to the Answer: The second chemical makes up three-quarters of the final mixture, so set up the equation $\frac{1}{4}(40) + \frac{3}{4}x = 16$. (Since all the values are in percents, there is no need to convert to decimals.) Solve to find that $\frac{3}{4}x = 16 - 10$, so $\frac{3}{4}x = 6$. Multiply both sides by $\frac{4}{3}$ to get x, which is 8%. Choice **(A)** is correct.

15. 75

Difficulty: Hard

Strategic Advice: Since the answer is in terms of seconds per lap, convert the given values to those units, then solve.

Getting to the Answer: The distance conversion is $\frac{440 \text{ yards}}{1 \text{ lap}} \times \frac{1 \text{ mi}}{5280 \text{ ft}} \times \frac{3 \text{ ft}}{1 \text{ yard}} = \frac{1 \text{ mile}}{4 \text{ laps}}$. The speed conversion is $\frac{1 \text{ hr}}{12 \text{ mi}} \times \frac{60 \text{ min}}{1 \text{ hr}} \times \frac{60 \text{ sec}}{1 \text{ min}} = \frac{300 \text{ sec}}{1 \text{ mi}}$. Combine these to get $\frac{300 \text{ sec}}{1 \text{ mi}} \times \frac{1 \text{ mi}}{4 \text{ laps}} = \frac{75 \text{ sec}}{1 \text{ lap}}$.

16. B

Difficulty: Hard

Strategic Advice: Mixtures questions can often be solved by setting up a system of equations.

Getting to the Answer: Set up two equations. Since you know that some portion of Yogurt A mixed with some portion of Yogurt B makes up one cup, you can set up the equation $A + B = 1$. The second equation is $490A + 625B = 517$.

Since you're trying to find B, start by isolating A in the first equation and then plug that value into the second equation:

$$A = 1 - B$$
$$490(1 - B) + 625B = 517$$
$$490 - 490B + 625B = 517$$
$$135B = 27$$
$$B = \frac{27}{135}$$
$$B = \frac{1}{5}$$

Choice **(B)** is correct.

17. B

Difficulty: Medium

Strategic Advice: Calculate Qing Qing's current rate per session, and then determine how many times per week she would need to work on puzzles to reach the new goal of 10 puzzles in 5 weeks. Compare this to the current number of puzzle-solving sessions per week.

Getting to the Answer: Qing Qing's current rate is $\frac{16}{12} = \frac{4}{3}$ puzzles per week. Since she has 4 puzzle-solving sessions per week, Qing Qing completes $\frac{4}{3} \div 4 = \frac{1}{3}$ of a puzzle per session. The inverse of this is 3 sessions per puzzle completed. The new rate of puzzles per week required is $\frac{10}{5} = 2$ puzzles per week. So, $\frac{2 \text{ puzzles}}{1 \text{ week}} \times \frac{3 \text{ sessions}}{1 \text{ puzzle}} = 6 \frac{\text{sessions}}{\text{week}}$. Her original rate was 4 sessions per week. Thus, Qing Qing would have to increase the number of sessions per week by $6 - 4 = 2$. Choice **(B)** is correct.

18. B

Difficulty: Medium

Strategic Advice: Use the rates given to solve for cars per hour, paying close attention to the units.

Getting to the Answer: If 100,000 facilities wash 8,000,000 cars per day, then the average is $\frac{8,000,000}{100,000} = 80$ for each facility. Since the question states that the facility is open 8 hours, that equates to $\frac{80}{8} = 10$ cars per hour. Choice **(B)** is correct.

19. 112

Difficulty: Medium

Strategic Advice: Convert the part-to-part ratio to a part-to-whole ratio for ingredient B, then use a proportion to solve for the number of ounces of ingredient B in 2 gallons of the mixture.

Getting to the Answer: The part-to-whole ratio for ingredient B is $\frac{7}{3+7+6} = \frac{7}{16}$. Set up the proportion for 2 gallons of the mixture: $\frac{7}{16} = \frac{x}{2(128)}$. So $16x = 7(2)(128)$, and $x = \mathbf{112}$.

20. A

Difficulty: Easy

Strategic Advice: Multiply the number of visitors in each category by the percentage who purchased memberships, and sum the two numbers. Since the question asks for the closest choice, use approximation.

Getting to the Answer: The approximation is $400 \times 0.25 + 100 \times 0.50 = 100 + 50 = 150$. Choice **(A)** is closest to this approximation.

CHAPTER 6

Tables, Statistics, and Probability

Two-Way Tables

A two-way table is a table that is used to summarize data that pertains to two variables, sometimes referred to as bivariate data. The information given in a two-way table can be used to assemble ratios, make comparisons, and find probabilities. For example, if you have a two-way table that summarizes book sales for three local bookshops over the course of one week, you can compare Store 1's sales to total sales, Monday sales to Tuesday sales, and so on. The key to properly using a two-way table is to focus only on the cell(s), row(s), and/or column(s) that pertain to the question being asked.

Statistics

Statistics is a part of almost every major in college and can be used in a variety of careers, which explains why there are entire high school and college courses devoted to the study of statistics. Fortunately, the SAT will only test you on a few basic statistical concepts. Suppose you took five tests in a world history class and earned scores of 85, 92, 85, 80, and 96. Descriptions of several common statistical measures that you can find for this data set are described below.

- **Mean** (also called average): The sum of the values divided by the number of values. For your history class, the mean of your test scores is $\frac{85 + 92 + 85 + 80 + 96}{5} = \frac{438}{5} = 87.6$.
- **Median:** The value that is in the middle of the set *when the values are arranged in ascending order*. The history scores in ascending order are 80, 85, 85, 92, and 96, making the median 85. To find the median of a data set that contains an even number of terms, find the mean of the two middle terms.
- **Mode:** The value that occurs most frequently. The test score that appears more than any other is 85, so it is the mode. If more than one value appears the most often, that's fine. A set of data can have more than one mode.
- **Range:** The difference between the highest and lowest values. The highest and lowest scores are 96 and 80, so the range is $96 - 80 = 16$.
- **Standard deviation:** A measure of how far a typical data point is from the mean of the data. A low standard deviation indicates that most values in the set are fairly close to the mean; a high standard deviation indicates that the values are more spread out.
- **Margin of error:** A description of the maximum expected difference between a true value for a data pool (e.g., mean) and a random sampling from the data pool. A lower margin of error is achieved by increasing the size of the data pool.

Note: On the SAT, you will need to understand what the standard deviation and margin of error tell you about a set of data, but you won't have to calculate either of them.

You might also be asked to describe or analyze the shape of a data set, which can be either symmetric or skewed (asymmetric). Many data sets have a head, where many data points are clustered in one area, and tails, where the number of data points slowly decreases to 0. A data set is skewed in the direction of its longer tail.

Symmetric	**Skewed to the Left**	**Skewed to the Right**
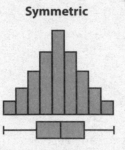	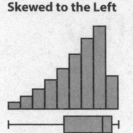	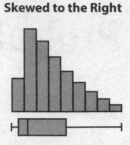
The data is evenly spread out.	The tail is longer on the left.	The tail is longer on the right.
mean ≈ median	mean < median	mean > median

Probability

Probability is a fraction or decimal between 0 and 1 comparing the number of desired outcomes to the number of total possible outcomes. A probability of 0 means that an event will never occur, while a probability of 1 means that it will always occur. The probability formula is as follows:

$$\text{Probability} = \frac{\text{Number of desired outcomes}}{\text{Total number of outcomes}}$$

From a two-way table, you can find the probability that a randomly selected data value (be it a person, object, etc.) will fit a certain profile (in a certain age range, married or single, etc.). The key to probability questions on the SAT is making sure that you select the right total to work from. The total number of possible outcomes in the formula is usually dictated by the question stem and is not necessarily the grand total of items in the table.

Statistics Drill

Set $A = \{1, 2, 2, 4, 5\}$
Set $B = \{2, 4, 4, 8, 10\}$

1. The mean of Set A

2. The median of Set A

3. The mode of Set A

4. The range of Set A

5. Which set has the greater standard deviation?

Tables, Statistics, and Probability Practice Set

PROBABILITY: Keep a calculator handy as you work through this practice set, but reserve it for those questions that have a calculator icon next to them—and even on those questions, use it only if you really need it. Questions without the icon are intended to be done without a calculator, to help you prepare for the no-calculator section of the SAT.

Test Score	Class A	Class B
91–100	11	8
81–90	17	13
71–80	16	20
below 70	6	4

1. The given table shows the test score breakdown of the students in Class A and in Class B. Which interval does the median test score for Class A fall into?

   A) 91–100

   B) 81–90

   C) 71–80

   D) below 70

List A	1	2	3	4	5
List B	3	4	5	6	7

2. Which of the following is true regarding the two lists of numbers shown in the table above?

   A) The means are the same, and the standard deviations are the same.

   B) The means are the same, and the standard deviations are different.

   C) The means are different, and the standard deviations are the same.

   D) The means are different, and the standard deviations are different.

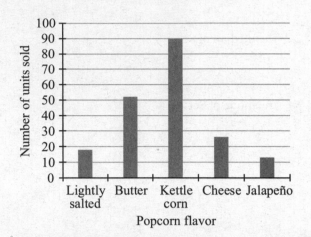

3. The given bar graph shows the number of units sold per popcorn flavor in one morning at the local farmers market. For which two popcorn flavors is the ratio of the number of units sold 1:5 ?

   A) Lightly salted:kettle corn

   B) Kettle corn:cheese

   C) Jalapeño:butter

   D) Cheese:butter

Number of Pins Knocked Down in
30 Frames

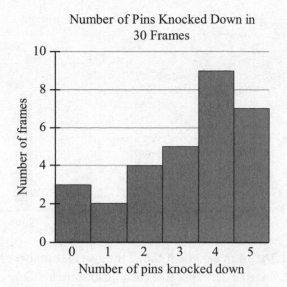

4. Rigo played 30 frames of five-pin bowling. Based on the given histogram, what was Rigo's average number of pins knocked down per frame?

Team	Score	Team	Score
Colts	212	Pirates	110
Cubs	185	Falcons	169
Archers	151	Bruins	199
Cougars	232	Giants	142

5. The given table shows the bowling scores for 8 teams. Based on the table, what is the mean score of the teams?

A) 169

B) 175

C) 177

D) 186

6. If to correct for an error, the score for Team Archers was changed to 251, how does the change affect the mean and median score of the teams?

A) Mean and median will both decrease.

B) Mean will decrease, and median will increase.

C) Mean will increase, and median will decrease.

D) Mean and median will both increase.

Number of Visits to Aquatic Center in One Week

	1–2	3–4	5 or more	Total
Resident	347	203	75	625
Nonresident	169	44	36	249
Total	516	247	111	874

7. The table shows the number of visits to the community aquatic center during one week. If a person is chosen at random from those who visited the aquatic center at least three times that week, what is the probability that person is a resident?

A) $\frac{139}{179}$

B) $\frac{179}{437}$

C) $\frac{625}{874}$

D) $\frac{203}{247}$

Questions 8 and 9 refer to the following stimulus.

Year	Spanish	French	German	Chinese	Total
Freshman	25	12	17	4	58
Sophomore	20	16	13	3	52
Junior	14	16	11	6	47
Senior	10	18	9	9	43
Total	69	62	50	19	200

A random sample of students at a 4-year high school were asked which foreign language class they were currently taking. The results are shown in the table above.

8. Which of the following categories accounts for 10 percent of all respondents?

   A) Freshman taking French

   B) Sophomore taking Spanish

   C) Junior taking German

   D) Senior taking Chinese

9. Which foreign language's senior to sophomore ratio is closest to 3:1 ?

   A) Spanish

   B) French

   C) German

   D) Chinese

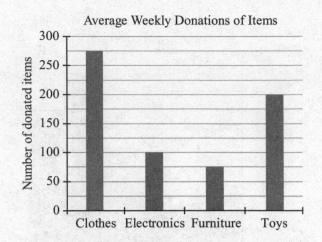

10. The given bar graph shows the average number of donated items per week at a thrift store for four categories. What is the positive difference between the median and the mean number of items donated per category?

11. The results of a nationwide survey of veterinarians reported that 5 percent of dogs that they treated had behavioral problems. Which of the following best explains why the results of the study are unlikely to represent the percentage of all dogs in the nation that have behavioral problems?

    A) Dog owners' descriptions of their pets' behavior are not always accurate.

    B) The survey included only state-licensed veterinarians.

    C) Dogs with behavioral problems could also have physical illnesses.

    D) Veterinarians are more likely to see dogs that have behavioral problems than those that do not.

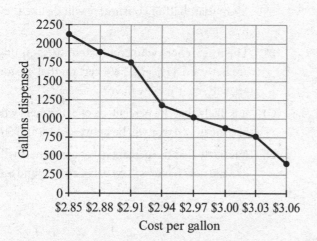

12. A gas station records the number of gallons of regular unleaded fuel dispensed over two weeks. The graph shows the number of gallons of fuel as a function of cost per gallon. For which price bracket is the range of gallons dispensed the greatest?

    A) $2.85 to $2.91

    B) $2.91 to $2.94

    C) $2.94 to $3.03

    D) $3.03 to $3.06

Number of Lunches Purchased per Week

Grade	0	1	2	3 or more	Total
First	14	3	13	47	77
Second	20	8	8	37	73
Third	29	5	2	39	75
Total	63	16	25	121	225

13. The table above records the number of school lunches purchased per week for a cohort of elementary school students. If a student is chosen at random, what is the probability that the student is either a first or second grader who did not buy school lunch that week?

    A) $\frac{34}{225}$

    B) $\frac{17}{77}$

    C) $\frac{63}{225}$

    D) $\frac{34}{63}$

14. The sum of the eight values in a data set is 40. If two additional values that total 20 are added to the data set, what is the change in the mean from the original data set?

    A) 1

    B) 2

    C) 3

    D) 5

15. A machine produces 200 products per hour at a constant rate. Which of the following sampling procedures would be the most effective in determining the overall quality of an eight-hour production run?

    A) Test 10 products at the beginning of the day and 10 at the end of the day.

    B) Test 6 consecutive products every hour.

    C) Test 20 products at some time during the production run.

    D) Test 6 products per hour at random intervals.

	Voted for Sam	Did not vote for Sam
Attended final debate	64	47
Did not attend final debate	80	24

16. The table shows the results of the student council president race. If a student is chosen at random, what is the probability that the student did not attend the final debate and voted for Sam?

    A) $\frac{24}{215}$

    B) $\frac{6}{31}$

    C) $\frac{24}{71}$

    D) $\frac{16}{43}$

Questions 17 and 18 refer to the following table.

Most Recently Watched Movie Genres

Age (years) of movie-goer	Action	Romance	Science Fiction	Comedy	Total
15–24	65	20	45	31	161
25–34	49	27	42	22	140
35–44	40	25	43	18	126
45–54	15	7	38	13	73
Total	169	79	168	84	500

17. Five hundred movie-goers were asked which movie genre they last watched. The results are shown in the table. What percent of the movie-goers surveyed were those aged 45–54 who last watched a romance or a comedy film?

    A) 4.0%

    B) 14.6%

    C) 27.4%

    D) 32.6%

18. Which age group's ratio of action to romance is closest to the total's ratio of action to romance?

    A) 15–24

    B) 25–34

    C) 35–44

    D) 45–54

19. A beverage company tested a new flavor of fruit drink on a random, representative sample of consumers. The company found that 47 percent of consumers surveyed liked the new flavor, with a margin of error of 6 percent. Which of the following is the most appropriate conclusion about how consumers in general will like the new flavor?

    A) More than half of consumers will dislike the new flavor.

    B) The researchers who conducted the sampling are between 41% and 53% certain that customers will like the new flavor.

    C) It is likely that the percentage of consumers who like the new flavor will be between 44% and 50%.

    D) It is likely that the percentage of consumers who like the new flavor will be between 41% and 53%.

Number of vehicles owned	Number of Company A employees	Number of Company B employees
0	2	5
1	8	4
2	12	15
3	3	1

20. Two companies each randomly selected 25 employees and asked each of them how many vehicles they own. The results are shown in the table above. If there are a total of 575 employees at Company A and 825 employees at Company B, which of the following statements is most accurate?

A) The total number of employees who own 3 vehicles at Company A is expected to be 2 more than at Company B.

B) The total number of employees who own 3 vehicles at Company A is expected to be 36 more than at Company B.

C) The total number of employees who own 3 vehicles at Company B is expected to be 36 more than at Company A.

D) The total number of employees who own 3 vehicles is expected to be equal at the two companies.

Answers and Explanations

Statistics Drill

1. $\dfrac{1+2+2+4+5}{5} = \dfrac{14}{5} = 2.8$

2. 2 is the middle number, so it is the median.

3. 2 is the only value that appears twice, so it is the mode.

4. The range is $5 - 1 = 4$.

5. Set *B* has a greater spread among the values and hence the greater standard deviation.

Tables, Statistics, and Probability Practice Set

1. B

Difficulty: Medium

Strategic Advice: Calculate the total number of students in Class A. The median will be the middle value when the scores are arranged in ascending or descending order.

Getting to the Answer: There are a total of $11 + 17 + 16 + 6 = 50$ students in Class A, so the median value will be the average of the 25th and 26th scores. There are 11 students who scored 91 or above and 17 who scored 81–90. Thus, the 12th through 29th highest scores fall in the 81–90 range. This includes the 25th and 26th highest scores, so **(B)** is correct.

2. C

Difficulty: Medium

Strategic Advice: The choices deal with the mean and standard deviation of the two lists, so evaluate those measures.

Getting to the Answer: Each number in List B is 2 greater than the corresponding value in List A, so the mean of List B is greater; eliminate (A) and (B). Standard deviation is a measure of the spread or dispersion of a group of values. In both lists, the values are all spaced one apart, so the standard deviations of the two lists are the same. Therefore, **(C)** is correct.

3. A

Difficulty: Medium

Strategic Advice: Notice that none of the values of the bars in the graph are over 100. This indicates that the part of the ratio, 1:5, that equals 1 must be less than $100 \div 5 = 20$ units sold.

Getting to the Answer: According to the graph, only lightly salted and jalapeño have less than 20 units sold. Eliminate (B) and (D). Try (A). The ratio of the number of units sold for lightly salted to kettle corn is approximately 18:90, which reduces to 1:5. Choice **(A)** is correct. Note that the ratio of jalapeño to butter is about 13:52, which reduces to 1:4. So (C) is incorrect.

4. 3.2

Difficulty: Medium

Strategic Advice: The average number of pins knocked down per frame is the total number of pins knocked down in the 30 frames divided by the total number of frames.

Getting to the Answer: Use the histogram to determine the total number of pins knocked down in Rigo's 30 frames of bowling. In 3 of the frames, Rigo knocked down 0 pins, which is a total of $0 \times 3 = 0$ pins. In 2 of the frames, Rigo knocked down 1 pin, which is a total of $1 \times 2 = 2$ pins. Thus, the total number of pins Rigo knocked down is $(0 \times 3) + (1 \times 2) + (2 \times 4) + (3 \times 5) + (4 \times 9) + (5 \times 7) = 96$. Since the total number of frames is 30, the average number of pins knocked down per frame is $\dfrac{96}{30} = 3.2$. Grid in **3.2**.

5. B

Difficulty: Easy

Strategic Advice: The mean is the average, which is the total of all the values divided by the number of values.

Getting to the Answer: For all 8 teams, the mean is $\dfrac{212 + 110 + 185 + 169 + 151 + 199 + 232 + 142}{8} = \dfrac{1,400}{8} = 175$. Choice **(B)** is correct.

6. D

Difficulty: Medium

Strategic Advice: The choices deal with mean and median, so examine the effect of the change on these measures.

Getting to the Answer: The effect on mean is straightforward; adding 100 points while not changing the number of teams will increase the mean. In order to analyze the effect of the change on the median, start by arranging all the original scores in order: 110, 142, 151, 169, 185, 199, 212, 232. The median is the average of 169 and 185. When the error is corrected, the lowest five scores are 110, 142, 169, 185, and 199. So, the new fourth and fifth terms are 185 and 199. The new median is the average of 185 and 199, so that is an increase. Choice **(D)** is correct.

You may have analyzed this by noting that changing 151 to 251 would result in a shift in the scores that make up the median. Because no scores are identical, this automatically increases the median.

7. A

Difficulty: Medium

Strategic Advice: Determine the applicable numbers of people who fit the desired parameters by referring to the applicable cells in the table, and then apply the probability formula, $P = \dfrac{\text{number of desired outcomes}}{\text{number of total outcomes}}$.

Getting to the Answer: The denominator of the probability calculation is the total number of people who visited 3 or more times, which is the total of the second and third columns of numbers, $247 + 111 = 358$. The numerator is the number of people in those two columns who are residents, $203 + 75 = 278$. The probability that a resident is chosen at random from the applicable group is $\dfrac{278}{358} = \dfrac{139}{179}$. The correct answer is **(A)**.

8. B

Difficulty: Easy

Strategic Advice: Calculate the number of students that represent 10% of all respondents, then examine the choices to see which cell equals that value.

Getting to the Answer: There are 200 respondents, so 10% of that is 20 students, since $200 \times 0.1 = 20$. There is only one cell with that value, Sophomores taking Spanish, so **(B)** is correct.

9. D

Difficulty: Easy

Strategic Advice: Calculate the ratios using data for the language in each choice. Unless one of the choices is exactly a 3:1 ratio, you'll need to check all the choices.

Getting to the Answer: The senior to sophomore ratio for Spanish is 10:20, or 1:2. Keep (A) for now. The ratio for French is 18:16, or 9:8. Eliminate (A) because (B) is closer. The ratio for German is 9:13. Eliminate (C). The ratio for Chinese is 9:3, or 3:1. Choice **(D)** is correct.

10. 12.5

Difficulty: Medium

Strategic Advice: The mean is the sum of the values divided by the number of values, and the median is the value that is in the middle of the set when the values are arranged in ascending order.

Getting to the Answer: According to the graph, the numbers of items donated per category are clothes, 275; electronics, 100; furniture, 75; and toys, 200. To find the median, list the data points in ascending order: 75, 100, 200, 275. Since there are an even number of data points, the median is the average of the two middle values: $\dfrac{100 + 200}{2} = \dfrac{300}{2} = 150$. The mean is the total number of items donated divided by the number of donation categories: $\dfrac{75 + 100 + 200 + 275}{4} = \dfrac{650}{4} = 162.5$. The positive difference is $|150 - 162.5| = \textbf{12.5}$.

11. D

Difficulty: Medium

Strategic Advice: Samples must be representative of the entire population, unbiased, and of sufficient size in order to be predictive of the entire population. Look for a choice that points out a discrepancy in one or more of these parameters.

Getting to the Answer: Choice **(D)** points out that dogs treated by veterinarians are more likely to have behavioral problems than dogs in general and is the correct choice.

12. B

Difficulty: Medium

Strategic Advice: You do not need to determine the exact values of the numbers of gallons dispensed for each price bracket listed in the answer choices. Use visual estimation to determine the range for each price bracket listed.

Getting to the Answer: Range is the difference between the highest and lowest values. Notice that the difference between the highest and lowest data points in the price bracket between $2.85 and $2.91 is less than two tick marks, which represents 500 gallons. For the interval $2.91 to $2.94, the difference between the data points is more than two tick marks, which is greater than 500. The range of gallons dispensed for both the $2.94 to $3.03 and $3.03 to $3.06 price brackets is also less than two tick marks. Thus, the greatest range occurs in the $2.91 to $2.94 price bracket. **(B)** is correct.

13. A

Difficulty: Medium

Strategic Advice: Refer to the cells in the table to calculate the number of desired outcomes and the number of total outcomes for the population being considered.

Getting to the Answer: The probability formula is probability $= \frac{\text{number of desired outcomes}}{\text{total number of outcomes}}$. The desired outcomes, first and second graders who didn't buy lunch, is $14 + 20 = 34$. The total number of outcomes from which the random student is selected is 225, all the students in the table. So the probability is $\frac{34}{225}$, which is **(A)**.

14. A

Difficulty: Medium

Strategic Advice: Use the average formula to determine the means before and after the two values are added, then find the difference between them.

Getting to the Answer: The average formula is average $= \frac{\text{sum of terms}}{\text{number of terms}}$. Before the new values were added, the average was $\frac{40}{8} = 5$. Adding two values that total 20 changes the average to $\frac{40 + 20}{8 + 2} = \frac{60}{10} = 6$. Thus, the increase is $6 - 5 = 1$, so **(A)** is correct.

15. D

Difficulty: Easy

Strategic Advice: In order to be predictive of the overall quality of the entire production run, the samples must be truly random and must be of sufficient size to be significant. Select the choice that best meets the requirements.

Getting to the Answer: Choice (A) is a sample size of 20, but the testing occurs only at the beginning and end of the day, so it is not random. Eliminate (A). There are more samples, 48, in (B), and the intervals are more random, so hold on to (B) for now. The procedure in (C) tests only 20 products, and they are all taken at the same time, so the sample size and randomness are less than in (B). The difference between (D) and (B) is crucial. Both involve testing 6 samples per hour, but the samples in (B) are consecutive while those in (D) are at random intervals. Therefore, the procedure in **(D)** is more random and thus more representative of the entire production run.

16. D

Difficulty: Easy

Strategic Advice: Find the cell in the table that reflects the number of students who did not attend the final debate and who voted for Sam. Divide that number by the total number of students.

Getting to the Answer: The number of students who did not attend the final debate and who voted for Sam is 80. The total number of students is $64 + 47 + 80 + 24 = 215$. So the probability is $\frac{80}{215} = \frac{16}{43}$, which matches **(D)**.

17. A

Difficulty: Medium

Strategic Advice: Find and add the numbers for romance and comedy among those aged 45–54, then divide that sum by the total population.

Getting to the Answer: In the row for ages 45–54, the cell for romance films is 7 and the cell for comedy films is 13, so there were a total of 20 movie-goers who met the question's criteria. The population from which the random sample is taken is that of the entire survey, 500. So the percent in question is $\frac{20}{500} = \frac{4}{100} = 4\%$. Choice **(A)** is correct.

18. D

Difficulty: Medium

Strategic Advice: Refer to the cells in the table to calculate the ratios for each age category. Then compare the results for each of the four age categories to the ratio for the total of all movie-goers sampled.

Getting to the Answer: The ratio of action to romance for the total sample is $\frac{169}{79}$, which is a bit greater than 2:1. The ratio for ages 15–24 is 65:20. For ages 25–34, the ratio is 49:27. The applicable ratio for ages 35–44 is 40:25. Finally, the ratio for ages 45–54 is 15:7. Eliminate (B) and (C) because they are much less than 2:1. (A) is greater than 3:1, and **(D)** is, like the overall ratio, just a bit more than 2:1, so that is the correct choice.

19. D

Difficulty: Medium

Strategic Advice: If a sampling is properly done, the results can be applied to the population as a whole, plus or minus the margin of error.

Getting to the Answer: The percentage of consumers in general is most likely to be between 47% less the margin of error and 47% plus the margin of error. This gives a range of 41% to 53%, which matches **(D)**. Choice (C) is actually a 3% margin of error.

20. B

Difficulty: Medium

Strategic Advice: To extrapolate sample results to a larger group, multiply the values in the sample by the ratio of the size of the total group to the size of the sample.

Getting to the Answer: For Company A, the ratio of total to sampled employees is $\frac{575}{25} = \frac{23}{1}$. The ratio for Company B is $\frac{825}{25} = \frac{33}{1}$.

The choices all involve a comparison between the predicted number of 3-car owners at the companies, so focus on the bottom row of the table. The number of sampled employees at Company A who own 3 vehicles is 3, so the expected value for all Company A employees is $23 \times 3 = 69$. The number of sampled employees at Company B who own 3 vehicles is 1, so the expected value for all Company B employees is $33 \times 1 = 33$, which is 36 less than the expected value for Company A. Choices (B) and (C) both cite a difference of 36, but **(B)** correctly states that the prediction for Company A is greater.

CHAPTER 7

Scatterplots

Scatterplot Basics

Some students tend to associate scatterplots with complicated statistical analyses and consequently become nervous when they hear they'll likely encounter them on test day. However, these seemingly difficult plots are usually straightforward—if you know what to look for. Below are the fundamental parts of a scatterplot:

- You're already familiar with *x*- and *y*-axes, but something that might be new is their **units**. Most scatterplots based on real data have units on the axes; these are important when drawing conclusions and inferences based on the data.

- The **line of best fit** is drawn through the approximate center of the data points to describe the relationship between the two variables. This line does not need to go through all, or even most, of the data points, but it should accurately reflect the trend of the data with about half the points above the line and half below.

- The **equation of the line of best fit** (also called the **regression equation**) describes the best fit line algebraically. On test day, you'll most likely encounter this equation as linear, quadratic, or exponential, though it can also be other types of equations.

- As with linear equations, lines of best fit associated with real-world data contain valuable information. For example, the **slope** of a linear line of best fit gives the **average rate of change**, and the *y*-intercept represents an **initial amount**.

Modeling Data

The relationship between two variables presented in the form of data may be modeled by functions or equations, which can be used for drawing conclusions and making predictions. Following are the three types of models you are most likely to see:

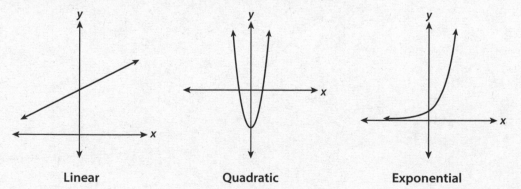

Linear   Quadratic   Exponential

- A **linear model** will always increase (when its slope is positive) or decrease (when its slope is negative) at a constant rate, making it easy to spot.

- A **quadratic model** is U-shaped and the trend of the data changes from decreasing to increasing, or vice versa. The graph of a quadratic equation takes the shape of a parabola, which has either a minimum or a maximum called the vertex (although it is sometimes not shown on the graph). A parabola opens upward when the coefficient of the x^2 term is positive, and it opens downward when the coefficient of the x^2 term is negative.

- An **exponential model** typically starts with a gradual rate of change that increases significantly over time. Unlike a quadratic model, the trend of the data does not change direction, and the graph does not have a vertex.

Scatterplots Practice Set

> **DIRECTIONS:** Keep a calculator handy as you work through this practice set, but reserve it for those questions that have a calculator icon next to them—and even on those questions, use it only if you really need it. Questions without the icon are intended to be done without a calculator, to help you prepare for the no-calculator section of the SAT.

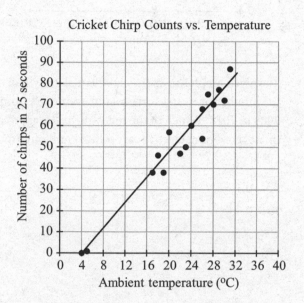

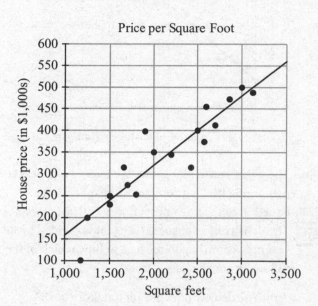

1. The given scatterplot shows cricket chirp counts at 16 temperatures. Based on the line of best fit, approximately how many chirp counts would there be in 75 seconds at 34 degrees Celsius?

   A) 15

   B) 90

   C) 180

   D) 270

2. The given scatterplot shows house prices per square foot. If f represents the number of square feet and p represents the house price in dollars, which of the following equations could be the line of best fit?

   A) $p = 0.16f$

   B) $p = 0.16f + 160$

   C) $p = 160f$

   D) $p = 160f + 160$

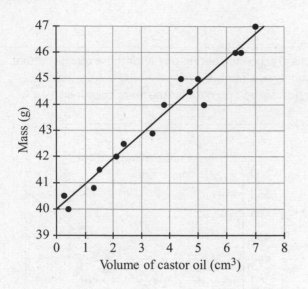

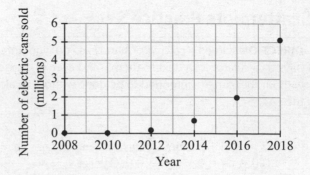

3. The given scatterplot shows the masses of a beaker containing varying volumes of castor oil. The equation of the line of best fit is $y = 0.961x + 40$. The density of a substance is its mass divided by its volume. According to the best fit line, which of the following conclusions is true?

   A) The density of castor oil is 0.961 g cm^{-3}.

   B) The density of castor oil is 40 g cm^{-3}.

   C) The density of the beaker is 40 g cm^{-3}.

   D) The mass of the beaker alone is 0.961 g cm^{-3}.

4. The given graph shows the exponential growth of the number of electric cars sold in even years from 2008 to 2018. Which of the following is the approximate number of electric cars sold, in millions, in 2015?

   A) 0.4

   B) 0.8

   C) 1.2

   D) 1.8

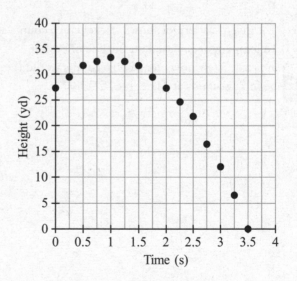

5. The given scatterplot shows the height of a diver above the water. Which of the following equations best describes the data in the scatterplot?

   A) $y = -5.294x^2 + 10.718x + 3.5$

   B) $y = -5.294x^2 + 10.718x + 27.438$

   C) $y = 5.294x^2 + 10.718x + 3.5$

   D) $y = 5.294x^2 + 10.718x + 27.438$

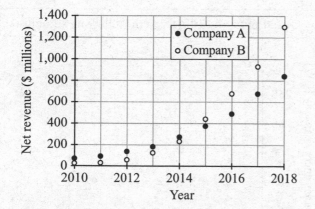

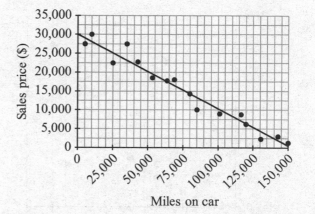

6. The given scatterplot shows the net revenue in millions of dollars for Company A and Company B from 2010 to 2018. Which of the following statements is true?

   A) Every 2 years from 2010 to 2018, the net revenue of Company A increases by 150 million dollars.

   B) The net revenue of Company B is greater than the net revenue of Company A for the even years from 2010 to 2014 inclusive.

   C) In the interval from 2014 to 2018, the rate of change of Company A's net revenue is of greater magnitude than the rate of change of Company B's net revenue.

   D) In the interval from 2014 to 2018, the rate of change of Company B's net revenue is of greater magnitude than the rate of change of Company A's net revenue.

7. The given scatterplot shows the sales price in dollars of cars sold in the past month at a used car lot as a function of the number of miles on the car. A linear model, represented by the line of best fit, $y = -0.197x + 29,995$, is used to predict a car's sales price. By how much did the model overpredict the sales price of the car that was sold for $10,000 ? (Ignore the dollar sign when gridding in your answer.)

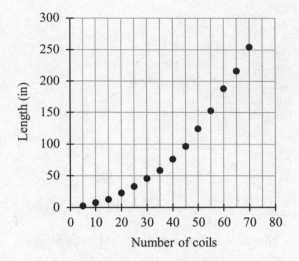

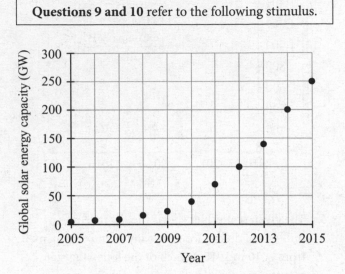

8. The given scatterplot shows the length of a hanging spring as a function of the number of coils. Which of the following statements correctly describes the data?

A) A linear model would best fit the data, while a quadratic model would underestimate the length of the spring when the number of coils is less than 20.

B) A linear model would best fit the data, while a quadratic model would overestimate the length of the spring when the number of coils is between 60 and 80.

C) A quadratic model would best fit the data, while a linear model would underestimate the length of the spring when the number of coils is between 60 and 80.

D) A quadratic model would best fit the data, while a linear model would overestimate the length of the spring when the number of coils is between 60 and 80.

9. The given graph shows the global solar energy capacity in gigawatts from 2005 to 2015.

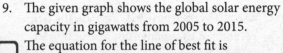 The equation for the line of best fit is $y = 23.682x - 47,522$. Which of the following statements correctly compares the value predicted by the equation and the actual global solar energy capacity value in the scatterplot?

A) The value predicted by the equation is less than the actual global solar energy capacity value in 2006.

B) The value predicted by the equation is less than the actual global solar energy capacity value in 2010.

C) The value predicted by the equation is less than the actual global solar energy capacity value in 2012.

D) The value predicted by the equation is greater than the actual global solar energy capacity value in 2015.

10. During which interval is the average rate of change for global solar energy capacity the greatest?

A) 2005–2009

B) 2010–2012

C) 2013–2014

D) 2014–2015

Answers and Explanations

Scatterplots Practice Set

1. D

Difficulty: Easy

Strategic Advice: Extrapolate the data by extending the line of best fit to 34°C. Then from that point, draw a horizontal line to the y-axis.

Getting to the Answer: The number of chirps in 25 seconds at 34°C is approximately 90. Thus, in 75 seconds, the number of chirps at 34°C would be approximately $3 \times 90 = 270$. Choice **(D)** is correct.

Alternatively, you could determine the equation of the line of best fit using two points on the line, for example, (4, 0) and (24, 60). The slope of the line of best fit is $m = \frac{60 - 0}{24 - 4} = \frac{60}{20} = 3$, and the y-intercept is $b = 0 - 4(3) = -12$. Thus, at 34°C, $y = 3(34) - 12 = 90$ chirps in 25 seconds. In 75 seconds, the number of chirps would approximately be $3 \times 90 = 270$.

2. C

Difficulty: Medium

Strategic Advice: To determine the equation of the line of best fit, use two points on the line such as (1,250, 200) and (2,500, 400).

Getting to the Answer: The slope of the line is $m = \frac{400 - 200}{2,500 - 1,250} = \frac{200}{1,250} = 0.16$. The axes on the scatterplot do not start at 0, so use the slope and one point to find the y-intercept. The y-intercept is $b = 400 - 0.16(2,500) = 0$. Note that p represents the house price in dollars, so you need to multiply the slope, 0.16, which is in thousands of dollars per square foot, by 1,000. Thus, the equation of the line of best fit could be $p = 160f$. Choice **(C)** is correct.

3. A

Difficulty: Medium

Strategic Advice: Recall that the y-intercept is the y-value when x is 0.

Getting to the Answer: The y-intercept of the equation of the line of best fit is 40 g when 0 g of castor oil have been added to the beaker. Thus, the y-intercept represents the mass of the beaker alone. The slope of the

equation of the line of best fit is mass over volume, or density, of castor oil. Thus, 0.961 g cm^{-3} represents the density of castor oil. Choice **(A)** is correct.

4. C

Difficulty: Easy

Strategic Advice: Draw a best fit curve to model the data and then interpolate.

Getting to the Answer: The curve of best fit models exponential growth. Draw a horizontal line from where the best fit curve intersects the line for 2015. According to the graph, the number of electric cars sold in 2015 falls between 1 and 2 but closer to 1. Choice **(C)** is correct.

5. B

Difficulty: Easy

Strategic Advice: Identify the shape of the data and y-intercept.

Getting to the Answer: The shape of the data is a downward opening parabola. For a quadratic in the form $ax^2 + bx + c$, c is the y-intercept, and the parabola opens downward when $a < 0$. Thus, the coefficient in front of x^2 is negative. Eliminate (C) and (D). According to the scatterplot, the y-intercept falls between positive 25 and 30, so **(B)** is correct. Note that 3.5 is the x-intercept.

6. D

Difficulty: Hard

Strategic Advice: For the interval given in each answer choice, draw a best fit line through the data and then compare the slopes to compare the rate of change.

Getting to the Answer: The rate of change of Company A's net revenue every 2 years is not constant, so eliminate (A). For the even years from 2010 to 2014 inclusive, the net revenue of Company A is greater than the net revenue of Company B, so eliminate (B). Choices (C) and (D) both compare the slopes from 2014 and 2018. According to the graph, the slopes for Company B are greater from 2014 to 2018. Thus, **(D)** is correct.

7.   3250

Difficulty: Medium

Strategic Advice: Determine how many miles were on the car that was sold for $10,000. Then calculate the predicted sale price using the equation for the line of best fit, and find the difference between the predicted and actual sale price.

Getting to the Answer: According to the scatterplot, the car that sold for $10,000 had 85,000 miles on it. Plug this value in for x in the equation $y = -0.197x + 29,995$ to calculate the predicated sale price: $y = -0.197(85,000) + 29,995 = 13,250$. The difference between the predicted and actual sale price is $13,250 - $10,000 = **$3,250**.

8.   C

Difficulty: Medium

Strategic Advice: Remember that the line (or curve) of best fit should be drawn so that about half the data points fall above it and about half fall below.

Getting to the Answer: The data points do not form a straight line; eliminate (A) and (B). The shape of the data can be modeled by the right side of an upward-opening parabola. To decide between (C) and (D), sketch a line of best fit through the data.

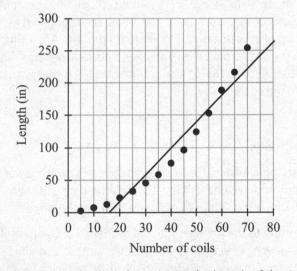

The linear model will underestimate the length of the coil when the number of coils is between 60 and 80. Thus, **(C)** is correct.

9.   A

Difficulty: Hard

Strategic Advice: Determine two points that fall on the graph of $y = 23.682x - 47,522$, and draw in the line on the scatterplot to compare the predicted values to the actual values.

Getting to the Answer: At 200, the equation predicts $23.682(200) - 47,522 = -15.908$, and at 2015, the equation predicts $23.682(2015) - 47,522 = 197.23$. The graph of the line is below the points before 2006, above the points from 2008 to 2013, and below the points after 2014.

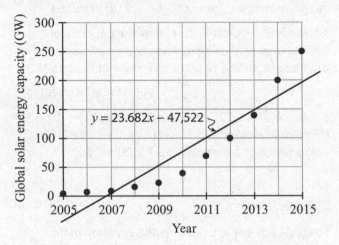

Thus, **(A)** is correct. The value predicted by the model is less than the actual global solar energy capacity value in 2006.

10.   C

Difficulty: Medium

Strategic Advice: Identify the general trend of the data, and use the endpoints of the intervals in the answer choices to estimate the rate of change for global solar energy capacity.

Getting to the Answer: The general trend of the data is that it increases in a nonlinear way, so the average rate of change appears to be greater after 2012. Eliminate (A) and (B). For (C), the vertical distance between the data points at 2013 and 2014 is greater than one tick mark, whereas for (D), the vertical distance between the data points at 2014 and 2015 is one tick mark. Since the horizontal interval for (C) and for (D) is the same (1 year), (C) has a greater average rate of change. Therefore, **(C)** is correct.

CHAPTER 8

Functions

Function Notation

Functions act as rules that transform inputs into outputs, and they differ from equations in that each input can have only one corresponding output. The **domain** of a function is the set of input values (typically x) for which the function is defined, and the **range** of a function is the set of corresponding output values (typically y). The notation $f(3)$ is read "f of 3," and it means the output value when 3 is substituted for x.

Graphical Representation of Functions

Graphically, an input and corresponding output create ordered pairs of the form $(x, f(x))$. If given the graph of a function and asked to evaluate $f(3)$, locate 3 along the x-axis, trace up (or down) to the function's graph, and find the corresponding y-value. Conversely, suppose you're given a graph and asked to find the value of x for which $f(x) = 3$. Because $f(x)$ represents the output value, or range, translate this as "When does the y-value equal 3 ?" To answer the question, find 3 on the y-axis this time, and trace over to the function's graph. The corresponding x-value is your answer.

Nested Functions

Questions involving nested functions require you to find the output of a function at a given input value and then plug the result into another function to get the final answer. Nested functions could be written as $f(g(x))$ or $(f \circ g)(x)$. Regardless of which form you're given, always start with the function that is closest to the x, and work your way outward. Keep in mind that $f(g(x))$ is very rarely the same as $g(f(x))$, so order definitely matters.

Relationships between Variables

When analyzing the graph of a function or an interval (a specific segment) of the function, the relationship between the x- and y-values can be described as follows:

- Increasing: The y-values *increase* as the corresponding x-values increase.
- Decreasing: The y-values *decrease* as the corresponding x-values increase.
- Constant: The y-values *remain the same* as the x-values increase. The graph of a constant function is a horizontal line.

Transformations

A transformation occurs when a change is made to a function's equation and/or graph. Transformations include translations (moving a graph up/down, left/right), reflections (flips about an axis or other line), and expansions/compressions (stretching or squashing horizontally or vertically). The following table provides transformation rules for altering a given function $f(x)$.

Algebraic Change	Corresponding Graphical Change
$f(x)$	N/A—original function
$f(x) + a$	$f(x)$ moves up a units
$f(x) - a$	$f(x)$ moves down a units
$f(x + a)$	$f(x)$ moves left a units
$f(x - a)$	$f(x)$ moves right a units
$-f(x)$	$f(x)$ is reflected vertically over the x-axis (top-to-bottom)
$f(-x)$	$f(x)$ is reflected horizontally over the y-axis (left-to-right)
$af(x)$ for $0 < a < 1$	$f(x)$ undergoes vertical compression
$af(x)$ for $a > 1$	$f(x)$ undergoes vertical expansion
$f(ax)$ for $0 < a < 1$	$f(x)$ undergoes horizontal expansion
$f(ax)$ for $a > 1$	$f(x)$ undergoes horizontal compression

Note: One way to think about transformations is that if the transformation is "with the x," then a horizontal change occurs. Keep in mind that horizontal changes are the opposite of what you might expect: $f(x + a)$ describes a move a units to the *left*, while $f(x - a)$ describes a move a units to the *right*. If the transformation is not "with the x," a vertical change occurs (vertical changes do work as you would expect).

Functions Drill

1. If $f(x) = x^2 - 5x + 8$, what is the value of $f(6)$?

2. A tutor charges a \$25 flat fee plus \$50 per hour. Write the function that describes her fees in terms of the number of hours, h.

3. If $f(x) = 2x^2 + 3x - 12$, what is $f(x - 4)$?

4. If $f(x) = 4(x - 3)$, for what value of x is $\dfrac{1}{f(x)}$ undefined?

5. If $f(x) = 3x^2 - kx + 5$, what is $f(4) - f(2)$?

6. If $f(x) = 3x^2 - kx + 5$, and $f(3) = 11$, what is the value of k ?

x	y
−1	−1
0	2
1	5
2	8

7. If y is a function of x, based on the data above, what is $f(x)$?

8. If $f(x) = \dfrac{x-1}{3}$ and $g(x) = 3x + 7$, what is $f(g(x))$?

9. $f(3) = 2, f(5) = 4, g(2) = 5$, and $g(4) = 3$. What is the value of $g(f(5))$?

10. $f(x) = ax^2 - 12, g(x) = 2x + 3$, and $f(3) = 24$. What is the value of $g(f(2))$?

Functions Practice Set

DIRECTIONS: Keep a calculator handy as you work through this practice set, but reserve it for those questions that have a calculator icon next to them—and even on those questions, use it only if you really need it. Questions without the icon are intended to be done without a calculator, to help you prepare for the no-calculator section of the SAT.

1. If $g(x) = -3x + 6$, what is $g(-3)$?

   A) 3

   B) 9

   C) 15

   D) 18

x	2	4	6	8
$g(x)$	−6	−7	−8	−9

2. The table above shows some values of the linear function g. Which of the following defines g ?

   A) $g(x) = -2x - 10$

   B) $g(x) = -\dfrac{x}{2} - 5$

   C) $g(x) = -\dfrac{x}{2} - 2$

   D) $g(x) = 4x - 10$

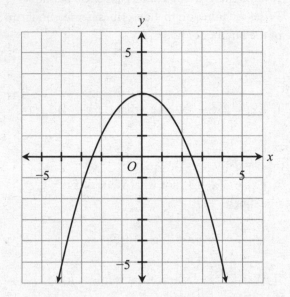

3. The figure above is the graph of $f(x)$ in the xy-plane. The function g is defined as $f(x - 2)$. At what value of x is $g(x) = 3$?

4. If for all non-zero values of y, $g(y) = \dfrac{8}{6y^2} - 7$, what is $g\left(\dfrac{2}{3}\right)$?

    A) -4

    B) 0

    C) 20

    D) 25

5. If function f satisfies $f(5) = 7$ and $f(6) = 10$, and function g satisfies $g(6) = 6$ and $g(10) = 5$, what is the value of $f(g(6))$?

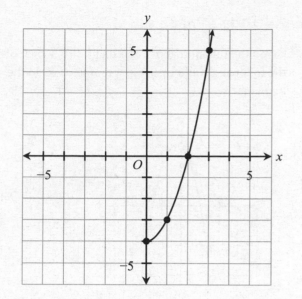

6. The graph of $y = f(x)$ is shown in the xy-plane. What is the value of $f(x)$ when $2x + 5 = 11$?

$$f(x) = \frac{-5}{x^2 - 2x - 15}$$

7. The function f above is undefined for which of the following values of x?

    A) -5

    B) 0

    C) 3

    D) 5

$$y = (x + k)(2 - x)$$

8. Given the function above and that $k > 0$, which of the following could be the graph of $y = f(x)$ in the xy-plane?

A)

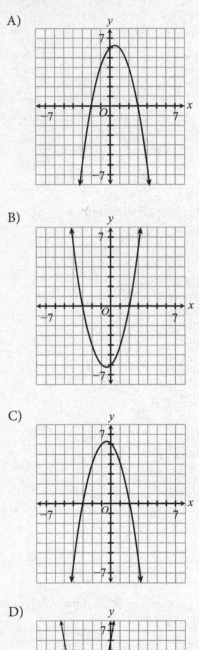

B)

C)

D)

$$g(t) = -16t^2 + 32t + x$$

9. In the function above, x is a constant. If $g(1) = 144$, what is the value of $g(3)$?

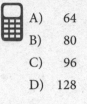

   A)   64

   B)   80

   C)   96

   D)   128

10. If $f(y) = -2^y - \dfrac{12}{y}$, what is $f(-4)$?

   A) $-3\dfrac{1}{16}$

   B) $-2\dfrac{15}{16}$

   C) $2\dfrac{1}{16}$

   D) $2\dfrac{15}{16}$

m	0	3	5	7	10
$k(m)$	−21	0	4	0	−21

11. The table above shows some values of the quadratic function k. Which of the following defines k ?

   A) $k(m) = -m^2 - 10m - 21$

   B) $k(m) = -m^2 + 10m - 21$

   C) $k(m) = -m^2 + 10m + 21$

   D) $k(m) = m^2 - 10m - 21$

$$f(x) = -3x + 5$$
$$g(x) = 2 + f(x)$$

12. For the given functions f and g, what is the value of $g(1)$?

   A)   1

   B)   2

   C)   3

   D)   4

$$f(x) = \frac{1}{(x+2)^2 - 3(x+2) - 10}$$

13. The function f above is undefined for which of the following values of x ?

    A) -4

    B) -3

    C) -2

    D) 4

x	0	1	2	3	4	5
f(x)	2	3	5	9	17	33

16. The table above shows some values of the exponential function f. Which of the following could be f ?

    A) $f(x) = x^2 + 1$

    B) $f(x) = x^2 + 2$

    C) $f(x) = 2^x + 1$

    D) $f(x) = 2^{x+1}$

x	−2	0	2	9
j(x)	26	18	0	0

14. The table above shows some values of the quadratic function j. Which of the following defines j ?

    A) $j(x) = (x+2)^2 + 26$

    B) $j(x) = (x-18)^2$

    C) $j(x) = (x+2)(x+9)$

    D) $j(x) = (x-9)(x-2)$

17. If $k(x) = \dfrac{6x}{-3x^2}$ for all values of x greater than 1, what is the value of $k(2x-1)$?

    A) $\dfrac{3(2x-1)}{-6x^2 + 6x - 1}$

    B) $\dfrac{2(2x-1)}{12x^2 - 12x + 3}$

    C) $\dfrac{2}{-2x+1}$

    D) $\dfrac{2}{-4x+1}$

a	3	4	8	11
f(a)	2.5	3	5	6.5

15. Some values of the linear function f are shown in the table above. What is the value of $f(6)$?

    A) 4

    B) 6

    C) 8.5

    D) 10

18. The graph of the function g in the xy-plane, where $y = g(x)$, has a y-intercept of $-k$, where k is a positive constant. Which of the following could define the function g ?

    A) $g(x) = -4dx$

    B) $g(x) = -4(d)^x$

    C) $g(x) = (-4d)^x$

    D) $g(x) = 2x^2$

19. If $f(x) = 7x + 3$ and $f(x - b) = 7x - 18$, what is the value of b?

20. Monique sets a cup of very hot coffee on the counter to cool. The rate at which a hot substance cools is directly proportional to the temperature difference between the substance and the surrounding environment. If $f(t)$ is the temperature of the coffee at different times, t, which of the following statements best describes the function f? (Assume that air circulation maintains a constant temperature of the air adjacent to the cup.)

A) The function f is a decreasing linear function.

B) The function f is an increasing linear function.

C) The function f is a decreasing exponential function.

D) The function f is an increasing exponential function.

Answers and Explanations

Functions Drill

1. $f(6) = 6^2 - 5(6) + 8 = 36 - 30 + 8 = 14$

2. $t(h) = 25 + 50h$

3. $f(x-4) = 2(x-4)^2 + 3(x-4) - 12$

   $\qquad = 2(x^2 - 8x + 16) + 3x - 12 - 12$

   $\qquad = 2x^2 - 16x + 32 + 3x - 24$

   $\qquad = 2x^2 - 13x + 8$

4. Undefined when $f(x) = 0$, which occurs at $x = 3$.

5. $\qquad f(4) = 3(4^2) - 4k + 5 = 53 - 4k$

   $\qquad f(2) = 3(2^2) - 2k + 5 = 17 - 2k$

   $f(4) - f(2) = 53 - 4k - (17 - 2k) = 36 - 2k$

6. $3(3^2) - 3k + 5 = 11$

   $\quad 27 - 11 + 5 = 3k$

   $\qquad\quad 21 = 3k$

   $\qquad\quad\ 7 = k$

7. Linear function with a slope of 3 and a y-intercept of 2, so $f(x) = 3x + 2$.

8. $f(g(x)) = \dfrac{(3x+7)-1}{3} = \dfrac{3x+6}{3} = x + 2$

9. $f(5) = 4 \rightarrow g(4) = 3$

10. $a(3^2) - 12 = 24$, so $9a = 36$ and $a = 4$.

    $f(2) = 4(2^2) - 12 = 16 - 12 = 4$. Finally,

    $g(4) = 2(4) + 3 = 11$.

Functions Practice Set

1. C

Difficulty: Easy

Strategic Advice: Plug the given value -3, into the function.

Getting to the Answer: For -3,
$g(-3) = -3(-3) + 6 = 9 + 6 = 15$. Choice (**C**) is correct.

2. B

Difficulty: Medium

Strategic Advice: Given that the function is linear, determine the slope, then plug in a value to find the intercept in order to get an equation in $y = mx + b$ form.

Getting to the Answer: Pick any two pairs of values to find the slope: $\dfrac{-7-(-6)}{4-2} = -\dfrac{1}{2}$. Both (B) and (C) have this slope, so find the y-intercept. Plug in values for x and y from the table, say $(2, -6)$:
$-6 = -\dfrac{1}{2}(2) + b$, and $-6 = -1 + b$. So, $b = -5$. Thus, $y = -\dfrac{1}{2}x - 5$, or $y = -\dfrac{x}{2} - 5$. Choice (**B**) is correct.

3. 2

Difficulty: Medium

Strategic Advice: The function $g(x)$ is merely $f(x)$ shifted 2 units to the right.

Getting to the Answer: The value of $f(x)$ is 3 when $x = 0$. Therefore, the value of $g(x)$ is 0 when $x = 2$.

If you didn't recognize the shift, you could solve with algebra. From the graph, $3 = f(x - 2)$, which is also $f(0)$. So, $x - 2 = 0$, and $x = $ **2**.

4. A

Difficulty: Medium

Getting to the Answer: Plug $\dfrac{2}{3}$ into the given function:

$$g\left(\frac{2}{3}\right) = \frac{8}{6\left(\frac{2}{3}\right)^2} - 7$$

$$= \frac{8\left(\frac{3}{2}\right)^2}{6} - 7$$

$$= \frac{8(9)}{6(4)} - 7$$

$$= 3 - 7 = -4$$

Choice (**A**) is correct.

5.   10

Difficulty: Medium

Strategic Advice: Evaluate the nested functions from inside out.

Getting to the Answer: The stems states that $g(6) = 6$, so $f(g(6))$ simplifies to $f(6)$. Again, per the stem, $f(6) = $ **10**.

6.   5

Difficulty: Medium

Strategic Advice: Solve the equation for x, then refer to the graph to locate the value of y for that x.

Getting to the Answer: The equation $2x + 5 = 11$ simplifies to $2x = 6$, so $x = 3$. Looking at the graph, $y = f(3) = $ **5**.

7.   D

Difficulty: Medium

Strategic Advice: The function is undefined when the denominator is 0. Backsolve to see which choice results in a value of 0 for the denominator.

Getting to the Answer: For (A),
$(-5)^2 - 2(-5) - 15 = 25 + 10 - 15 = 20$.
For (B), $0^2 - 2(0) - 15 = -15$.
For (C), $3^2 - 2(3) - 15 = 9 - 6 - 15 = -12$. So **(D)** is correct; on test day, you would choose it and move on.
For the record, $5^2 - 2(5) - 15 = 25 - 10 - 15 = 0$.

8.   C

Difficulty: Medium

Strategic Advice: Determine whether the coefficient of the x^2 term would be positive or negative if the equation were expanded into the $y = ax^2 + bx + c$ form in order to see whether the parabola should open upward or downward. Then use the x-intercepts to find the correct choice.

Getting to the Answer: Since the x^2 term would be $(x)(-x) = -x^2$, the parabola must open downward; eliminate (B) and (D). The x-intercepts correspond to $y = 0$, which occurs when either factor of the function is 0. For the given equation, that would be when $x = 2$ or $-k$. Only **(C)** has an intercept of $+2$.

9.   B

Difficulty: Hard

Strategic Advice: To find the value of x, solve $g(1) = 144$ for x. Then plug 3 into the complete function.

Getting to the Answer: The equation $g(1) = 144$ is $144 = -16(1^2) + 32(1) + x$, so $x = 144 + 16 - 32 = 128$.
Now solve for $g(3)$:
$g(3) = -16(3^2) + 32(3) + 128 = -144 + 96 + 128 = 80$.
Choice **(B)** is correct.

10.   D

Difficulty: Medium

Strategic Advice: Plug -4 into the function.

Getting to the Answer:
$$f(-4) = -(2^{-4}) - \frac{12}{-4} = -\frac{1}{16} + 3 = 2\frac{15}{16}$$
Choice **(D)** is correct.

11.   B

Difficulty: Hard

Strategic Advice: Choose a pair of values from the table, then plug them into the choices to see which creates a valid equation.

Getting to the Answer: Starting with $m = 0$ and $k(m) = -21$, the constant term is -21 for all but (C). Eliminate (C). Try $m = 3$ and $k(m) = 0$.
For (A), $-(3^2) - 10(3) - 21 = -9 - 30 - 21 = -60$. This is not 0, so eliminate (A).
For (B), $-(3^2) + 10(3) - 21 = -9 + 30 - 21 = 0$, so this could be the correct choice.
For (D), $(3^2) - 10(3) - 21 = 9 - 30 - 21 = -42$. This is not 0, so **(B)** is correct.

12.   D

Difficulty: Medium

Strategic Advice: Solve for $f(1)$, then add 2 to get $g(1)$.

Getting to the Answer: The value of $f(1)$ is $-3(1) + 5 = 2$, so $g(1) = 2 + 2 = 4$. Choice **(D)** is correct.

13. A

Difficulty: Medium

Strategic Advice: The function will be undefined when the denominator is 0. Backsolve by plugging in the choices.

Getting to the Answer: Plug -4 into the denominator: $(-4+2)^2 - 3(-4+2) - 10 = (-2)^2 - 3(-2) - 10 = 4 + 6 - 10 = 0$. No need to proceed further; **(A)** is correct.

14. D

Difficulty: Hard

Strategic Advice: Plug a value for x into the equations for the function shown in the choices to see which produces the correct value for $j(x)$.

Getting to the Answer: Picking 0 for x could be the easiest to calculate. For (A), $j(x) = (0+2)^2 + 26 = 4 + 26 = 30$. This result is not 18, so eliminate (A). $(0 - 18)^2$ clearly isn't 18, so eliminate (B). For (C), $(0 + 2)(0 + 9) = 18$, so (C) could be correct. Finally, (D) is $(0 - 2)(0 - 9) = (-2)(-9) = 18$, so this could also be the correct choice.

Try $x = 2$, in which case $j(x)$ should be 0. For (C), this is $(2 + 2)(2 + 9)$, which clearly isn't zero. **(D)** must be correct. Double-checking (D), you get $(2 - 9)(2 - 2) = (-7)(0) = 0$.

15. A

Difficulty: Medium

Strategic Advice: Since the function is linear, interpolate between known values.

Getting to the Answer: The slope of the function is $\frac{5-3}{8-4} = \frac{2}{4} = \frac{1}{2}$. So since 6 is 2 greater than 4, $f(6)$ is 1 greater than 3, which is 4. Alternatively, you could have noticed that 6 is halfway between 4 and 8, and 4 is halfway between 3 and 5. Choice **(A)** is correct.

16. C

Difficulty: Hard

Strategic Advice: Plug a value for x into the equations for the function shown in the choices to see which produces the correct value for $f(x)$.

Getting to the Answer: Start with the first column, $x = 0$ and $f(x) = 2$.

A) $0^2 + 1 \neq 2$; eliminate.
B) $0^2 + 2 = 2$; keep for now.
C) $2^0 + 1 = 1 + 1 = 2$; keep for now.
D) $2^{0+1} = 2^1 = 2$; keep for now.

You've eliminated only (A), so try the values from another column in the table to test the remaining choices; say $x = 3$ and $f(x) = 9$:

B) $3^2 + 2 \neq 9$; eliminate.
C) $2^3 + 1 = 8 + 1 = 9$; keep.
D) $2^{3+1} = 2^4 \neq 9$; eliminate.

The correct answer is **(C)**.

17. C

Difficulty: Medium

Strategic Advice: Simplify the function, then plug in the given term for x.

Getting to the Answer: The function $\frac{6x}{-3x^2}$ simplifies to $\frac{6}{-3x} = \frac{2}{-x}$. Plugging in $(2x - 1)$ results in $\frac{2}{-(2x-1)} = \frac{2}{-2x+1}$, which is **(C)**.

18. B

Difficulty: Medium

Strategic Advice: At the y-intercept, x is 0. Plug that in as a test for the y-intercept value to see if it can be a negative number, $-k$ given that k is positive.

Getting to the Answer: For (A), the value of $-4dx$ at $x = 0$, must be 0, not $-k$. Eliminate (A). For **(B)**, plugging in $x = 0$ yields $-4(d)^0 = -4(1) = -4$. This is a permissible value for $-k$. For (C), $(-4d)^0 = 1$, and for (D), $2(0)^2 = 0$, so these are both incorrect.

19. 3

Difficulty: Medium

Strategic Advice: Plug $(x - b)$ into the function, $f(x)$, set that equal to $7x - 18$, and solve for b.

Getting to the Answer: Substitute $(x - b)$ for x into $f(x)$ to get $f(x - b) = 7(x - b) + 3$. So $7x - 7b + 3 = 7x - 18$. This simplifies to $-7b + 3 = -18$. Subtract 3 from both sides to get $-7b = -21$, so $b = $ **3**.

20. C

Difficulty: Medium

Strategic Advice: Evaluate the statements using the given information to determine whether the function is increasing or decreasing and whether it is linear or exponential.

Getting to the Answer: Since the coffee is cooling, the temperature is decreasing, so eliminate (B) and (D). The function is exponential because the rate of cooling slows as temperature differential decreases. If the function were linear, the rate of cooling would be constant. Choice **(C)** is correct.

CHAPTER 9

Exponents, Radicals, Polynomials, and Rational Expressions

Exponents

Questions involving exponents often look intimidating, but knowing the rules of exponents provides plenty of shortcuts. Make sure you're comfortable with the following rules and terminology before test day:

- Terminology: The **base** is the value being multiplied by itself, and the **exponent** (written as a superscript) tells you how many times to multiply ($3^5 = 3 \times 3 \times 3 \times 3 \times 3$).
- Multiplying terms with the same base: $a^b \times a^c = a^{(b+c)}$
- Dividing terms with the same base: $\dfrac{a^b}{a^c} = a^{(b-c)}$
- Raising a power to a power: $\left(a^b\right)^c = a^{bc}$
- Raising a product or quotient to a power: $(ab)^c = a^c \times b^c$ and $\left(\dfrac{a}{b}\right)^c = \dfrac{a^c}{b^c}$
- Raising a quantity to the zero power: $a^0 = 1$
- Raising a quantity to a negative power: $a^{-b} = \dfrac{1}{a^b}$ and $\dfrac{1}{a^{-b}} = a^b$

Radicals

Radicals (square roots, cube roots, etc.) can be written using fractional exponents (for example, $\sqrt{x} = x^{\frac{1}{2}}$, $\sqrt[3]{x} = x^{\frac{1}{3}}$, and so on). Fortunately, this means that radicals follow the same rules as exponents:

- Multiplying: $\sqrt{ab} = \sqrt{a} \times \sqrt{b}$ $\left(\text{because } \sqrt{ab} = (ab)^{\frac{1}{2}} = a^{\frac{1}{2}}b^{\frac{1}{2}} = \sqrt{a} \times \sqrt{b}\right)$
- Dividing: $\sqrt{\dfrac{a}{b}} = \dfrac{\sqrt{a}}{\sqrt{b}}$ $\left(\text{because } \sqrt{\dfrac{a}{b}} = \left(\dfrac{a}{b}\right)^{\frac{1}{2}} = \dfrac{a^{\frac{1}{2}}}{b^{\frac{1}{2}}} = \dfrac{\sqrt{a}}{\sqrt{b}}\right)$
- Powers: $a^{\frac{b}{c}} = \sqrt[c]{a^b}$ $\left(\text{because } a^{\frac{b}{c}} = \left(a^{\frac{1}{c}}\right)^b = \left(\sqrt[c]{a}\right)^b\right)$
- Rationalizing a denominator: When a fraction contains a radical in the denominator, multiply the numerator and denominator by the radical in the denominator.

Note: Radicals with different indices (square root versus cube root) can only be multiplied (or divided) by first writing the radicals using fractional exponents. For example, $\sqrt{7} \times \sqrt[3]{7} = 7^{\frac{1}{2}} \times 7^{\frac{1}{3}} = 7^{\frac{1}{2}+\frac{1}{3}} = 7^{\frac{5}{6}} = \sqrt[6]{7^5}$.

Solving Radical Equations

To solve a radical equation, follow these steps:

- Isolate the radical part of the equation.
- Remove the radical using an inverse operation. For example, to remove a square root, square both sides of the equation; to remove a cube root, cube both sides; and so on.
- Solve for the variable. Note: If $x^2 = 81$, then $x = \pm 9$, BUT $\sqrt{81} = 9$ only.
- Check for extraneous (invalid) solutions.

Polynomials

A **polynomial** is an expression or equation with one or more terms consisting of variables with nonnegative integer exponents and coefficients, joined by addition, subtraction, and multiplication. You can combine like terms in polynomials as you did with linear expressions and equations. Adding and subtracting polynomials is straightforward—simply combine like terms, paying careful attention to negative signs. Multiplying polynomials is slightly more involved, requiring a careful distribution of terms followed by combining like terms if possible. You can use FOIL (First, Outer, Inner, Last) when you multiply two binomials.

When a polynomial is written in descending order, the term with the highest power (called the leading term) tells you the basic shape of its graph and how many x-intercepts (also called roots or zeros) its graph can have. To find the zeros of a polynomial equation, factor the equation and set each factor equal to 0. You can have simple zeros and/or multiple zeros. For example, in the equation $y = (x + 6)(x - 3)^2$, the factor $x + 6$ gives a simple zero of $x = -6$, while the factor $(x - 3)^2$ gives a double zero of $x = 3$ (because technically, the factor is $(x - 3)(x - 3)$). Graphically, when a polynomial has a simple zero (multiplicity 1) or any zero with an odd multiplicity, its graph will cross through the x-axis. When a polynomial has a double zero (multiplicity 2) or any zero with an even multiplicity, its graph just touches the x-axis, creating a turning point in the graph.

Rational Expressions

A **rational expression** is a fraction that contains one or more variables in the denominator (basically a polynomial over a polynomial). The rules that govern fractions and polynomials also govern rational expressions (e.g., finding common denominators and factoring to simplify). However, rational expressions have a few extra features that should be considered:

- Because rational expressions, by definition, have variables in the denominator, they are often undefined for certain values. Watch for expressions that could lead to a denominator of 0. For example, the expression $\dfrac{4x}{x - 11}$ is undefined at $x = 11$.
- Factors in a rational expression can be canceled when simplifying, but under no circumstances can you do the same with individual terms. For example, $\dfrac{(x + 3)(x - 4)}{2(x + 3)}$ is allowed, but $\dfrac{x^2 + 2x + 3}{2x}$ is NOT allowed.

Division of Multi-Term Polynomials

Dividing polynomial expressions requires a fairly involved process called **polynomial long division**. Polynomial long division is just like regular long division except, as the name suggests, you use polynomials instead of numbers.

Suppose you wish to divide $x^3 + 3x + 7$ by $x + 4$. You can set this up as a long division problem:

$$x + 4 \overline{)x^3 + 0x^2 + 3x + 7}$$

Notice that even though the dividend does not have an x^2 term, a placeholder is used to keep the terms organized. Because $0x^2$ is equal to 0, adding this placeholder term doesn't change the value of the polynomial. Start by dividing the first term of the dividend ($x^3 + 3x + 7$) by the first term of the divisor ($x + 4$) to get x^2. Multiply the entire divisor by x^2, and then subtract this product from the dividend. Bring down leftover terms as needed:

$$\begin{array}{r} x^2 \\ x+4 \overline{\smash{\big)}\ x^3 + 0x^2 + 3x + 7} \\ \underline{-(x^3 + 4x^2)} \\ -4x^2 + 3x + 7 \end{array}$$

Continue by dividing the next term, $-4x^2$, by the first term of the divisor. Bring down leftover terms as needed. Multiply the quotient, $-4x$, by the entire divisor and subtract. Then repeat the process for the resulting x term:

$$\begin{array}{r} x^2 - 4x + 19 \\ x+4 \overline{\smash{\big)}\ x^3 + 0x^2 + 3x + 7} \\ \underline{-(x^3 + 4x^2)} \\ -4x^2 + 3x + 7 \\ \underline{-(-4x^2 - 16x)} \\ 19x + 7 \\ \underline{-(19x + 76)} \\ -69 \end{array}$$

The quotient is $x^2 - 4x + 19$ with a remainder of -69; the remainder is written over the divisor in a separate term. The final answer is $x^2 - 4x + 19 - \dfrac{69}{x + 4}$.

Note: For a polynomial to be evenly divisible by another polynomial, the remainder must be 0.

Solving Rational Equations

Rational equations are just like rational expressions except for one difference: they have an equal sign. They follow the same rules as rational expressions and can be solved (just like linear equations) using inverse operations. However, there are often extra steps involved, which makes solving them more intimidating. Here are a few strategies for solving rational equations:

- If there are only two nonzero terms in the equation, separate the terms on opposite sides of the equal sign and cross-multiply.
- If there are more than two nonzero terms, find a common denominator, multiply all the terms in the equation by the common denominator (which "clears" the fractions), and then solve the resulting equation.
- Beware of extraneous solutions (solutions that don't actually satisfy the original equation). When a solution to a rational equation produces a 0 denominator in *any* of the terms in the equation, the solution is invalid (because division by 0 is not possible).

You might also be asked to match a graph to a rational equation or vice versa. To do this, make note of any x-values that cause the equation to be undefined, which will appear as open dots on the graph or, in more complicated equations, dashed vertical lines (called **asymptotes**). Then, plot a few key points to see how the graph behaves on each side of the undefined value(s).

Growth and Decay

Growth and decay can be **linear** (which graphs as a straight line) or **exponential** (which graphs as a curve):

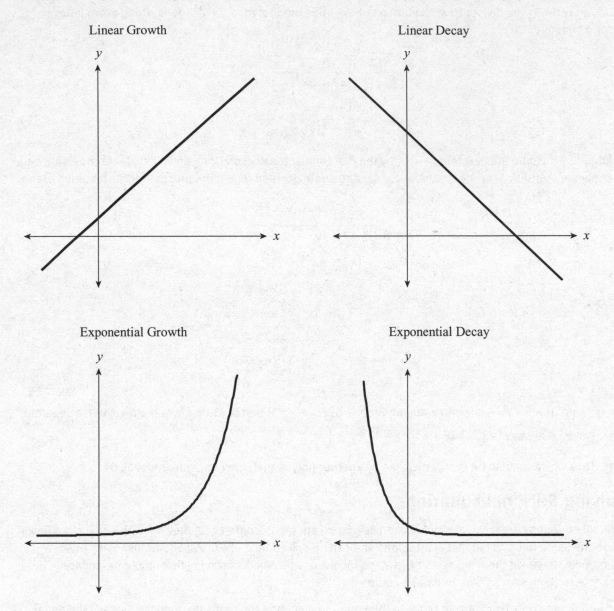

Examples of growth and decay questions include questions asking about interest rates, the growth of bacteria in a petri dish, or the decay rate of a radioactive isotope. You may see the following types of equations:

- Linear growth: $y = mx + b$, where b is the starting amount and m is the amount added or subtracted each time x increases by 1.
- Exponential growth (general form): $y = ab^x$, where a is the y-intercept and b is the amount multiplied each time x increases by 1.
- Exponential growth/decay over time: $f(x) = f(0)(1 + r)^t$, where $f(0)$ is the amount at time $t = 0$ and r is the growth rate (or decay rate, if negative) expressed as a decimal.

Exponents Drill

Simplify the following.

1. $2a^3 \times 3a^2$

2. $2a^3 + 3a^3$

3. $\dfrac{4b^3}{2b^2}$

4. $\left(4a^3\right)^2$

5. $2a^3 + 3a^2$

6. $4 + a^0$

7. $\dfrac{6a^5}{3a^{-2}}$

8. $(6x)^2 + (2x)^2$

9. $\left(x^4 y^2\right)^{\frac{1}{2}}$

10. $\dfrac{x^{\frac{3}{2}} y^{\frac{1}{2}} z^{-\frac{1}{2}}}{x^{-\frac{1}{2}} y^{\frac{1}{2}} z^{\frac{1}{2}}}$

Polynomials Drill

Expand questions 1–3, factor questions 4–7, and simplify questions 8–10.

1. $(2x + 3)(5x - 4)$

2. $(2x + 3y)(x - 2y)$

3. $(x + 3)(x - 1)(x)$

4. $3x^3 + 9x^2 - 12x$

5. $\dfrac{3xy - 3xz}{y - z}$

6. $6x^3 y^2 z^4 + 4xy^2 z - 2xyz^3$

7. $2x^2 + 6x + xy + 3y$

8. $\dfrac{x^2 + 2x}{x + 2}$

9. $\dfrac{x^3 + x^2 - 5x - 2}{x - 2}$

10. $\dfrac{4x^3 + 5x^2 + 3x + 2}{x^2 + 2}$

Exponents, Radicals, Polynomials, and Rational Expressions Practice Set

> **DIRECTIONS:** Keep a calculator handy as you work through this practice set, but reserve it for those questions that have a calculator icon next to them—and even on those questions, use it only if you really need it. Questions without the icon are intended to be done without a calculator, to help you prepare for the no-calculator section of the SAT.

1. Ronnie opened a bank account that earns 2 percent interest compounded annually. Her initial deposit was $100, and she uses the expression $100(x)^t$ to find the value of the account after t years. What is the value of x in the equation?

   A) 0.02
   B) 1
   C) 1.02
   D) 2

$$\sqrt[3]{8x^3}$$

2. If $x < 0$, which of the following is equivalent to the expression above?

   A) $-8x$
   B) $-2x$
   C) $2x$
   D) $2x^3$

$$\sqrt{x} = x - 2$$

3. What is the greatest value of x that satisfies the above equation?

4. If $a = \dfrac{3\sqrt{7}}{4}$ and $4a = \sqrt{3b}$, what is the value of b ?

   A) $\dfrac{4}{3}$
   B) 7
   C) 21
   D) 63

5. If $3y = 2(x - 1)$, what is the value of $\dfrac{3^{2x}}{27^y}$?

6. If $2x^2 + x^2y - 2xy - 4x - 15y - 30 = 0$, and $x > 5$, what is the value of y ?

A) -5

B) -2

C) 2

D) The value cannot be determined from the information given.

7. What is the value of x if $3\sqrt{x - 20} = 2\sqrt{x}$?

A) 12

B) 24

C) 36

D) 60

8. If $x^3 - 5x^2 - 29x + k$ is evenly divisible by $x - 7$, what is the value of k ?

A) 7

B) 15

C) 35

D) 105

9. If $a + b = 4$, $a - b = 2$, $x > 1$, and $\dfrac{x^{a^2}}{x^{b^2}} = x^c$, what is the value of c ?

10. Cecily observed x bacterial specimens in a lab culture on the first day of an experiment. The number of specimens in the lab culture doubled each day, and Cecily observed 2,560 specimens on the fifth day of the experiment. What is the value of x ?

A) 2

B) 80

C) 160

D) 512

11. Radioisotopes are unstable forms of chemical elements that decay at a steady rate into more stable forms. Half-life is the most common way to measure this decay; 1 half-life is the length of time it takes for half of the original amount of the isotope to decay. Gold-195 is the most stable radioisotope of the element gold. It has a half-life of 186 days, which happens to be about one-half of 365 days, or 1 year. Xavier uses the expression $s\left(1-\frac{1}{2}\right)^4$ to estimate how many grams of gold-195 remains from a sample of s grams after 2 years. In the equation, what does 4 represent?

    A) The number of grams in the sample that are left after 4 years

    B) The number of years it takes for one-half of the original sample to decay

    C) The estimated number of half-lives that gold-195 undergoes in 2 years

    D) The rate of decay for a radioisotope during 1 half-life

12. If $s = 4\sqrt{5}$ and $3s = \sqrt{5t}$, what is the value of t?

    A)   12

    B)   64

    C)   144

    D)   256

13. Which of the following is NOT a solution to the equation $x^3 + 3x^2 - 4x = 0$?

    A)   −4

    B)   0

    C)   1

    D)   2

$$\sqrt{2c^2 - 4} + d = 1$$

14. If in the equation above, $c > 0$ and $d = -1$, what is the value of c?

    A)   2

    B)   3

    C)   4

    D)   5

15. Garret invests in a restaurant that earns a 6 percent return annually, which he reinvests in the restaurant for the same rate of return. His initial investment is $20,000, and he uses the expression $20,000(x)^t$ to find the value of his investment, in dollars, after t years.

    Garret's friend Helga invests in a small business that earns 18 percent return annually, which she reinvests in the small business for the same rate of return. Helga makes an initial investment of $5,000 in the small business at the same time that Garret makes his initial investment in the restaurant. After 4 years, what is the positive difference between the amounts, rounded to the nearest dollar, that Garret and Helga have each gained from their initial investments?

    A) $556

    B) $4,694

    C) $5,250

    D) $15,556

$$(ax - 2)(3x^2 + bx - 5) = 9x^3 - 3x^2 - 17x + 10$$

16. The equation above is true for all x, where a and b are constants. What is the value of $a + b$?

Answers and Explanations

Exponents Drill

1. $6a^5$

2. $5a^3$

3. $2b$

4. $16a^6$

5. $2a^3 + 3a^2$. No further simplification is possible.

6. $4 + 1 = 5$

7. $2a^{5-(-2)} = 2a^7$

8. $36x^2 + 4x^2 = 40x^2$

9. x^2y

10. $x^{\left(\frac{3}{2}-\left(-\frac{1}{2}\right)\right)}y^{\left(\frac{1}{2}-\frac{1}{2}\right)}z^{\left(-\frac{1}{2}-\frac{1}{2}\right)} = x^2(1)z^{-1} = \dfrac{x^2}{z}$

Polynomials Drill

1. $10x^2 - 8x + 15x - 12 = 10x^2 + 7x - 12$

2. $2x^2 - 4xy + 3xy - 6y^2 = 2x^2 - xy - 6y^2$

3. $\left(x^2 - x + 3x - 3\right)x = x^3 + 2x^2 - 3x$

4. $3x\left(x^2 + 3x - 4\right) = 3x(x + 4)(x - 1)$

5. $\dfrac{3x\left(y - z\right)}{y - z} = 3x$

6. $2xyz\left(3x^2yz^3 + 2y - z^2\right)$

7. $2x(x + 3) + y(x + 3) = (2x + y)(x + 3)$

8. $\dfrac{x\left(x + 2\right)}{x + 2} = x$

9.
$$
\begin{array}{r}
x^2 + 3x + 1 \\
x - 2 \overline{\smash{\big)}\, x^3 + x^2 - 5x - 2} \\
\underline{-\left(x^3 - 2x^2\right)} \\
3x^2 - 5x \\
\underline{-\left(3x^2 - 6x\right)} \\
x - 2 \\
\underline{-(x - 2)} \\
0
\end{array}
$$

10.
$$
\begin{array}{r}
4x + 5 \\
x^2 + 2 \overline{\smash{\big)}\, 4x^3 + 5x^2 + 3x + 2} \\
\underline{-\left(4x^3 + 0x^2 + 8x\right)} \\
5x^2 - 5x + 2 \\
\underline{-\left(5x^2 + 0x + 10\right)} \\
-5x - 8
\end{array}
$$

Exponents, Radicals, Polynomials, and Rational Expressions Practice Set

1. C

Difficulty: Easy

Strategic Advice: Keep in mind that x must be greater than 1 to make the value of the account grow.

Getting to the Answer: The x term is 1 plus the decimal equivalent of 2%, or 1.02. This is because at the end of each compounding period, all of the money in the account remains (100%), and the interest (2%) is applied: $100\% + 2\% = 102\% = 1.02$. Because the compounding happens once a year, the number 1.02 must be raised to the number of years the account has been open to find the factor by which the original deposit has grown. Choice **(C)** is correct.

2. C

Difficulty: Medium

Strategic Advice: Don't be sidetracked by the fact that x is negative. The cube root of a negative number is simply another negative number.

Getting to the Answer: The cube root of the product of two terms is the product of their cube roots. The cube root of 8 is 2, and the cube root of x^3 is x, so the cube root of their product is $2x$.

You could pick -1 for x to double-check this. Because $(-1)^3 = -1$, the question asks for $\sqrt[3]{-8}$, which is -2. This result matches **(C)**, since $2x = -2$ when $x = -1$.

3. 4

Difficulty: Medium

Strategic Advice: Square both sides of the equation to eliminate the radical and solve for x.

Getting to the Answer: Square both sides: $\left(\sqrt{x}\right)^2 = (x - 2)^2$. Expand to get $x = x^2 - 4x + 4$. Subtract x from both sides: $x^2 - 5x + 4 = 0$. Since $1 \times 4 = 4$ and $1 + 4 = 5$, this quadratic factors to $(x - 4)(x - 1) = 0$. Therefore, $x = 1$ or $x = 4$, but since $x = 1$ does not satisfy the original equation, the correct answer is **4**.

4. C

Difficulty: Medium

Strategic Advice: Substitute the value of a from the first equation into the second equation and solve for b.

Getting to the Answer: With substitution, you get $4\left(\dfrac{3\sqrt{7}}{4}\right) = 3\sqrt{7}$, so $3\sqrt{7} = \sqrt{3b}$. Square both sides to get $9(7) = 3b$. So, $b = 3(7) = 21$. Choice **(C)** is correct.

5. 9

Difficulty: Medium

Strategic Advice: Express both the numerator and denominator with a common base so that their exponents can be combined, then use the given equation to evaluate the result.

Getting to the Answer: Since 27 is 3^3, the denominator is $\left(3^3\right)^y = 3^{3y}$ and the fraction is $\dfrac{3^{2x}}{3^{3y}}$. The exponents can be combined by subtracting the exponent in the denominator from that of the numerator to get 3^{2x-3y}.

Expand and rearrange $3y = 2(x - 1)$ to see that $3y = 2x - 2$ and $2x - 3y = 2$. Therefore, $3^{2x-3y} = 3^2 = \mathbf{9}$.

6. B

Difficulty: Hard

Strategic Advice: Look for common factors among the terms and regroup the equation.

Getting to the Answer: The first two terms have a common factor of x^2, the next two terms have a common factor of $-2x$, and the last two terms are divisible by 15. So rewrite the equation as $x^2(2 + y) - 2x(y + 2) - 15(y + 2) = 0$. Combine the factors of $(2 + y)$ to get $(x^2 - 2x - 15)(y + 2) = 0$. Factor the quadratic: $(x - 5)(x + 3)(y + 2) = 0$. Since $x > 5$, neither of the first two terms can be 0, so y must be -2 in order for the last term to be 0. Choice **(B)** is correct.

7. C

Difficulty: Medium

Strategic Advice: Square both sides of the equation, then solve the resulting equation for x.

Getting to the Answer: Square both sides: $9(x - 20) = 4x$, so $9x - 180 = 4x$. Thus, $5x = 180$ and $x = 36$. Choice **(C)** is correct.

8. D

Difficulty: Medium

Strategic Advice: Use polynomial long division to determine the value of k.

Getting to the Answer:

$$
\begin{array}{r}
x^2 + 2x - 15 \\
x - 7 \overline{) x^3 - 5x^2 - 29x + k} \\
\underline{-(x^3 - 7x^2)} \\
2x^2 - 29x \\
\underline{-(2x^2 - 14x)} \\
-15x + k \\
\underline{-(-15x + 105)} \\
k - 105
\end{array}
$$

In order for the difference of the two terms at the bottom to be 0, leaving no remainder, k must be 105. Choice **(D)** is correct.

9. 8

Difficulty: Hard

Strategic Advice: Combine the exponents in the fraction, simplify, and use the equations for a and b to solve for c.

Getting to the Answer: Since the bases are the same, simplify $\frac{x^{a^2}}{x^{b^2}} = x^c$ to $x^{a^2 - b^2} = x^c$. So $a^2 - b^2 = c$. Solve for a and b using combination:

$$
\begin{array}{r}
a + b = 4 \\
+(a - b = 2) \\
\hline
2a \quad\;\; = 6 \\
a \quad\;\; = 3
\end{array}
$$

Now use either $a + b = 4$ or $a - b = 2$ and $a = 3$ to find $b = 1$. Then $c = a^2 - b^2 = 3^2 - 1^2 = 9 - 1 = 8$. Alternatively, you may have noticed that $(a + b)(a - b) = a^2 - ab + ab - b^2 = a^2 - b^2$. Therefore, $a^2 - b^2 = (4)(2) = \mathbf{8}$.

10. C

Difficulty: Medium

Strategic Advice: Since the number of specimens doubles each day, that means that the number for a prior day is half the current number. Work backward four days to determine the original number.

Getting to the Answer: Half of 2,560 is 1,280, which is the number of specimens on day 4. Similarly, there were 640 on day 3, 320 on day 2, and 160 on day 1. Choice **(C)** is correct.

11. C

Difficulty: Medium

Strategic Advice: The equation describes an exponential decay at a rate of $1 - \frac{1}{2} = \frac{1}{2}$ per period. The exponent, 4, represents the number of periods over which the decay of the sample occurs. Look for a choice that conforms to these parameters.

Getting to the Answer: The stem states that the half-life of gold-195 is about half a year, so the compounding occurs twice per year. In 2 years, that is 4 times. Choice **(C)** correctly describes an estimated compounding of twice per year for 2 years. Note that (A) implies that the estimated half-life is a full year.

12. C

Difficulty: Medium

Strategic Advice: Multiply both sides of the first equation by 3 so that both equations start with 3s.

Getting to the Answer: If $s = 4\sqrt{5}$, then $3s = 12\sqrt{5}$. Set the two terms that are equal to $3s$ equal to each other and solve for t: $12\sqrt{5} = \sqrt{5t} = (\sqrt{5})(\sqrt{t})$. The $\sqrt{5}$ terms cancel out, so $12 = \sqrt{t}$. Square both sides to get $t = 144$. Choice **(C)** is correct.

13. D

Difficulty: Medium

Strategic Advice: Backsolving is an efficient approach to this "NOT" question. Plug the values of the choices into the equation until you find one that does not work.

Getting to the Answer: For (A), -4, the equation is $(-4)^3 + 3(-4)^2 - 4(-4) = -64 + 48 + 16 = 0$, so this is a solution. For (B), 0, both sides of the equation are 0, so this is also a solution. For (C), 1, the equation is $(1)^3 + 3(1)^2 - 4(1) = 1 + 3 - 4 = 0$. Thus, (C) is also a solution, and **(D)** is the correct choice.

Alternatively, you could factor the equation to $x(x + 4)(x - 1) = 0$. Setting each of the three factors equal to 0 gives you 0, -4, and 1 as the solutions.

14. A

Difficulty: Medium

Strategic Advice: Substitute the given value for d and solve the resulting equation for c.

Getting to the Answer: Substituting -1 for d and adding 1 to both sides of the equation results in the equation $\sqrt{2c^2 - 4} = 2$. Square both sides to get $2c^2 - 4 = 4$. So $2c^2 = 8$, $c^2 = 4$, and $c = \pm 2$. The stem states that $c > 0$, so $c = 2$. Choice **(A)** is correct.

15. A

Difficulty: Hard

Strategic Advice: Use the compound interest formula to calculate the value of each person's investment and find the difference between the two. The formula is given in the description of Garret's investment, with x being 1 plus the rate of return.

Getting to the Answer: Garret's investment is worth $20,000(1.06)^4 \approx \$25,250$ after 4 years. Since Garret's original investment was \$20,000, he gained \$5,250. Helga's is worth $\$5,000(1.18)^4 \approx \$9,694$ after 4 years. This is a gain of \$4,694 above her original \$5,000 investment. The difference between the two gains is $\$5,250 - \$4,694 = \$556$. Choice **(A)** is correct.

16. 4

Difficulty: Hard

Strategic Advice: Expand the left side of the equation, then use the fact that the coefficients for like terms must be the same on both sides to set up and solve equations for a and b.

Getting to the Answer: Use the distributive property to expand the left side of the equation, $ax(3x^2 + bx - 5) - 2(3x^2 + bx - 5)$, to get $3ax^3 + abx^2 - 5ax - 6x^2 - 2bx + 10$. Combine like terms to get $3ax^3 + (ab - 6)x^2 - (5a + 2b)x + 10$. The only x^3 term on the right side of the equation is $9x^3$, so $3a = 9$, and $a = 3$. Looking at the x^2 coefficients, $-3 = ab - 6$. Since a is 3, this means that $3b - 6 = -3$, so $3b = 3$ and $b = 1$. Thus, $a + b = 3 + 1 = \mathbf{4}$.

CHAPTER 10

Quadratics

Introduction to Quadratic Equations

A quadratic equation or expression is one that contains a squared variable (x^2) as the highest-order term. In standard form, a quadratic equation is written as $y = ax^2 + bx + c$, where a, b, and c are constants. A quadratic equation can have zero, one, or two real solutions, which are also called roots, x-intercepts (because solutions are where the graph of an equation crosses the x-axis), or zeros.

Solving Quadratic Equations

In most cases, before you can solve a quadratic equation, you must set the equation equal to 0. In other words, move everything to one side of the equal sign so that 0 is the only thing remaining on the other side. Once complete, you can use a variety of algebraic techniques, the quadratic formula, or graphing to find the solutions.

Factoring

Factoring, also known as reverse-FOIL, allows you to go from a quadratic equation written in standard form to a product of two binomials. Once you have a pair of binomials, set each factor equal to 0 and solve for the variable. Here are some general rules for factoring:

- Factoring is easiest when $a = 1$, so whenever possible, try to simplify your expression so that this is the case.

- If you see nice-looking numbers (integers or simple fractions) in the answer choices, this is a clue that factoring is possible.

- To factor a quadratic expression that is written in the form $x^2 + bx + c$, look for the factors of c that add up to b.

- To factor a quadratic expression that is written in the form $ax^2 + bx + c$, multiply a times c, look for the factors of ac that add up to b, use those factors to break the middle term into two pieces, and then factor by grouping.

- If you're ever not sure that you've factored correctly, use FOIL to check your work. You should get the equation you started with.

Square Rooting and Completing the Square

Occasionally, a quadratic equation is already set up perfectly to use *square rooting*, which simply means taking the square root of both sides. For example, $(x + 3)^2 = 49$ is ready to square root because both sides of the equation are perfect squares. For more difficult quadratic equations, you can *complete the square* and then use square rooting. To complete the square, start by putting the quadratic equation in standard form. Once there, divide b by 2 and square the result. Then, add the result to both sides of the equation, factor, and solve by square rooting.

The Quadratic Formula

The quadratic formula can be used to solve any quadratic equation. However, because the math can often get complicated, use it as a last resort or when you need to find exact solutions (or when you see radicals in the answer choices). Be sure to write the equation in standard form before plugging the values of a, b, and c into the formula. Memorize the formula before test day:

$$x = \frac{-b \pm \sqrt{b^2 - 4ac}}{2a}$$

The expression under the radical ($b^2 - 4ac$) is called the *discriminant*, and its sign dictates the number of real solutions that the equation has. If this quantity is positive, there are two distinct real solutions; if it is equal to 0, there is just one distinct real solution; and if it is negative, there are no real solutions.

Finding Solutions by Graphing

To solve a quadratic equation in the Calculator section of the SAT, you might also consider graphing the equation and finding its x-intercepts. Be sure you are familiar with your calculator's graphing capabilities in advance.

Graphing Parabolas

All quadratic equations and functions graph as parabolas (U-shaped), opening either up or down. The graph of a quadratic equation written in standard form will open down when $a < 0$ (negative) and up when $a > 0$ (positive). You should have a foundational knowledge of the structure of a parabola for test day. Some of the basic pieces you could be asked about are shown in the following figure:

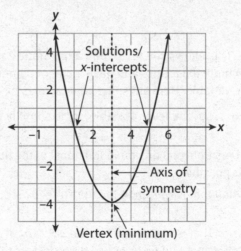

Along with the standard and factored forms of quadratic equations, you might also see them written in vertex form, $y = a(x - h)^2 + k$, where h and k are the x- and y-coordinates of the parabola's vertex, respectively, and the equation $x = h$ gives the axis of symmetry. From standard form, you can find the x-coordinate of the vertex (and therefore the location of the axis of symmetry) by plugging the appropriate values into the equation $x = \frac{-b}{2a}$ (the quadratic formula without the square root part). To find the y-coordinate of the vertex (which tells you the maximum or minimum value of the parabola), plug the x-coordinate into the original equation and solve for y.

Quadratics Drill

For questions 1 to 7, solve for x.

1. $x^2 + 3x - 10 = 0$

2. $4x^2 - 36 = 0$

3. $6x = -\left(x^2 + 8\right)$

4. $6x^2 + x - 12 = 0$

5. $2x^2 - 7x + 4 = 0$ (Use the quadratic formula.)

6. $x^2 + 4x - 1 = 0$ (Complete the square.)

7. $y = x^2 + 4x + 3$ and $y = 2x + 2$ (Solve for the point or points of intersection.)

8. What is the axis of symmetry for $x^2 - 3x - 4 = 0$?

9. How many real solutions are there for $x^2 + 3x + 5 = 0$?

10. What are the coordinates of the vertex for $y = x^2 + 6x + 16$?

Quadratics Practice Set

> **DIRECTIONS:** Keep a calculator handy as you work through this practice set, but reserve it for those questions that have a calculator icon next to them—and even on those questions, use it only if you really need it. Questions without the icon are intended to be done without a calculator, to help you prepare for the no-calculator section of the SAT.

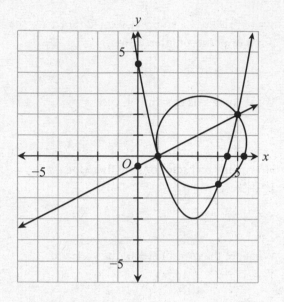

1. What is the number of solutions to the system of equations in the given graph?

   A) 2

   B) 3

   C) 4

   D) 5

$$3x^2 - 9x + 4 = 0$$

2. What are the values of x that satisfy the given equation?

   A) $-9 \pm 3\sqrt{11}$

   B) $3 \pm \dfrac{\sqrt{33}}{2}$

   C) $\dfrac{3}{2} \pm \dfrac{\sqrt{33}}{6}$

   D) $\dfrac{9}{2} \pm \dfrac{3\sqrt{11}}{2}$

3. In the xy-plane, the quadratic function $g(x)$ passes through the points $(a, 1)$ and $(b, 1)$. If $g(x) = f(x) + 1$, and $a < 0$ and $b > 0$, which of the following could define f?

   A) $(x - a)(x - b)$

   B) $(x - a)(x + b)$

   C) $(x + a)(x - b)$

   D) $x(x - a)(x - b)$

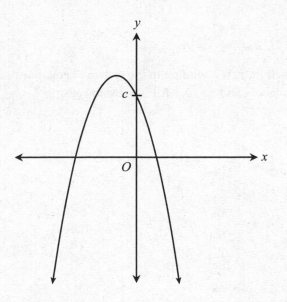

4. The given graph shows $y = -(x+1)^2 + 4$. What is the value of c ?

5. Which of the following equivalent forms gives the x-intercepts of the parabola given by the equation above?

$$y = x^2 - 10x + 24$$

A) $y - 24 = x^2 - 10x$

B) $y + 1 = (x - 5)^2$

C) $y = (x - 4)(x - 6)$

D) $y = x(x - 10) + 24$

$$-2x(x - 5) + 7(x - 5) = ax^2 + bx + c$$

6. In the given equation, a, b, and c are constants. What is the value of b ?

A) -35

B) -2

C) 3

D) 17

$$y = a(x - 3)(x + 5)$$

7. In the given equation, a is a nonzero constant. If the vertex of the graph of the equation is (c, d), what is the value of d ?

A) $-16a$

B) $-12a$

C) $-a$

D) $2a$

8. The formula for the distance an accelerating object travels is $d = v_0 t + \frac{1}{2}at^2$, for which v_0 is the initial velocity, t is time, and a is the rate of acceleration. An airplane is traveling at a horizontal velocity of 100 meters per second and a vertical velocity of 10 meters per second downward when it releases an object. The plane releases the object when it is 2,200 meters directly above point A, and the object strikes the ground at point B. The acceleration due to gravity is approximately 10 meters per second per second. If the ground is level between points A and B, what is the approximate distance, in meters, between the two points? (Assume that air resistance is negligible.)

A)   200

B)   1,000

C)   2,000

D)   2,200

9. The equation $\dfrac{20x^2 - ax + 9}{4x + 1} = 5x - 3 + \dfrac{12}{4x + 1}$ is true for all values of x except $x = -\dfrac{1}{4}$, where a is a constant. What is the value of a?

A) -7

B) -4

C) 4

D) 7

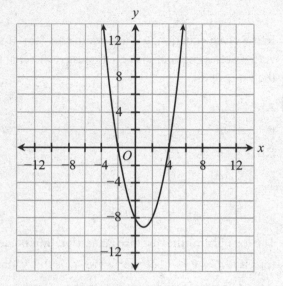

10. For the given graph, which of the following is the equation of the parabola?

A) $x^2 - x - 2$

B) $x^2 + x - 2$

C) $x^2 - 2x - 8$

D) $x^2 + 2x - 8$

$$y = x^2 - 3$$
$$y + 5 = 5x + 16$$

11. If (x, y) is a solution to the system of equations above and $x < 0$, what is the value of $x^2 y^2$?

A) 1

B) 4

C) 9

D) 16

$$y = -2\left(x^2 - 2x\right)$$
$$2x = y - 5$$

12. How many real solutions are there to the system of equations above?

A) There are exactly 3 solutions.

B) There are exactly 2 solutions.

C) There is exactly 1 solution.

D) There are no solutions.

$$\dfrac{4\left(x^2 - 6x + 9\right)}{(x - 3)} = 6$$

13. If x does not equal 3, then what value of x satisfies the equation above?

A) $-1\dfrac{1}{2}$

B) 3

C) $4\dfrac{1}{2}$

D) 9

$$y = 3(x - 5)^2 + 4$$

14. The graph of the equation above in the xy-plane is a parabola. Which of the following is true about that parabola?

    A) The maximum occurs at $(5, 4)$.

    B) The minimum occurs at $(-5, 4)$.

    C) The minimum occurs at $(5, -4)$.

    D) The minimum occurs at $(5, 4)$.

15. What is the distance between the x-intercepts in the xy-plane for the graph of the function $f(x) = x^2 - 3x - 28$?

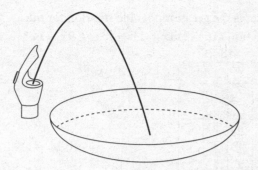

16. The parabolic path of water in the drinking fountain pictured above can be described by the function $h(x) = -\frac{4}{5}x^2 + 3x + 6$, where $h(x)$ is the height of the water and x is the horizontal distance from the spout. Which of the following best describes the meaning of the constant term 6?

    A) The initial angle of the water stream

    B) The maximum height of the water stream

    C) The distance from the spout at which the water stream reaches its maximum height

    D) The vertical distance between the spout and the basin

$$3x^2 + 4x - 3 = 2x^2 + 5x + 17$$

17. If b is a solution to the equation above and $b < 0$, what is the value of b?

    A) -12

    B) -5

    C) -4

    D) -2

18. What is the greatest possible solution for the equation $11x^2 - 11x + 11 = 7x^2 + 9x - 14$?

19. The line represented by the equation $y = 49$ intersects the parabola given by the equation $y = (x - 12)^2$ at two points, A and B. What is the distance between A and B?

    A)   7

    B)   12

    C)   14

    D)   24

20. Each investor in a group of n investors contributes an equal amount to a pool of funds totaling $10,000. The group unanimously decides to give an investment adviser an equal share in the pool for free in return for her advice. If this action reduces the value of each of the original contributors' share of the pool by $500, what is the number of original investors?

    A)   4

    B)   5

    C)   8

    D)   10

Answers and Explanations

Quadratics Drill

1. $5 \times (-2) = -10$ and $5 + (-2) = 3$:
$x^2 + 3x - 10 = (x+5)(x-2) = 0$. So $x = 2$ or -5.

2. Classic Quadratic: $(2x+6)(2x-6) = 0$. So,
$2x = \pm 6$ and $x = 3$ or -3. Alternatively,
$\frac{4x^2 - 36}{4} = x^2 - 9 = (x+3)(x-3)$.

3. $x^2 + 6x + 8 = 0$; $4 \times 2 = 8$ and $4 + 2 = 6$: $(x+4)$
$(x+2) = 0$. So $x = -4$ or -2.

4. Factors of 6: 1, 2, 3, 6; factors of 12: 1, 2, 3, 4, 6,
12. $(3 \times 3) + (2 \times (-4)) = 9 - 8 = 1$ and
$3(-4) = -12$: $(2x+3)(3x-4) = 0$, so
$x = -\frac{3}{2}$ or $\frac{4}{3}$.

5. $x = \frac{-(-7) \pm \sqrt{(-7)^2 - 4(2)(4)}}{2(2)}$

$= \frac{7 \pm \sqrt{49 - 32}}{4}$

$= \frac{7 + \sqrt{17}}{4}$ or $\frac{7 - \sqrt{17}}{4}$

6. $x^2 + 4x + 4 = 5$
$(x+2)^2 = 5$
$x + 2 = \pm\sqrt{5}$
$x = -2 \pm \sqrt{5}$

7. $x^2 + 4x + 3 = 2x + 2$
$x^2 + 2x + 1 = 0$
$(x+1)^2 = 0$
$x = -1$

8. $x = \frac{-(-3)}{2(1)} = \frac{3}{2}$

9. $3^2 - 4(1)(5) = 9 - 20 = -11$. The discriminant is
negative, so there are no real solutions.

10. $y = x^2 + 6x + 9 + 7$
$y = (x+3)^2 + 7$
Once you have the equation in vertex form, you're
done. The vertex is $(-3, 7)$.

Quadratics Practice Set

1. **A**
Difficulty: Easy

Strategic Advice: Identify the number of times the
graphs of all three equations intersect.

Getting to the Answer: The line, parabola, and circle all
intersect at $(1, 0)$ and $(5, 2)$. Thus, $(1, 0)$ and $(5, 2)$ are
solutions for each equation, and there are two solutions
to the system of equations. Choice **(A)** is correct.

2. **C**
Difficulty: Medium

Strategic Advice: A quick glance at the choices shows
that using the quadratic formula, rather than factoring,
is the way to solve this one.

Getting to the Answer: The coefficients to enter in the
quadratic formula are $a = 3$, $b = -9$, and $c = 4$. So the
quadratic formula for this equation is:
$$x = \frac{-(-9) \pm \sqrt{(-9)^2 - 4(3)(4)}}{2(3)} = \frac{9 \pm \sqrt{81 - 48}}{6}$$
$$= \frac{3}{2} \pm \frac{\sqrt{33}}{6}$$

Choice **(C)** is correct.

3. **A**
Difficulty: Hard

Strategic Advice: That $g(x) = f(x) + 1$ means that for any
value of x, the value of $g(x)$ is 1 greater than the value of
$f(x)$. By subtracting 1 from the y-coordinate of the given
points for $g(x)$, you can determine that the two points at
which $f(x)$ crosses the x-axis are $(a, 0)$ and $(b, 0)$, which
occur when $f(a) = 0$ and $f(b) = 0$, respectively. The
choices are given in the form of factored quadratics, so
when either factor is 0, the value of $f(x)$ is 0.

Getting to the Answer: For (A), when $x = a$, the function is
$f(a) = (a-a)(a-b)$. Regardless of whether a is positive
or negative, the first factor is 0. When $x = b$, the function is
$f(b) = (b-a)(b-b)$, in which case the second factor is 0.
So **(A)** is correct. Choice (D) is incorrect because it isn't a
quadratic: $f(x)$ intercepts the x-axis a third time when $x = 0$.

4.   3

Difficulty: Medium

Strategic Advice: Find the value of the y-intercept.

Getting to the Answer: The y-intercept of the parabola is at $x = 0$. Plug 0 in for x in the equation $y = -(x + 1)^2 + 4$ to find c. Thus, c is $y = -(0 + 1)^2 + 4 = \mathbf{3}$.

5.   C

Difficulty: Medium

Strategic Advice: The x-intercepts are at points where $y = 0$, so the correct choice will clearly show that.

Getting to the Answer: The variable y expressed as the product of two factors clearly reveals the two values for which $y = 0$. Choice **(C)** is correct.

6.   D

Difficulty: Medium

Strategic Advice: Distribute the factors, then combine like terms to create a quadratic. The numerical coefficient of the x term is b.

Getting to the Answer: Since all the you need to answer the question is the coefficient of the x term, take a shortcut and only bother evaluating that part of the equation: $(-2x)(-5) = 10x$, and $7(x) = 7x$. The sum of these two terms is $17x$. Choice **(D)** is correct.

7.   A

Difficulty: Hard

Strategic Advice: State the equation in vertex form and set that equal to the given equation. Solve this for the value of d.

Getting to the Answer: Start with $a(x - 3)(x + 5) = a(x - c)^2 + d$. Expand the quadratics on both sides: $a(x^2 + 2x - 15) = a(x^2 - 2cx + c^2) + d$. The coefficients of x in both equations must be equal, so $2ax = -2cax$. Thus, $c = -1$. Paying close attention to the sign, the $x - c$ term in the vertex form is $x + 1$. Plugging this in results in the equation $a(x^2 + 2x - 15) = a(x^2 + 2x + 1) + d$. Deleting identical terms on both sides yields $-15a = a(1) + d$. Subtract a from both sides to see that $-16a = d$. Choice **(A)** is correct.

8.   C

Difficulty: Hard

Strategic Advice: Find the time that it takes for the object to hit the ground using the given formula. Then use $d = r \times t$ to find the horizontal distance the object travels.

Getting to the Answer: The vertical distance traveled is 2,200 meters. Since the plane is moving downward at 10 meters per second, that is the initial downward velocity of the object. The acceleration due to gravity, a, is stated to be about 10 meters per second per second. Plug these values into the formula to get $2{,}200 = 10t + \frac{1}{2}(10)t^2$. Setting the quadratic equal to 0, this becomes $5t^2 + 10t - 2{,}200 = 0$. Divide by the common factor of 5 to get $t^2 + 2t - 440 = 0$. This factors to $(t - 20)(t + 22) = 0$. Since the time must be positive, $t = 20$.

The horizontal velocity is 100 meters per second, so during the 20 second drop, the object travels $100 \times 20 = 2{,}000$ meters. This is the distance between points A and B. Choice **(C)** is correct.

9.   D

Difficulty: Medium

Strategic Advice: Clear the fractions by multiplying both sides by $4x + 1$. Then compare coefficients of a common term of the resulting equation to solve for a.

Getting to the Answer: Multiplying both sides of the original equation by $4x + 1$ results in the new equation $20x^2 - ax + 9 = 20x^2 - 12x + 5x - 3 + 12$. This simplifies to $20x^2 - ax + 9 = 20x^2 - 7x + 9$, so $a = 7$. Choice **(D)** is correct.

10.   C

Difficulty: Hard

Strategic Advice: Identify the x-intercepts on the graph. Then write the equation in the form $ax^2 + bx + c$.

Getting to the Answer: The parabola crosses the x-axis at $x = -2$ and $x = 4$. Note that each tick mark represents 2 units. Thus, in factored form, the quadratic is $y = (x + 2)(x - 4)$. Use FOIL and then simplify to get the equation:

$$
\begin{aligned}
y &= (x + 2)(x - 4) \\
&= x^2 - 4x + 2x - 8 \\
&= x^2 - 2x - 8
\end{aligned}
$$

The correct answer could be a multiple of this quadratic equation. In this case, only **(C)** matches.

11. B

Difficulty: Hard

Strategic Advice: Since the first equation provides the value of y in terms of x, substitute $x^2 - 3$ for y in the second equation, then solve for x and y.

Getting to the Answer: With substitution, the second equation becomes $x^2 - 3 + 5 = 5x + 16$. Rearrange this to $x^2 - 5x - 14 = 0$. This equation factors to $(x - 7)(x + 2) = 0$. Since x is negative, $x = -2$. Plug this value into the first equation to get $y = (-2)^2 - 3 = 4 - 3 = 1$. So, $x^2 y^2 = (-2)^2 (1)^2 = 4$. Choice **(B)** is correct.

12. D

Difficulty: Hard

Strategic Advice: Since the y-coordinates at any point of intersection will be equal, restate the second equation in terms of y, set the two expressions for y equal to each other, and solve for x.

Getting to the Answer: The second equation converts to $y = 2x + 5$, so $2x + 5 = -2(x^2 - 2x) = -2x^2 + 4x$. Combine like terms and rearrange the equation to equal zero: $2x^2 - 2x + 5 = 0$. To determine how many real solutions there are to this equation, use the discriminant, $b^2 - 4ac = (-2)^2 - 4(2)(5) = 4 - 40 = -36$. Because the discriminant is negative, there are no real solutions to this equation. Choice **(D)** is correct.

13. C

Difficulty: Medium

Strategic Advice: Factor the term inside the parentheses in the numerator to see if the equation can be simplified without having to multiply both sides by $x - 3$ to clear the fraction.

Getting to the Answer: The term $x^2 - 6x + 9$ is a classic quadratic, $(x - 3)^2$. So the equation can be written as $\dfrac{4(x - 3)(x - 3)}{x - 3} = 6$, which simplifies to $4(x - 3) = 6$. Thus, $4x = 18$, and $x = 4\frac{1}{2}$. Choice **(C)** is correct.

14. D

Difficulty: Medium

Strategic Advice: The equation is written in vertex form, $y = a(x - h)^2 + k$. In this form, if a is positive, the parabola opens upward. The variable h is the x-coordinate of the vertex, and k is the y-coordinate of the vertex.

Getting to the Answer: The given equation is an upward opening parabola because a is positive; thus, the vertex represents the minimum. Eliminate (A). The coordinates of the vertex are $(5, 4)$. Eliminate (B) and (C). The correct answer is **(D)**.

15. 11

Difficulty: Medium

Strategic Advice: Set $f(x)$ equal to 0, and factor that quadratic to find the x-intercepts. The difference between these two values is the positive distance between them.

Getting to the Answer: The product of the two numeric terms is -28, and their sum is -3. The numbers that produce these results are -7 and $+4$, so $(x - 7)(x + 4) = 0$. Therefore, the x-intercepts are 7 and -4. The distance between them is **11**.

16. D

Difficulty: Medium

Strategic Advice: When quadratic functions model real-life situations, match each part of the situation to its corresponding term in the equation.

Getting to the Answer: The equation is provided in standard form, so recall how each part of the equation corresponds to the real-life situation. The coefficient of the squared term, $-\dfrac{4}{5}$, indicates that the parabola is opening down, and the constant term, 6, is the y-intercept. This is a positive number because the spout is higher than the basin. Choice **(D)** is correct.

17. C

Difficulty: Medium

Strategic Advice: Combine like terms to get a quadratic expression set equal to zero in order to find the solutions.

Getting to the Answer: Subtract the right side of the equation from the left side: $3x^2 - 2x^2 + 4x - 5x - 3 - 17 = 2x^2 - 2x^2 + 5x - 5x + 17 - 17$. Thus, $x^2 - x - 20 = 0$. Factor this using reverse FOIL to get $(x + 4)(x - 5) = 0$. Hence, the two solutions are -4 and 5, but only -4 is less than 0. Choice **(C)** is correct.

18. 2.5 or 5/2

Difficulty: Hard

Strategic Advice: Rearrange the equation to get a quadratic equal to zero, then factor to solve.

Getting to the Answer: Subtracting the right side from the left side of the equation $11x^2 - 11x + 11 = 7x^2 + 9x - 14$ yields $4x^2 - 20x + 25$. Notice that the first term is $(2x)^2$, the middle term is $-2(2x)(5)$, and the third term is $(5)^2$. Since the middle term is negative, this pattern quadratic is $(2x - 5)^2 = 0$. Thus, $2x = 5$ and the single solution is $x = $ **2.5** or $\frac{5}{2}$.

19. C

Difficulty: Medium

Strategic Advice: Set the right side of the two equations equal and solve for x.

Getting to the Answer: Substitute 49 for y in the equation for the parabola: $(x - 12)^2 = 49$. Take the square root of both sides of the equation to get $x - 12 = \pm 7$. So, the x-values at the two points of intersection are $12 - 7 = 5$ and $12 + 7 = 19$. The distance between those points is $19 - 5 = 14$. Choice **(C)** is correct.

20. A

Difficulty: Medium

Strategic Advice: Translate the given scenario into an equation, and solve for the original number of investors.

Getting to the Answer: The original investors' individual contribution to the pool of funds is $\frac{\$10,000}{n}$ each. When the adviser is brought into the group, each share of the pool is worth $\frac{\$10,000}{n + 1}$. Since this amount is $500 less than the original value of each person's share of the pool, set up the equation $\frac{10,000}{n} - 500 = \frac{10,000}{n + 1}$. Multiply both sides by the denominators to clear the fractions:
$$(n + 1)(\not{n})\frac{10,000}{\not{n}} - (n + 1)(n)500 = (\not{n+1})(n)\frac{10,000}{\not{n+1}}.$$
So $10,000n + 10,000 - 500n^2 - 500n = 10,000n$. Divide all terms by 500 to get $20 - n^2 - n = 0$. Multiply both sides by -1 so that $n^2 + n - 20 = 0$. This factors to $(n + 5)(n - 4) = 0$. Since the solution cannot be a negative number, $n = 4$.

Alternatively, you could solve by testing the choices. If you started with (B), 5 investors, that would be an initial contribution of $\frac{\$10,000}{5} = \$2,000$ each. Adding the adviser would reduce each person's share to $\frac{\$10,000}{6} \approx \$1,667$. Each person's reduction is about $333, but you're looking for a $500 reduction. Since this is too small a per-person reduction and increasing the number of investors would further decrease the per-person reduction, 4 must be the correct value for n. Choice **(A)** is correct.

CHAPTER 11

Lines, Angles, and Triangles

Lines and Angles

Lines and angles are the foundation of SAT geometry. Reviewing a few basic definitions and rules will make answering these questions, as well as related geometry questions, much easier:

- **Acute angle:** an angle that measures between 0 and 90 degrees
- **Obtuse angle:** angle that measures between 90 and 180 degrees
- **Right angle** (formed by perpendicular lines): an angle that measures exactly 90 degrees
- **Complementary angles:** angles that sum to 90 degrees
- **Supplementary angles:** angles that sum to 180 degrees
- **Vertical angles:** angles opposite to each other when two lines intersect. Vertical angles have equal measures.

Parallel Lines Cut by a Transversal

When two parallel lines are intersected by another line (called a **transversal**), all acute angles are equal, and all obtuse angles are equal:

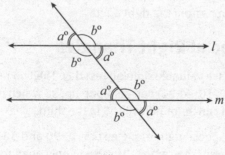

$l \parallel m$

Triangles

Lines and angles form the basis of triangles—some of the most commonly occurring shapes on the SAT. The following facts apply to all triangles:

- The sum of the measures of the interior angles of a triangle is 180 degrees.
- A side opposite a greater angle is longer than a side opposite a smaller angle.
- Triangle inequality theorem: The length of any side of a triangle is less than the sum of the other two sides and greater than the positive difference of the other two sides. This can be represented by $a - b < c < a + b$, where a, b, and c are the side lengths of the triangle.
- An exterior angle of a triangle is equal to the sum of the two opposite interior angles, as in the image below:

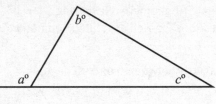

Finding the Area of a Triangle

The formula for finding the area of a triangle is $A = \frac{1}{2}bh$, where b is the length of the base of the triangle and h is the height. When you have a right triangle, you can use the legs as the base and the height. If the triangle isn't a right triangle, you'll need to draw in the height (sometimes called an altitude) from the angle opposite the base. Remember that the height *must* be perpendicular to the base.

The Pythagorean Theorem

If you know any two side lengths of a right triangle, you can use the Pythagorean theorem to find the missing side. The theorem states that $a^2 + b^2 = c^2$, where a and b are the shorter sides of the triangle (called legs) and c is the hypotenuse, which is always across from the right angle.

Pythagorean Triples and Special Right Triangles

Knowing common Pythagorean triples can save valuable time on test day. The two most common are 3-4-5 and 5-12-13. Multiples of these (e.g., 6-8-10, 10-24-26) can also pop up, so watch out for those, too. If you see any two sides in one of these ratios, you can automatically fill in the third.

Another time-saving strategy is recognizing special right triangles (45-45-90 and 30-60-90). The lengths of the sides of these special triangles are always in the same ratio, so you only need to know one side in order to calculate the other two. The ratios are shown below:

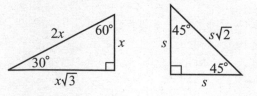

While the Pythagorean theorem can almost always be used to solve right triangle questions, it is often not the most efficient way to proceed. Recognizing Pythagorean triples and special right triangles allows you to save time, so use them whenever possible!

Additional Triangle Theorems

In the following table, you'll find several more triangle theorems that you may find useful on test day.

Triangle Theorems	Definition
Isosceles triangle theorems	• Angles opposite congruent sides have equal measures. • Sides opposite congruent angles have equal lengths.
Mid-segment theorems	• The mid-segment (or midline) of a triangle is parallel to one side of the triangle and joins the midpoints of the other two sides. • The length of the mid-segment is half the length of the side to which it is parallel.

Similarity and Congruence

Knowing when two figures are similar (or congruent) allows you to use what you know about one figure to derive information about the other figure:

- Two triangles are **similar** if the measures of the angles of one triangle are equal to the measures of the angles of the other triangle or if all pairs of corresponding sides of the two triangles are in the same proportion.

- Two triangles are **congruent** if and only if they have the same angle measures AND the same side lengths.

Notation

The order of the vertices in a similarity ($\sim$) or congruence ($\cong$) statement is key to understanding which parts are corresponding parts. For example, if $\triangle CAT \sim \triangle DOG$, then $\angle C$ corresponds to $\angle D$, $\angle A$ corresponds to $\angle O$, and $\angle T$ corresponds to $\angle G$. Similarly, side CA corresponds to side DO, side CT corresponds to side DG, and side AT corresponds to side OG.

Complex Figures

Unusual shapes, comprised of multiple familiar shapes, which can be obvious or cleverly hidden, can always be broken down into squares, rectangles, triangles, and/or circles:

- Start by transferring information from the question stem to the figure. If a figure isn't provided, draw one!

- Break the figure into familiar shapes.

- Determine how one line segment can play multiple roles in a figure. For example, if a right triangle is inscribed in a circle, the diameter of the circle will also be the hypotenuse of the triangle.

- Work from the shape with the most information to the shape with the least information.

Lines, Angles, and Triangles Drill

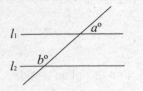

1. If $a = 42$, then what is the value of b ?

2. The three interior angles of a triangle are $(x + 10)°$, $(x - 20)°$, and $(x + 40)°$. What is the value of x ?

3. In triangle ABC, side AB is 8 and side BC is 5. What are the minimum and maximum possible lengths of side AC ?

4. In triangle ABC, the interior angles at A and B are 65 degrees and 45 degrees, respectively. What is the measure of the exterior angle at C ?

5. A triangle has a base 12 and height 3. What is the area of the triangle?

6. The vertices A, B, and C of triangle ABC correspond to the vertices D, E, and F of similar triangle DEF. If the length of side AB is 8, the length of side AC is 14, and the length of side DE is 12, what is the length of side DF ?

7. The lengths of the legs of a right triangle are 12 and 16. What is the length of the hypotenuse?

8. What is the area of a 30-60-90 right triangle if the hypotenuse is 12 cm long?

9. What is the hypotenuse of a right triangle with one leg of 20 and an area of 100 ?

10. The sides of equilateral triangle A are twice those of equilateral triangle B. If the area of triangle B is 50, what is the area of triangle A ?

Lines, Angles, and Triangles Practice Set

DIRECTIONS: Keep a calculator handy as you work through this practice set, but reserve it for those questions that have a calculator icon next to them—and even on those questions, use it only if you really need it. Questions without the icon are intended to be done without a calculator, to help you prepare for the no-calculator section of the SAT.

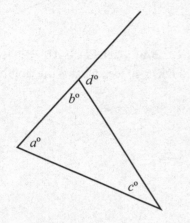

1. In the figure above, $d = 105$. If $a = 2c$, what is the value of $a + b$?

   A) 105
   B) 120
   C) 130
   D) 145

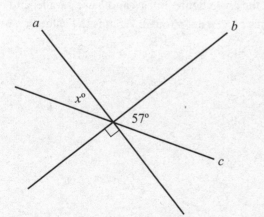

2. In the given figure, lines a, b, and c intersect at one point. What is the value of x?

   A) 33
   B) 43
   C) 57
   D) 90

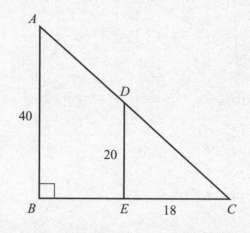

3. In the given figure, AB and DE are parallel. What is the length of AC?

   A) $2\sqrt{181}$
   B) 36
   C) 54
   D) $4\sqrt{181}$

4. What is the value of c if the number of radians in a 630-degree angle can be written as $c\pi$, where c is a constant?

   A) $\frac{1}{6}$
   B) $\frac{5}{6}$
   C) $\frac{3}{2}$
   D) $\frac{7}{2}$

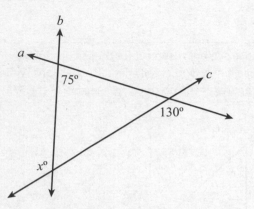

5. In the figure above, what is the value of x ?

A)   75

B)   105

C)   125

D)   130

6. The sum of the measures of the exterior angles of a polygon is equal to 360 degrees. If the shape is a regular polygon, all the exterior angles are equal. What is the positive difference, in degrees, between the degree measure of an exterior angle of a regular pentagon and the degree measure of an exterior measure of a regular hexagon?

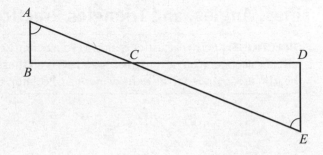

7. In the given figure, $\angle BAC = \angle CED$. If $AB = 20$ feet, $BC = 48$ feet, and $DE = 40$ feet, what is the length, in feet, of CD ?

A)   17

B)   24

C)   96

D)   104

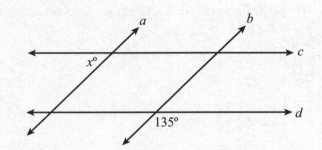

8. In the given figure, lines a and b are parallel and lines c and d are parallel. What is the value of x ?

A)   45

B)   55

C)   135

D)   145

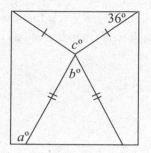

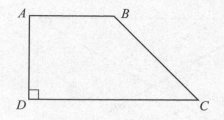

9. The given figure shows two isosceles triangles within a rectangle. If *b* is half of *c*, what is the value of *a* ?

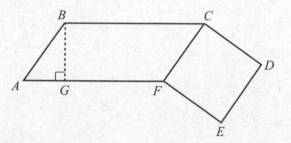

11. In the figure given, *AD* is perpendicular and equal to *AB*. If *DC* = 2*AB*, what is the degree measure of angle *ABC* ?

A) 125

B) 135

C) 145

D) 155

12. A rectangular garden with length *s* and width 0.5*s* is surrounded on all four sides by a walkway of width 0.1*s*. If the width of the walkway is increased by 50 percent by expanding into the garden, what is the percent decrease in the area of the garden?

10. In the figure above, square *CDEF* shares the common side *CF* with parallelogram *ABCF*. The area of the square is 225, the length of *AG* is 9, and the length of *FG* is 21. What is the area of the parallelogram?

A) 240

B) 300

C) 360

D) 480

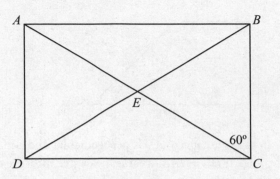

13. In the figure given, *ABCD* is a rectangle. If *DE* is 3, what is the length of *AB* ?

A) $3\sqrt{2}$

B) $2\sqrt{3}$

C) $3\sqrt{3}$

D) $6\sqrt{3}$

15. What is the diameter of the largest circle that can be inscribed within an equilateral triangle that has sides of 10 centimeters?

A) $\dfrac{5\sqrt{3}}{3}$

B) 5

C) $\dfrac{10\sqrt{3}}{3}$

D) $5\sqrt{3}$

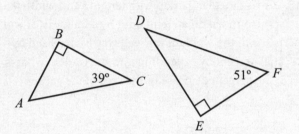

14. Based on the given figure, which of the following equals $\dfrac{BA}{EF}$?

A) $\dfrac{BA}{DF}$

B) $\dfrac{CB}{DE}$

C) $\dfrac{CB}{EF}$

D) $\dfrac{AC}{DE}$

Answers and Explanations

Lines, Angles, and Triangles Drill

1. $180° − 42° = 138°$

2. $(x + 10)° + (x − 20)° + (x + 40)° = 180°$. So, $3x + 30 = 180$, $3x = 150$, and $x = 50$.

3. $AC < (8 + 5)$ and $AC > (8 − 5)$, so $3 < AC < 13$.

4. The exterior angle is equal to the sum of the other two interior angles: $65° + 45° = 110°$.

5. $A = \frac{1}{2}bh = \frac{1}{2}(12)(3) = 18$

6. $\frac{DE}{AB} = \frac{12}{8} = 1.5$, and $AC \times 1.5 = DF = 14 \times 1.5 = 21$.

7. This is a 3:4:5 Pythagorean triple multiplied by 4 to get 12:16:20, so 20 is the length of the hypotenuse.

8. Side ratio of $1:\sqrt{3}:2$ multiplied by 6, so legs are 6 and $6\sqrt{3}$. Area $= \frac{1}{2}bh = \frac{1}{2}(6)(6\sqrt{3}) = 18\sqrt{3}$.

9. $100 = \frac{1}{2}(20)h$, so $h = 10$.

   Hypotenuse$^2 = 10^2 + 20^2 = 500$, so the length of the hypotenuse is $\sqrt{500} = 10\sqrt{5}$.

10. $A = \frac{1}{2}(2b)(2h) = 2bh$ and $B = \frac{1}{2}bh$, so the area of A is 4 times that of B; thus, the area of A is 200.

Lines, Angles, and Triangles Practice Set

1. D

Difficulty: Medium

Strategic Advice: Use angle rules to derive the values of a and b.

Getting to the Answer: Since angles b and d form a straight line, their sum is $180°$. So $b = 180 − 105 = 75$. The interior angles of a triangle total $180°$, so the sum of a, b, and c is 180. Substituting 75 for b and $2c$ for a, write that as $2c + 75 + c = 180$. So $3c = 105$, and $c = 35$. Thus, $a = 2(35) = 70$, and $a + b = 70 + 75 = 145$. Choice **(D)** is correct.

2. A

Difficulty: Easy

Strategic Advice: Use the angle properties to fill in the necessary missing values.

Getting to the Answer: The angle at the bottom of the intersection is a right angle, so the vertical angle to the right of x must also be 90°. Angle x and the 90° and 57° angles form a straight line, so they must total 180°. Therefore, $x° = 180° − 90° − 57° = 33°$. Choice **(A)** is correct.

3. D

Difficulty: Medium

Strategic Advice: Because AB is parallel to DE, triangles ACB and DCE have the same angles and are, therefore, similar. Determine the length of DC using the Pythagorean theorem, then use the side ratio of the triangles to obtain the length of AC.

Getting to the Answer: Side DC is the hypotenuse of triangle DCE, so $DC^2 = 18^2 + 20^2 = 324 + 400 = 724$, which factors to 4×181. So $DC = \sqrt{4(181)} = 2\sqrt{181}$. Sides AB and DE are corresponding sides. Since $AB = 40$ and $DE = 20$, the side ratio of the triangles is 2:1. Therefore, $AC = 2DC = 4\sqrt{181}$. Choice **(D)** is correct.

4. D

Difficulty: Medium

Strategic Advice: There are 2π radians in a complete circle, which is 360°. Set up a proportion to solve for c.

Getting to the Answer: The proportion is $\frac{630}{360} = \frac{c\pi}{2\pi}$, so $1{,}260 = 360c$. The math appears quite cumbersome without a calculator, but 1,260 is more than 3 times 360, and the only choice that is greater than 3 is **(D)**. (For the record, $1{,}260 \div 360 = 3.5$.)

5. C

Difficulty: Medium

Strategic Advice: Use the angle properties to fill in the necessary missing values needed to find the value of x.

Getting to the Answer: The 130° angle and the interior angle of the triangle adjacent to it form a straight line, so that angle is $180° - 130° = 50°$. The interior angles of a triangle total 180°, so the interior angle of the triangle adjacent to x is $180° - 50° - 75° = 55°$. That angle and x form a straight line, so $x° = 180° - 55° = 125°$. (If you recalled that the measure of an exterior angle of a triangle is the sum of the other two interior angles, you could have saved a step.) Choice **(C)** is correct.

6. 12

Difficulty: Hard

Strategic Advice: Convert the wording into an equation, then solve for the measures of the exterior angles of a five-sided and a six-sided regular polygon.

Getting to the Answer: Set n as the number of sides and a as the exterior angle measure. Since the exterior angles of a regular polygon are all equal and add up to 360°, write the equation $a = \frac{360}{n}$. The exterior angles of a pentagon, or a regular polygon with five sides, each have a degree measure of $\frac{360}{5} = 72$. The exterior angles of a hexagon, or a regular polygon with six sides, each have a degree measure of $\frac{360}{6} = 60$. The positive difference is $72 - 60 = \mathbf{12}$.

7. C

Difficulty: Medium

Strategic Advice: Since the angles at vertices A and E are the same, and the vertical angles at C are equal, the two triangles are similar. The side-to-side ratio can be used to calculate the length of CD.

Getting to the Answer: Side AB, 20 feet, corresponds to side DE, 40 feet, so the dimensions of triangle CDE are twice those of triangle ACB. Side CD corresponds to side BC, so the length of CD is $2 \times 48 = 96$. Choice **(C)** is correct.

8. A

Difficulty: Easy

Strategic Advice: Use the angle properties of parallel transversals to get the value of x.

Getting to the Answer: Since the lines and transversals are parallel, the measure of x is the same as that of the angle to the left of the 135° angle. The 135° angle and the angle to its left make up a straight line, so that angle is $180° - 135° = 45°$. Choice **(A)** is correct.

9. 117

Difficulty: Medium

Strategic Advice: Note that a is supplementary to the angle in the bottom isosceles triangle. Recall that the angles opposite the equal sides in an isosceles triangle are equal.

Getting to the Answer: To find a, you need b; b is half of c. Therefore, first determine the value of c in the top triangle. Since the triangle is isosceles, the other acute angle is also 36°. The sum of the interior angles in a triangle sum to 180°, so $c° + 36° + 36° = 180°$. Solving for c gives, $c = 180° - 72° = 108°$. b is half of c, so $b = 108° \div 2 = 54°$. The measure of the two other angles in the bottom isosceles triangle are equal. Thus, they are $(180° - 54°) \div 2 = 63°$. Since $a°$ is supplementary to that angle, $a° = 180° - 63° = \mathbf{117°}$.

10. C

Difficulty: Medium

Strategic Advice: Use the formula for the area of a square to find the length of CF, which will be the same as the length of AB, then calculate the height of the parallelogram and use that to obtain the area of the parallelogram.

Getting to the Answer: The area of a square is the side length squared. So $CF = \sqrt{225} = 15$. Opposite sides of a parallelogram are equal, so $AB = 15$. Triangle ABG has a hypotenuse of 15 and one leg of 9. This fits the 3:4:5 Pythagorean triple pattern multiplied by 3, so BG, the height of the parallelogram, is 12. The length of the parallelogram is $21 + 9 = 30$. Thus, the area of the parallelogram, base times height, is $30 \times 12 = 360$. Choice **(C)** is correct.

11. B

Difficulty: Medium

Strategic Advice: Identify common shapes within the trapezoid.

Getting to the Answer: Since AD is perpendicular and equal to AB and $DC = 2AB$, the trapezoid can be divided into a square and a 45-45-90 degree triangle:

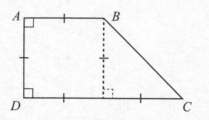

Thus, the measure of angle ABC is $90° + 45° = 135°$. Choice **(B)** is correct.

12. 28

Difficulty: Hard

Strategic Advice: Determine the new dimensions of the garden when the width of the walkway is increased. Calculate the before and after areas, and use the percentage change formula for the decrease.

Getting to the Answer: The walkway is originally $0.1s$ wide; a 50% increase in width equates to $0.05s$. However, the encroachment into the garden occurs on all four sides, so both the width and length of the original rectangular garden will decrease by $2 \times 0.05s = 0.1s$. The new dimensions are $0.9s$ and $0.4s$, so the new area is $0.9s \times 0.4s = 0.36s^2$. The original area is $s \times 0.5s = 0.5s^2$, so the percent decrease is $\frac{0.50 - 0.36}{0.50} = \frac{0.14}{0.50} = 0.28$, or **28**%.

13. C

Difficulty: Medium

Strategic Advice: Note that rectangle $ABCD$ is composed of two 30-60-90 triangles DAB and BCD (or ADC and ABC). Use the ratio of the sides of a 30-60-90 triangle to determine the length of AB.

Getting to the Answer: Diagonals in a rectangle bisect each other, so DE is half of DB. Since DE is 3, DB is 6. Triangles DAB and ABC are congruent, so angle ADB, opposite side AB, is also 60°. Set up a proportion using the ratio of the sides of a 30-60-90 triangle, $x:x\sqrt{3}:2x$, to solve for the length of AB:

$$\frac{AB}{6} = \frac{\sqrt{3}}{2}$$
$$2AB = 6\sqrt{3}$$
$$AB = 3\sqrt{3}$$

(C) is correct.

Alternatively, if you noticed triangles ADE and BEC are equilateral triangles, then $AD = DE = 3$. AD is the side opposite 30° in triangle DAB. According to the ratio of the sides of a 30-60-90 triangle, AB is thus $x\sqrt{3} = 3\sqrt{3}$.

14. B

Difficulty: Medium

Strategic Advice: The interior angles of a triangle total 180°, so both triangles have the same angles, 31°, 59°, and 90°; therefore, they are similar triangles. Sides BA and EF are corresponding sides since they are both opposite 39° angles. Their ratio is the same as the ratio of any two corresponding sides.

Getting to the Answer: Sides CB and DE are both opposite 51° angles, so they are corresponding sides with the same ratio as BA and EF. Choice **(B)** is correct.

15. C

Difficulty: Hard

Strategic Advice: Draw a sketch to help interpret this question. The circle will be tangent to each side of the triangle. Both figures are symmetrical, so lines drawn perpendicular to the points of tangency will meet at the center of the circle:

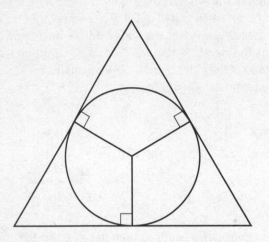

Getting to the Answer: The interior angles of an equilateral triangle are 60°, so a line from a vertex of the triangle to the center of the circle bisects that angle and is part of a 30-60-90 triangle. The longer leg of that triangle is half the length of a side of the triangle, or 5. The shorter leg is the radius of the circle. The ratio of the sides is $1:\sqrt{3}:2$. Since the long leg is 5, multiply the ratio by $\frac{5}{\sqrt{3}}$ to get the actual lengths of $\frac{5}{\sqrt{3}}:5:\frac{10}{\sqrt{3}}$. So the radius of the circle is $\frac{5}{\sqrt{3}}$, and the diameter is twice that, or $\frac{10}{\sqrt{3}}$. Rationalizing the denominator gives $\frac{10}{\sqrt{3}}\left(\frac{\sqrt{3}}{\sqrt{3}}\right) = \frac{10\sqrt{3}}{3}$.

Choice **(C)** is correct.

CHAPTER 12

Circles

Terminology and Basic Formulas

The SAT Math Test includes questions that test your knowledge of circles, including circles drawn on a coordinate plane. Here are some key features that you should review before test day:

- **Radius (r):** the distance from the center of a circle to its edge
- **Chord:** a line segment that connects two points on a circle
- **Diameter (d):** a chord that passes through the center of a circle. The diameter is always the longest chord a circle can have and is twice the length of the radius.
- **Circumference (C):** the distance around a circle given by the formula $C = 2\pi r = \pi d$
- **Area (A):** the space a circle takes up given by the formula $A = \pi r^2$
- Total number of **degrees in a circle:** 360 degrees

Tip: Finding the radius of a circle is often the key to unlocking several other components of the circle. Therefore, your first step for many circle questions will be to find the radius.

Angles, Arcs, and Sectors

The SAT can also ask you about parts of a circle. These parts include angles, arcs, and sectors. You'll need to be familiar with the following terms:

- When radii cut a circle into multiple (but not necessarily equal) pieces, the angle at the center of the circle contained by the radii is the **central angle**. The measure of a central angle cannot be greater than the number of degrees in a circle (360 degrees).
- When two chords share a common endpoint on the circumference of a circle, the angle between the chords is an **inscribed angle**.
- An **arc** is part of a circle's circumference. Thus, an arc length can never be greater than the circumference. Both chords and radii can cut a circle into arcs. The number of arcs present depends on how many chords and/or radii are present. If only two arcs are present, the smaller arc is called the **minor arc**, and the larger one is the **major arc**. On the SAT, if an arc is named with only its two endpoints (such as $\overarc{PQ}$), then you can assume it is a minor arc, which always has a measure that is less than 180 degrees. If a diameter cuts a circle in half, the two arcs formed are called **semicircles** and measure exactly 180 degrees.
- A **sector** is a pie-shaped piece of a circle enclosed by two radii and an arc. The area of a sector cannot be greater than the total area of the circle.

The following ratios can be used to find the size of part of a circle based on what you know about the whole circle:

$$\frac{\text{arc length}}{\text{circumference}} = \frac{\text{central angle}}{360°} = \frac{\text{area of sector}}{\text{area of circle}}$$

Radian Measure

Radians, like degrees, are a measure of the size of angles. There are 2π radians in a circle, which means $2\pi = 360°$, or $\pi = 180°$. To convert between radians and degrees, use the conversion factor $\frac{\pi}{180°}$ or $\frac{180°}{\pi}$, whichever is needed to cancel the unit that you are trying to eliminate. For example, to change 60 degrees to radians, use the conversion factor with degrees in the denominator so that the degrees cancel:

$$60° \times \frac{\pi}{180°} = \frac{60\pi}{180} = \frac{\pi}{3}$$

Knowing how to work with radians also allows you to use these additional properties of circles:

- The length of an arc is equal to the radian measure of the central angle that subtends (forms) the arc.
- The length of an arc is equal to twice the radian measure of the inscribed angle that subtends the arc.

Tangent Lines

A tangent line touches a circle at exactly one point and is perpendicular to the radius of the circle at the point of contact. The following diagram demonstrates what this looks like:

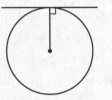

Tip: The presence of a right angle opens up the opportunity to draw otherwise hidden shapes, so pay special attention to tangent lines when they're mentioned in a question.

Circles on the Coordinate Plane and Their Equations

When a circle is drawn on a coordinate plane, its equation is given by $(x - h)^2 + (y - k)^2 = r^2$. This is called standard form. The variables h and k represent the x- and y-coordinates of the center of the circle, and r is the length of the radius. You might also be given the general form of a circle, which is $x^2 + y^2 + Cx + Dy + E = 0$, where C, D, and E are constants. Here are some tips for working with equations of circles:

- To convert from standard form to general form, square the two binomials, $(x - h)^2$ and $(y - k)^2$, square r, move everything to the left side of the equal sign, and simplify as much as possible.
- To convert from general form to standard form, complete the square for the x terms, and then repeat for the y terms.
- To find the center or radius of a circle, write the equation in standard form.

Circles Drill

1. What is the area of a circle with a diameter of 12 ?

2. What is the radius of a circle with a circumference of 36π ?

Questions 3–8 refer to the following figure.

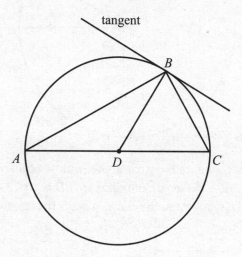

Diameter *AC* is 12, and ∠*CAB* = 30°.

3. What is the measure of ∠*ABC* ?

4. What is the measure of ∠*BDC* ?

5. What is the length of minor arc *BC* ?

6. What is the area of the sector created by ∠*BDC* ?

7. What is the measure of the angle formed by radius *DB* and the tangent line?

8. What is the measure of ∠*BDC* in radians?

9. What is the measure, in radians, of an angle of 135 degrees?

10. What is the measure, in degrees, of the smaller reference angle formed by an angle of 2.25π radians?

Circles Practice Set

DIRECTIONS: Keep a calculator handy as you work through this practice set, but reserve it for those questions that have a calculator icon next to them—and even on those questions, use it only if you really need it. Questions without the icon are intended to be done without a calculator, to help you prepare for the no-calculator section of the SAT.

1. Which of the following equations is the equation of a circle that is centered at $(2, -1)$ in the xy-plane and passes through the point $(6, -1)$?

   A) $(x - 2)^2 + (y + 1)^2 = 4$

   B) $(x + 2)^2 + (y - 1)^2 = 4$

   C) $(x - 2)^2 + (y + 1)^2 = 16$

   D) $(x + 2)^2 + (y - 1)^2 = 16$

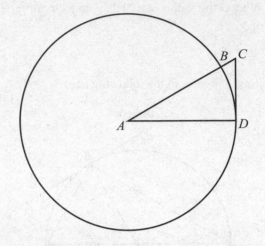

2. The radius of the circle above, with the center at A, is $36\sqrt{3}$, the length of minor arc BD is $6\pi\sqrt{3}$, and CD is tangent to the circle. What is the length of CD ?

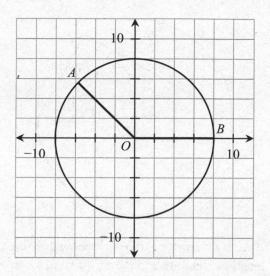

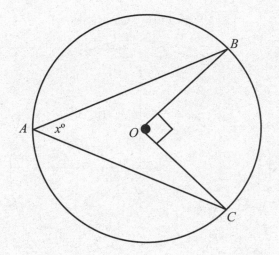

3. In the *xy*-plane above, *O* is the center of the circle, and the measure of ∠*AOB* is $\frac{3\pi}{4}$ radians. If the radius of the circle is 8, what is the *y*-coordinate of point *A* ?

   A) 4

   B) $4\sqrt{2}$

   C) $4\sqrt{3}$

   D) $8\sqrt{2}$

5. In the given figure, point *O* is the center of the circle. What is the value of *x* ?

   A) 45

   B) 60

   C) 75

   D) 90

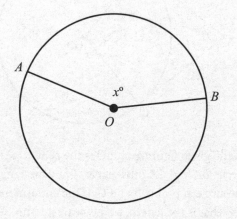

4. In the given figure, point *O* is the center of the circle. If the radius is 6 and the area of minor sector *AOB* is 15π, what is the value of *x* ?

   A)   90

   B)   120

   C)   130

   D)   150

Type of Bird Observed

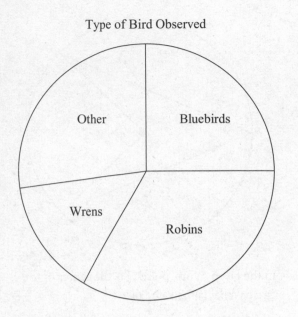

6. A group of birders recorded the results of an afternoon of birding in the form of the pie chart above. If the central angle for the sector "Bluebirds" is 90 degrees, the central angle for "Robins" is 120 degrees, and a total of 96 birds were observed, how many more robins than bluebirds were seen?

A) 8
B) 12
C) 18
D) 30

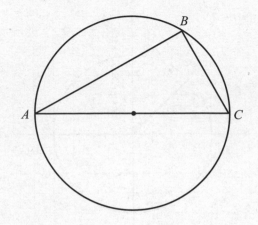

7. If AC is a diameter of the circle above and the lengths of lines AB and BC are $6\sqrt{3}$ and 6, respectively, what is the length of minor arc BC?

A) π
B) 2π
C) 10
D) 4π

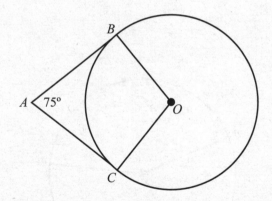

8. In the given figure, point O is the center of the circle. BA and CA intersect at A and are tangent to the circle at points B and C. If the circumference is 50, what is the length, to the nearest tenth, of minor arc BC?

A) 7.3
B) 10.4
C) 14.6
D) 37.5

9. A circle has a radius of 10, and the x-coordinate of the center in the xy-plane is -2. Two points on the circumference of the circle are $(6, 9)$ and $(-8, -5)$. What is the y-coordinate of the center?

   A) -3

   B) 0

   C) 3

   D) 8

$$x(x-6)=47-y(y+10)$$

10. The equation above describes a circle in the xy-plane in a nonstandard form. What is the radius of the circle?

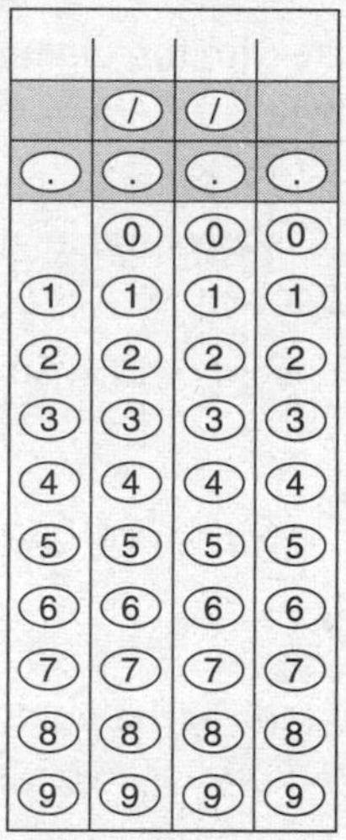

Answers and Explanations

Circles Drill

1. Area $= \pi r^2 = \pi \left(\frac{12}{2}\right)^2 = \pi\left(6^2\right) = 36\pi$

2. Circumference $= 2\pi r$, so $36\pi = 2\pi r$, and $r = 18$.

3. Any triangle inscribed in a circle with the diameter as the long side is a right triangle, so $\angle ABC = 90°$.

4. Angles BDC and BAC connect to the same points on the circumference. Since $\angle BDC$ is a central angle, its measure is twice that of $\angle BAC$: $30° \times 2 = 60°$.

5. The circumference of the circle is $\pi d = 12\pi$. So the length of arc BC is $\frac{60}{360} \times 12\pi = 2\pi$.

6. The area of the circle is $\pi r^2 = \pi\left(6^2\right) = 36\pi$. So the area of the sector is $\frac{60}{360} \times 36\pi = 6\pi$.

7. Tangents are perpendicular to radii at the point where they touch, so $90°$.

8. $360° = 2\pi$ radians, so $\angle BDC$ is
$\frac{60}{360} \times 2\pi = \frac{\pi}{3}$ radians.

9. $\frac{135}{360} = \frac{x}{2\pi}$. So, $270\pi = 360x$, and $x = \frac{3}{4}\pi$.

10. 2π radians is a complete circle, so the angle is
$2.25\pi - 2\pi = 0.25\pi$ radians. $\frac{0.25\pi}{2\pi} = \frac{x}{360°}$, so
$90° = 2x$, and $x = 45°$.

Circles Practice Set

1. C

Difficulty: Medium

Strategic Advice: Determine the radius of the circle, then use the coordinates of the center of the circle to state the equation in the standard format for a circle.

Getting to the Answer: The distance between the center of the circle and the point $(6, -1)$ is $6 - 2 = 4$, since the two points have the same y-coordinate. This is the radius. The equation for a circle with a center at (h, k) and a radius r is $(x - h)^2 + (y - k)^2 = r^2$. The coordinates of the center are given, so the equation for this circle is $(x - 2)^2 + (y + 1)^2 = 4^2 = 16$. Choice **(C)** is correct.

2. 36

Difficulty: Hard

Strategic Advice: Determine the central angle that defines the arc BD. Since CD is tangent to the circle, triangle ACD is a right triangle. Use the properties of right triangles to determine the length of CD.

Getting to the Answer: The proportion to determine the central angle for an arc, in which a is the number of degrees, is $\frac{a}{360} = \frac{\text{arc length}}{\text{circumference}}$. Since the circumference of a circle is $2\pi r$, the proportion is $\frac{a}{360} = \frac{6\pi\sqrt{3}}{2\pi\left(36\sqrt{3}\right)}$. This simplifies to $\frac{a}{360} = \frac{1}{12}$. So, $12a = 360$, and $a = 30$. This means that triangle ACD is a 30-60-90 triangle with the side ratio $1:\sqrt{3}:2$. The length of AD is $36\sqrt{3}$, so the length of CD is **36**.

3. B

Difficulty: Hard

Strategic Advice: Determine the central angle of angle AOB, then use the properties of triangles to get the y-coordinate of point A. (Note that the scale of the graph is 2 units for each grid.)

Getting to the Answer: Since 2π radians is $360°$, write the proportion $\frac{\angle AOB}{360} = \frac{\frac{3}{4}\pi}{2\pi}$. So, $2(\angle AOB) = \frac{3}{4}(360) = 270$, and $\angle AOB = 135$. This is $45 + 90$, so a horizontal line from A to the y-axis creates a 45-45-90 right triangle with the hypotenuse being the radius, 8.

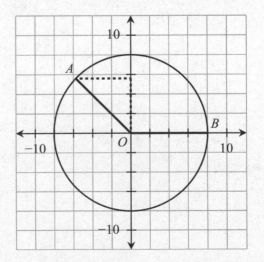

Since the side ratio of this triangle is $1:1:\sqrt{2}$ and the radius is 8, the length of the vertical leg is $\frac{8}{\sqrt{2}} = 4\sqrt{2}$, which is also the y-coordinate of point A. Choice **(B)** is correct.

4. D

Difficulty: Medium

Strategic Advice: Use the ratio of the area of the sector to the area of the circle to set up a proportion for the angles.

Getting to the Answer: The proportion is $\frac{15\pi}{\pi(6^2)} = \frac{x°}{360°}$. To make the math easier, multiply both sides by 36, so $15 = \frac{x}{10}$, and $x = 150$. Choice **(D)** is correct.

5. A

Difficulty: Hard

Strategic Advice: The central angle theorem states that the central angle from two points on a circle is twice the inscribed angle from those points.

Getting to the Answer: The central angle in this question is $90°$, so $x°$ is half that, or $45°$. Choice **(A)** is correct.

6. A

Difficulty: Medium

Strategic Advice: The area of a sector is the central angle as a fraction of $360°$ times the area of the circle. For this pie chart, think of the area as the total number of observations. Use this property to calculate the difference between the numbers of bluebirds and robins.

Getting to the Answer: Instead of calculating the number of each type of bird, note that the difference in the central angles for robins and bluebirds is $120° - 90° = 30°$. This is $\frac{30}{360} = \frac{1}{12}$ the area of the circle. Since the entire circle represents 96 birds spotted, and $\frac{1}{12}(96) = 8$, there were 8 more robins than bluebirds. Choice **(A)** is correct.

7. B

Difficulty: Medium

Strategic Advice: A triangle inscribed in a circle with one side being a diameter is a right triangle. Use the properties of right triangles to determine the diameter and the angle at vertex A. Apply the central angle theorem to find the central angle that defines arc BC, and use the diameter to calculate the arc length.

Getting to the Answer: The leg ratios are consistent with the $1:\sqrt{3}:2$ ratio of a 30-60-90 triangle. So the angle at vertex A is $30°$, and the length of diameter AC is $6 \times 2 = 12$. Per the central angle theorem, the central angle subtended by arc BC is twice the inscribed angle subtended by arc BC: $2 \times 30° = 60°$. Set up a proportion to find the arc length: $\frac{60°}{360°} = \frac{\overset{\frown}{BC}}{\pi d}$. So the length of arc BC is $\frac{1}{6}(12\pi) = 2\pi$. Choice **(B)** is correct.

8. C

Difficulty: Hard

Strategic Advice: Use the properties of tangents to a circle and the interior angles of a quadrilateral to calculate the central angle at O. Use that value and the circumference to find the arc length.

Getting to the Answer: The tangents create right angles at their intersection with the radii at B and C. The sum of the interior angles of quadrilateral $ABOC$ is $360°$. Since the measure of three of the angles is known, the measure of the central angle is $360° - 90° - 90° - 75° = 105°$. Set up a proportion to determine the arc length: $\frac{105}{360} = \frac{BC}{50}$. So, $50 \times 105 = 360 \times BC$, and $BC \approx 14.6$. Choice **(C)** is correct.

9.   C

Difficulty: Hard

Strategic Advice: Write the equation for a circle given the *x*-coordinate of the center and the radius. Plug in the given points and solve for the *y*-coordinate of the center.

Getting to the Answer: The equation for a circle is $(x - h)^2 + (y - k)^2 = r^2$, so $(x + 2)^2 + (y - b)^2 = 100$. Plug in the point (6, 9): $(6 + 2)^2 + (9 - b)^2 = 100$. So, $(9 - b)^2 = 100 - 64 = 36$. Take the square root of both sides of $(9 - b)^2 = 36$ to get $(9 - b) = \pm 6$. This means that *b* could be either 3 or 15.

Plug in the point (−8, −5): $(-8 + 2)^2 + (-5 - b)^2 = 100$. So, $(-5 - b)^2 = 100 - 36 = 64$. Thus, $(-5 - b) = \pm 8$, which means that *b* could be 3 or −13. The common value for *b* in the two solutions is 3, so that is the *y*-coordinate of the center. Choice **(C)** is correct.

10.   9

Difficulty: Hard

Strategic Advice: Convert the equation to the standard format for a circle. The radius of the circle will be the square root of the constant term on the right side.

Getting to the Answer: Start by distributing the multiplication to get $x^2 - 6x = 47 - y^2 - 10y$. Move the *y* terms to the left side: $x^2 - 6x + y^2 + 10y = 47$. Look at the coefficients of the *x* and *y* terms to determine the center coordinates. The −6 coefficient of *x* means that the *x*-coordinate of the center is $-\frac{b}{2a} = \frac{-6}{2(1)} = 3$. Similarly, the *y*-coefficient of the center is $-\frac{10}{2(1)} = -5$. When squared, you get 9 and 25, respectively; these become the constants that are added to complete the square.

Now the equation can be written as $\left(x^2 - 6x + 9\right) + \left(y^2 + 10y + 25\right) = 47 + 9 + 25$. Restated in standard format, this becomes $(x - 3)^2 + (y + 5)^2 = 81$. The radius is $\sqrt{81} = 9$. Grid in **9**.

CHAPTER 13

Three-Dimensional Figures

Introduction to 3-D Shapes

In addition to expertise in two-dimensional geometry, you'll also want to have a good understanding of **solids**, or three-dimensional shapes. You'll want to be familiar with both the terminology and formulas related to these shapes.

Terminology

A **face** is one of the sides of a solid. Two faces meet at a line segment called an **edge**, and three faces meet at a single point called a **vertex**.

The following diagram illustrates these terms:

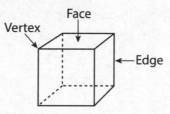

Volume

Volume is the amount of 3-D space occupied by a solid. This is analogous to the area of a 2-D shape like a triangle or circle. You can find the volume of many 3-D shapes by finding the area of the base and multiplying it by the height. We've highlighted the base area components of the formulas in the following table with parentheses. You'll be given the volume formulas on test day, so you don't absolutely have to memorize them all; however, knowing the formulas in advance will save valuable time.

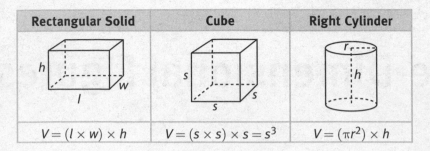

Rectangular Solid	Cube	Right Cylinder
$V = (l \times w) \times h$	$V = (s \times s) \times s = s^3$	$V = (\pi r^2) \times h$

The rectangular solid and cube in the table above are **prisms**. Almost all prisms on the SAT are right prisms; that is, all faces are perpendicular to those with which they share edges. Less commonly seen prisms (e.g., triangular, hexagonal, octagonal, etc.) have the same general volume formula as these: $V = A_{base} \times h$.

More complicated 3-D shapes include the right pyramid, right cone, and sphere. The vertex of a right pyramid or right cone will always be centered above the middle of the base. Their volume formulas are similar to those of prisms, with an added coefficient.

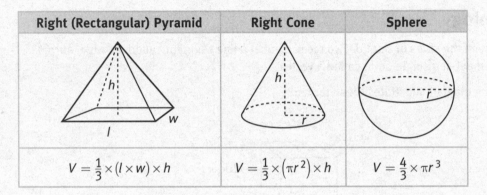

Right (Rectangular) Pyramid	Right Cone	Sphere
$V = \frac{1}{3} \times (l \times w) \times h$	$V = \frac{1}{3} \times (\pi r^2) \times h$	$V = \frac{4}{3} \times \pi r^3$

Surface Area

Surface area is the sum of the areas of all faces of a solid. You might compare this to determining the amount of paper needed to cover all sides of a box. To calculate the surface area of a solid, simply find the area of each face using your 2-D geometry skills, and then add them all together. Formulas for calculating surface area are NOT provided on the reference page.

You might think that finding the surface area of a solid with many faces, such as a 10-faced right octagonal prism, is a tall order. However, you can save time by noticing a vital trait: the prism has two identical octagonal faces and eight identical rectangular faces. Don't waste time finding the area of each of the 10 faces; find the area of one octagonal face and one rectangular face instead. Once complete, multiply the area of the octagonal face by 2 and the area of the rectangular face by 8, add the products together, and you're done! The same is true for other 3-D shapes, such as rectangular solids (including cubes), other right prisms, and certain pyramids.

Three-Dimensional Figures Practice Set

DIRECTIONS: Keep a calculator handy as you work through this practice set, but reserve it for those questions that have a calculator icon next to them—and even on those questions, use it only if you really need it. Questions without the icon are intended to be done without a calculator, to help you prepare for the no-calculator section of the SAT.

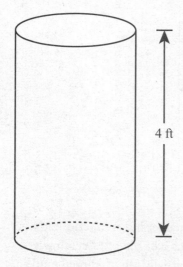

4 ft

1. In the figure given, the volume of the right circular cylinder is 4π cubic feet. What is the diameter, in feet, of the base of the cylinder?

    A) 1
    B) 2
    C) 4
    D) 8

2. An aquarium in the shape of a rectangular prism is 36 inches long, 24 inches wide, and 19 inches deep. The tank is filled with water to a level 1 inch below the top. If the density of water is 62.4 pounds per cubic foot, what is the weight of the water to the nearest pound? (Note: 1 foot = 12 inches.)

3. A right circular cone has a volume of 96π cubic centimeters. If the radius of the cone is 4 centimeters, what is the height, in centimeters, of the cone?

    A) 9
    B) 12
    C) 16
    D) 18

4. If the volume of a sphere is the same as that of a cylinder with radius 4 feet and height 18 feet, what is the radius, in feet, of the sphere?

A) 2

B) 3

C) 6

D) 12

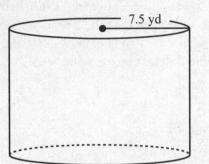

7.5 yd

5. In the figure given, if the height of the right circular cylinder is 12 yards, what is the volume, in cubic feet, of the cylinder? (Note: 1 yard = 3 feet.)

A) 675π

B) 2,025π

C) 6,075π

D) 18,225π

6. The volume of a cube is $\frac{1}{8}$ m³. What is the perimeter, in meters, of one face of the cube?

7. A cylindrical container has an interior radius of 12 centimeters and a height of 14 centimeters. The cylinder is partially full of a liquid until an additional 2,200 cubic centimeters are added to completely fill it. Approximately what percentage of the capacity of the container was filled before the additional liquid was added?

A) 35%

B) 58%

C) 62%

D) 65%

8. A cylindrical tank with a radius of 10 inches is partially filled with water. A sphere with radius k is placed in the tank and is fully submerged, thus displacing an amount of water equal to its volume. How many inches will this raise the water level in the cylinder?

A) $\frac{2k^2}{25}$

B) $\frac{k^3}{30\pi}$

C) $\frac{k^3}{75}$

D) $\frac{8k^3}{3}$

9. Air is pumped into a spherical balloon at a constant rate. Which of the following graphs best illustrates the radius of the balloon as it expands?

A)

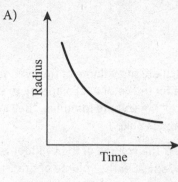

B)

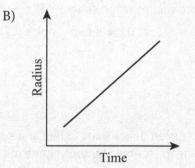

C)

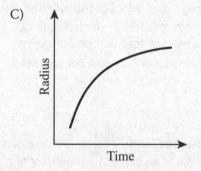

D)

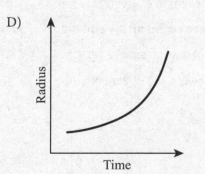

10. A sphere with a radius of 8 centimeters is inscribed within a cube such that the sphere is tangent to all the faces of the cube. Which of the following is closest to the volume, in cubic centimeters, within the cube but outside the sphere?

A) 1,950

B) 2,000

C) 3,900

D) 5,850

Answers and Explanations

Three-Dimensional Figures Practice Set

1. B

Difficulty: Easy

Strategic Advice: Plug the height and volume into the formula for the volume of a cylinder (available on the reference page on test day) and solve for the radius.

Getting to the Answer: The volume of a cylinder is given by $V = (\pi r^2) \times h$, so the volume equation is $4\pi = \pi r^2(4)$. So, $r^2 = 1$ and $r = 1$ since the radius cannot be negative. The diameter is twice the radius, or 2. Choice **(B)** is correct.

2. 562

Difficulty: Hard

Strategic Advice: Convert the dimensions to feet, calculate the volume of the water, and then multiply or divide (as appropriate for the units) by the density to get the weight.

Getting to the Answer: The length of the tank is $\frac{36 \text{ in}}{12 \text{ in/ft}} = 3$ ft, and the width is 2 feet. The height is 19 inches, but the tank is only filled to a depth of 18 inches, which is 1.5 feet. Thus, the volume of the water is 3 ft $\times$ 2 ft $\times$ 1.5 ft = 9 cubic feet. The weight is $9 \text{ ft}^3 \times \frac{62.4 \text{ lb}}{\text{ft}^3} = 561.6$ lb. This rounds to **562**.

3. D

Difficulty: Easy

Strategic Advice: Use the formula for the volume of a cone to solve for h.

Getting to the Answer: The formula for the volume of a cone (which will be given on the reference page on test day) is $V = \frac{1}{3}\pi r^2 h$. Plug in the known values for the cone, $96\pi = \frac{1}{3}\pi(4)^2 h$; then solve for h: $h = \frac{3(96\pi)}{16\pi} = 18$ centimeters. Choice **(D)** is correct.

4. C

Difficulty: Medium

Strategic Advice: Calculate the volume of the cylinder. Then use the formula for the volume of a sphere to solve for r. (If you don't recall the volume formulas, they are available on the reference page.)

Getting to the Answer: The volume of the cylinder is $\pi r^2 h = \pi(4)^2(18) = 288\pi$. Set the volume of the cylinder equal to the volume of the sphere: $288\pi = \frac{4}{3}\pi r^3$. So, $r^3 = \frac{3(288\pi)}{4\pi} = 216$, and $r = 6$ feet. Choice **(C)** is correct.

5. D

Difficulty: Medium

Strategic Advice: Convert dimensions to feet and solve for the volume using the formula for the volume of a cylinder, $V = (\pi r^2) \times h$.

Getting to the Answer: The radius of the cylinder is 7.5 yards, which equates to 22.5 feet. Similarly, the height of 12 yards is 36 feet. So the volume is $V = \pi(22.5)^2 \times 36 = 18,225\pi$. Choice **(D)** is correct.

6. 2

Difficulty: Easy

Strategic Advice: Use the formula for the volume of a cube to get the length of an edge. The perimeter of a face is 4 times the length of an edge.

Getting to the Answer: Set up the equation $V = s^3 = \frac{1}{8}$. Take the cube root of each side to get $s = \frac{\sqrt[3]{1}}{\sqrt[3]{8}} = \frac{1}{2}$. The perimeter of a face is $4 \times \frac{1}{2} = $ **2** meters.

7. D

Difficulty: Medium

Strategic Advice: Use the formula for the volume of a cylinder, $V = (\pi r^2) \times h$, to solve for the total volume, set up a proportion to determine the percentage of capacity that was the additional liquid, and subtract that from 100%. Since the question asks for an approximate value, you can use estimation shortcuts.

Getting to the Answer: The total volume of the cylinder is $\pi(12)^2 14 \approx 6333$. Set up a proportion to find what percentage of the capacity of the cylinder was added: $\frac{2,200}{6,333} = \frac{x}{100\%}$. Cross-multiply to get $6,333x = 220,000\%$, so $x \approx 34.7\%$. Subtract this from 100% to get the original percentage of the capacity of the container that was filled before additional liquid was added: $100\% - 34.7\% = 65.3\%$. Choice **(D)** is closest to this result.

8. C

Difficulty: Hard

Strategic Advice: Placing the sphere in the tank has the same effect on the height of the water in the tank as would adding that much water. Use the formula for the volume of a cylinder to determine how high that much water would fill the cylinder; this is the amount by which the height will be raised.

Getting to the Answer: The volume of the sphere is $\frac{4}{3}\pi k^3$. The equation for the volume of the cylinder is $V = \pi(10)^2 h$. Set these two equal to each other and solve for h, the height that the water level will increase. Thus, $\frac{4}{3}\pi k^3 = 100\pi h$. The π terms cancel out, so $h = \frac{4k^3}{300} = \frac{k^3}{75}$. Choice **(C)** is correct.

9. C

Difficulty: Medium

Strategic Advice: The volume of a sphere is $\frac{4}{3}\pi r^3$. Consequently, the volume depends on the cube of the radius.

Getting to the Answer: As the radius increases, it takes ever-greater volumes of air to continue to increase the radius. Because air is being added at a constant rate, the radius should be increasing at a decreasing rate over time, which matches the shape of **(C)**.

10. A

Difficulty: Hard

Strategic Advice: The length of the side of the cube is the diameter of the sphere. The volume within the cube but outside the sphere is the volume of the cube minus the volume of the sphere. Since the question asks for the choice that is closest to that volume, you can approximate as needed.

Getting to the Answer: The radius of the sphere is 8, so the diameter, which is the same length as a side of the cube, is 16. The volume of the cube is thus $s^3 = 16^3 = 4,096$. The volume of the sphere is $\frac{4}{3}\pi r^3 = \frac{4}{3}\pi(8)^3 \approx 2,145$. Thus, the approximate volume within the cube but outside the sphere is $4,096 - 2,145 = 1,951$ cubic centimeters. Choice **(A)** is closest to this result.

CHAPTER 14

Trigonometry

Introduction to Trigonometry

The word *trigonometry* comes from Greek words meaning "triangle" and "measure." The one or two trig questions that you may encounter on test day will probably be based on a triangle, and more specifically, a right triangle.

Trigonometric Ratios

You may recall learning the acronym SOH-CAH-TOA, a mnemonic device for remembering the **sine, cosine,** and **tangent** ratios. These are the trigonometric ratios you may see on the SAT. They are summarized in the following table:

Sine (sin)	Cosine (cos)	Tangent (tan)
$\dfrac{\text{opposite}}{\text{hypotenuse}}$	$\dfrac{\text{adjacent}}{\text{hypotenuse}}$	$\dfrac{\text{opposite}}{\text{adjacent}}$

The following example shows how to set up these trig ratios for a specific angle:

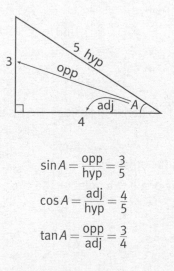

$$\sin A = \frac{\text{opp}}{\text{hyp}} = \frac{3}{5}$$

$$\cos A = \frac{\text{adj}}{\text{hyp}} = \frac{4}{5}$$

$$\tan A = \frac{\text{opp}}{\text{adj}} = \frac{3}{4}$$

Complementary Angle Relationship

Besides the sine, cosine, and tangent ratios, the SAT tests one other trigonometric property: the fact that the sine of an acute angle is equal to the cosine of its complement. (Remember that complementary angles sum to 90 degrees.) For example, $\sin(20°) = \cos(70°)$ because 20 degrees and 70 degrees are complementary angles. The same is true in reverse: $\cos(20°) = \sin(70°)$. This can be stated mathematically as $\sin(x°) = \cos(90° - x°)$ or $\cos(x°) = \sin(90° - x°)$.

Radians

Most geometry questions present angle measures in degrees. In trigonometry (and in some circle questions), you may encounter a different unit: the radian. In the chapter on circles, you learned that $180° = \pi$ radians and that you can use the conversion factor $\dfrac{\pi}{180°}$ or $\dfrac{180°}{\pi}$ to convert between units, whichever is needed to cancel the unit that you are trying to eliminate.

Benchmark Angles

Knowing the trig functions for the most commonly tested "benchmark" angles will save time on test day. You will not be asked to evaluate trig functions for angles that require a calculator. The table below gives the most commonly tested angles in degrees, their radian equivalents, and their trig values. (Note: "Und" means undefined.)

x	$0°\ (0\pi)$	$30°\left(\dfrac{\pi}{6}\right)$	$45°\left(\dfrac{\pi}{6}\right)$	$60°\left(\dfrac{\pi}{3}\right)$	$90°\left(\dfrac{\pi}{2}\right)$	$180°\ (\pi)$	$270°\left(\dfrac{3\pi}{2}\right)$	$360°\ (2\pi)$
$\sin x$	0	$\dfrac{1}{2}$	$\dfrac{\sqrt{2}}{2}$	$\dfrac{\sqrt{3}}{2}$	1	0	-1	0
$\cos x$	1	$\dfrac{\sqrt{3}}{2}$	$\dfrac{\sqrt{2}}{2}$	$\dfrac{1}{2}$	0	-1	0	1
$\tan x$	0	$\dfrac{\sqrt{3}}{3}$	1	$\sqrt{3}$	Und	0	Und	0

The Unit Circle

You can also use a unit circle (a circle of radius 1) to derive trig values. Here's an example:

For a 60-degree angle:

- Draw a circle with a radius of 1 centered at the origin.
- In the first quadrant, draw a radius from the origin to a point on the circle in such a way that it forms a 60-degree angle with the x-axis.

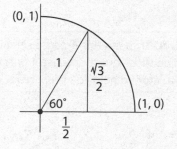

- Recall that the ratio for the sides of a 30-60-90 triangle is $x:x\sqrt{3}:2x$ Use the length of the hypotenuse (which is 1 because it is the radius of the circle) to find the lengths of the legs. If $2x = 1$, then $x = \frac{1}{2}$ and $x\sqrt{3} = \frac{1}{2}\left(\sqrt{3}\right) = \frac{\sqrt{3}}{2}$.

- Use SOH-CAH-TOA: $\sin(60°) = \frac{\frac{\sqrt{3}}{2}}{1} = \frac{\sqrt{3}}{2}$, $\cos(60°) = \frac{\frac{1}{2}}{1} = \frac{1}{2}$, $\tan(60°) = \frac{\frac{\sqrt{3}}{2}}{\frac{1}{2}} = \sqrt{3}$.

- You can use this same process for any of the benchmark angles (or multiples of these angles) using either a 30-60-90 triangle or a 45-45-90 triangle.

The legs of the triangle also give the coordinates of the point where the radius intersects the circle: $(x, y) = (\cos A, \sin A)$. Knowing the signs of the x- and y-values in each of the quadrants of the coordinate plane gives the signs of the trig values. For example, for any angle that lands in quadrant II, the cosine will be negative (because the x-coordinate of any point in quadrant II is negative) and the sine will be positive (because the y-coordinate of any point in quadrant II is positive).

Trigonometry Practice Set

DIRECTIONS: Keep a calculator handy as you work through this practice set, but reserve it for those questions that have a calculator icon next to them—and even on those questions, use it only if you really need it. Questions without the icon are intended to be done without a calculator, to help you prepare for the no-calculator section of the SAT.

1. If $\sin x° = a$ and $\cos x° = b$, what is the value of $2\cos x° + \cos(90° - x°) + 2\sin(90° - x°) - \sin x°$?

    A) $2a - 2b$

    B) $2a + 2b$

    C) $4a$

    D) $4b$

2. If $\tan a = \frac{3}{4}$ and $\cos a = \frac{4}{5}$, what is the value of $\sin a$?

    A) $\frac{5}{3}$

    B) $\frac{4}{3}$

    C) $\frac{5}{4}$

    D) $\frac{3}{5}$

3. The acute interior angles of a right triangle are a and b. If $\sin a = 0.6$, what is $2\cos b$?

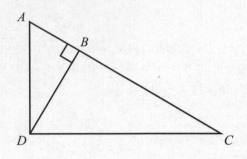

4. In the figure above, angle $ADC = 90°$, the length of AC is 50, and $\cos C = 0.8$. What is the length of BC ?

    A) 18

    B) 30

    C) 32

    D) 36

5. Triangle ABC has a right angle at vertex A. If $\sin C = \frac{5}{13}$, what is the value of $\tan B$?

    A) $\frac{5}{12}$

    B) $\frac{8}{13}$

    C) $\frac{8}{5}$

    D) $\frac{12}{5}$

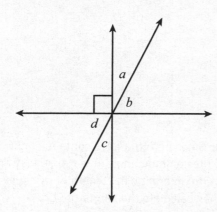

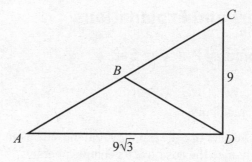

6. In the figure above, the measure of angle a is less than the measure of angle b. Which of the following statements is NOT true?

   A) $\sin a = \cos b$

   B) $\sin a = \cos d$

   C) $\sin d = \cos b$

   D) $\sin d = \cos a$

8. In the figure above, angle ADC is a right angle. If $\cos \angle BDA = \dfrac{\sqrt{3}}{2}$, what is $\sin \angle CDB$?

   A) $\dfrac{\sqrt{3}}{2}$

   B) $\dfrac{\sqrt{2}}{2}$

   C) $\dfrac{1}{2}$

   D) $\dfrac{\sqrt{3}}{4}$

7. Triangles ABC and DEF are similar; vertices D, E, and F correspond to vertices A, B, and C. The measure of angle B is 90 degrees, the length of BC is $24\sqrt{3}$, and $\sin C = 0.5$. The lengths of the sides of triangle ABC are 1.5 times those of triangle DEF. What is the length of side DE?

Answers and Explanations

Trigonometry Practice Set

1. D

Difficulty: Medium

Strategic Advice: Use the property that the sine of an angle is equal to the cosine of its complementary angle in order to restate all terms as a or b, then solve that expression.

Getting to the Answer: Replace $\sin x°$ and $\cos(90° - x°)$ with a, and replace $\cos x°$ and $\sin(90° - x°)$ with b, and solve that expression: $2\cos x° + \cos(90° - x°) + 2\sin(90° - x°) - \sin x° = 2b + a + 2b - a = 4b$. Choice **(D)** is correct.

2. D

Difficulty: Medium

Strategic Advice: Use the definitions of sine, cosine, and tangent to set up an equation and solve that for $\sin a$.

Getting to the Answer: Since $\tan = \dfrac{\text{opposite}}{\text{adjacent}}$, $\sin = \dfrac{\text{opposite}}{\text{hypotenuse}}$ and $\cos = \dfrac{\text{adjacent}}{\text{hypotenuse}}$, you can write that $\dfrac{\text{opposite}}{\text{adjacent}} = \dfrac{\frac{\text{opposite}}{\text{hypotenuse}}}{\frac{\text{adjacent}}{\text{hypotenuse}}}$, since both top and bottom of the fraction have the same numerator, hypotenuse. Thus, $\tan a = \dfrac{\sin a}{\cos a}$. Plug in the known values to get

$\dfrac{3}{4} = \dfrac{\sin a}{\frac{4}{5}}$. So, $\sin a = \dfrac{3}{4} \times \dfrac{4}{5} = \dfrac{3}{5}$. Choice **(D)** is correct.

3. 1.2

Difficulty: Medium

Strategic Advice: Since the angle other than a and b is $90°$, angles a and b are complementary. Use the property that the sine of an angle is equal to the cosine of its complementary angle to solve for $2\cos b$.

Getting to the Answer: If $\sin a = \cos b$, then $2\cos b = 2(0.6) =$ **1.2.**

4. C

Difficulty: Hard

Strategic Advice: Since both triangles contain a right angle and share the common angle at vertex A, they are similar. Use $\cos C$ to determine the length of DC, from which you can then calculate the length of BC.

Getting to the Answer: Using SOH-CAH-TOA, $\cos C = \dfrac{DC}{AC}$, so $DC = 0.8(50) = 40$. Use $\cos C = \dfrac{BC}{DC}$ to solve directly for BC: $0.8 = \dfrac{BC}{40}$, so $BC = 32$.

Alternatively, since ACD is a right triangle with a hypotenuse of 50 and one leg of 40, it is a 3:4:5 Pythagorean triple triangle. Therefore, $AD = 30$. Because triangle ABD is also a 3:4:5 Pythagorean triple triangle, $AB = \dfrac{3}{5}AD = 0.6(30) = 18$. So $BC = 50 - 18 = 32$. Choice **(C)** is correct.

5. D

Difficulty: Medium

Strategic Advice: Use SOH-CAH-TOA and the Pythagorean theorem to determine the value of $\tan B$.

Getting to the Answer: Draw a sketch to help visualize the triangle:

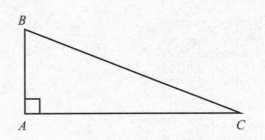

Because $\sin C$ is opposite over hypotenuse, those sides must be some multiple of 5 and 13. Those lengths are two parts of a Pythagorean triple, 5:12:13. The other side must be the same multiple of 12. (If you didn't recognize the triple, you could still determine the length of the other leg using the Pythagorean theorem.) The side opposite vertex C, which is a multiple of 5, is the side adjacent to vertex B. The side that is a multiple of 12 must, therefore, be the side opposite vertex B. Tangent $= \dfrac{\text{opposite}}{\text{adjacent}}$, so $\tan B = \dfrac{12}{5}$. Choice **(D)** is correct.

6.   **C**

Difficulty: Medium

Strategic Advice: Because two of the lines are perpendicular, angles a and b are complementary as are angles c and d. Because they are vertical angles, angles a and c are equal and angles b and d are also equal.

Getting to the Answer: For (A), because a and b are complementary, $a + b = 90°$, and $\sin x = \cos (90° - x)$, this is correct. Similarly, since b and d are equal, (B) is also true. For **(C)**, since angles b and d are equal, $\sin d$ does not equal $\cos b$, so this is an incorrect equation.

7.   **16**

Difficulty: Medium

Strategic Advice: Determine the length of side AB. Then use the ratios of the lengths of the sides of triangle ABC to those of DEF to calculate the length of DE. Draw a sketch to understand the given values and their relationships:

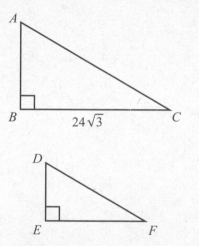

Getting to the Answer: Since $\sin C = 0.5$, the short leg is half the hypotenuse and both triangles are 30-60-90 right triangles. So their side ratio is $1:\sqrt{3}:2$. Because $BC = 24\sqrt{3}$, the length of AB is 24. The given side ratio means that $AB = 1.5DE$, so $DE = \frac{24}{1.5} = $ **16**.

8.   **A**

Difficulty: Medium

Strategic Advice: The sine of an acute angle equals the cosine of its complement.

Getting to the Answer: Angle ADC is said to be equal to $90°$. Thus, angles BDA and CDB are complementary, and the sine of angle CDB equals the cosine of angle BDA. Since $\cos \angle BDA = \frac{\sqrt{3}}{2}$, $\sin \angle CDB = \frac{\sqrt{3}}{2}$. Choice **(A)** is correct.

CHAPTER 15

Imaginary Numbers

Introduction to Imaginary Numbers

Until you reached more advanced math classes like Algebra 2, Pre-Calculus, or Trigonometry, you were likely taught that it is impossible to take the square root of a negative number. There is some truth to this, as the result isn't a real number. However, it is mathematically possible, and what you'll get is an imaginary number.

To take the square root of a negative number, it is necessary to use i, which is defined in math as the square root of -1. For example, to find $\sqrt{-49}$, rewrite it as $\sqrt{-1 \times 49}$, take the square root of -1 (which is by definition i), and then take the square root of 49, which is 7. The end result is $7i$.

Powers of i

When an imaginary number is raised to a power, you can use the pattern shown below to determine what the resulting term will be. Here are the first several in the pattern:

- $i^1 = i$
- $i^2 = -1$ (by definition because $\sqrt{-1} = i$)
- $i^3 = i^2 \times i = -1 \times i = -i$
- $i^4 = i^2 \times i^2 = -1 \times -1 = 1$
- $i^5 = i^4 \times i = 1 \times i = i$
- $i^6 = i^4 \times i^2 = 1 \times -1 = -1$

If you continued the pattern indefinitely, you would see that it repeats over and over in cycles of four ($i, -1, -i, 1, i, -1, -i, 1, \dots$). To simplify a large power of i, divide the exponent by 4 (the number of terms in the cycle) and look at the remainder. The remainder tells you which term in the cycle the number is equivalent to. For example, to evaluate i^{35}, divide 35 by 4 to get 8, remainder 3. This means that i^{35} is equivalent to i^3, which is $-i$.

Multiplying Radicals

Be particularly careful when multiplying two radicals that both contain negative numbers. The first step is *always* to rewrite each quantity as the square root of the product of -1 and a positive number. Take the square root of -1, and then multiply the resulting expressions together. For example, if asked to multiply $\sqrt{-16} \times \sqrt{-25}$, you must first rewrite the expression as $i\sqrt{16} \times i\sqrt{25}$, which becomes $4i \times 5i = 20i^2 = 20(-1) = -20$. Combining the two radicals into a single one and canceling the negative signs to give $\sqrt{16 \times 25}$ is incorrect and will likely lead to a trap answer.

Complex Numbers

When a number is written in the form $a + bi$, where a is the real component and bi is the imaginary component, it is referred to as a *complex number*. You can add, subtract, multiply, and divide complex numbers. Here are a few rules:

- To add (or subtract) complex numbers, simply add (or subtract) the real parts and then add (or subtract) the imaginary parts.
- To multiply complex numbers, treat them as binomials and use FOIL. To simplify the product, use the definition $i^2 = -1$ and combine like terms.
- To divide complex numbers, write them in fraction form, and then *rationalize the denominator* (just as you would a fraction with a radical in the denominator) by multiplying top and bottom by the conjugate of the complex number in the denominator. For example, if asked to divide $21 \div (3 + 5i)$, start by writing it as $\frac{21}{3 + 5i}$. Then multiply top and bottom by the conjugate of $3 + 5i$, which is $3 - 5i$.

Quadratic Equations with Imaginary Solutions

In addition to real solutions, quadratic equations can have imaginary solutions, which you can find by using the quadratic formula. Recall from the previous practice set that the quadratic formula is $x = \dfrac{-b \pm \sqrt{b^2 - 4ac}}{2a}$ and that the sign of the discriminant $\left(b^2 - 4ac\right)$ dictates the nature of the solutions. When $b^2 - 4ac < 0$, the equation will have two imaginary solutions because you are taking the square root of a negative quantity.

Graphically, a quadratic equation has imaginary solutions when its vertex is above the x-axis and the parabola opens upward, or when its vertex is below the x-axis and the parabola opens downward. In either case, the graph does not cross the x-axis and therefore has no real solutions.

Imaginary Numbers Practice Set

DIRECTIONS: Questions testing imaginary numbers typically show up on the no-calculator section, so put your calculator aside while working on this practice set.

1. For $i = \sqrt{-1}$, what is $(-4 + 3i) + (-5 + 9i)$?

   A) $-9 + 12i$

   B) $-9 - 6i$

   C) $1 + 12i$

   D) $1 - 6i$

2. For $i = \sqrt{-1}$, what is $(-3 - 5i) - (-9 + 2i)$?

   A) $-12 - 7i$

   B) $-12 - 3i$

   C) $6 - 7i$

   D) $6 - 3i$

3. For $i = \sqrt{-1}$, what is the sum of $3(-i + 4) + 5(2i - 3)$?

   A) $4i + 1$

   B) $7i - 3$

   C) $7i + 15$

   D) $13i + 27$

4. For $i = \sqrt{-1}$, what is the value of $9 + i(6i)$?

5. For $i = \sqrt{-1}$, what is the value of $\dfrac{6i^4 - i^3}{3i^2}$?

   A) $-2 + i$

   B) $-2 - \dfrac{1}{3}i$

   C) $-2 + \dfrac{1}{3}i$

   D) $2 - \dfrac{1}{3}i$

6. Which of the following complex numbers is equivalent to $\dfrac{3 + i}{4 - 3i}$? (Note: $i = \sqrt{-1}$.)

   A) $\dfrac{9}{25} + \dfrac{13}{25}i$

   B) $\dfrac{15}{25} + \dfrac{7}{25}i$

   C) $\dfrac{9}{7} + i$

   D) $\dfrac{15}{7} + i$

7. If the expression $\dfrac{-3-2i}{2+3i}$ is rewritten in the form $a + bi$, where a and b are real numbers, what is the value of b ? (Note: $i = \sqrt{-1}$.)

A) $\dfrac{-5}{13}$

B) $\dfrac{5}{13}$

C) $\dfrac{7}{13}$

D) $\dfrac{5}{7}$

8. For $i = \sqrt{-1}$, what is the value of $\dfrac{(i-2)(i+3)}{2i}$?

A) $-\dfrac{1}{2} - \dfrac{7}{2}i$

B) $-\dfrac{1}{2} + \dfrac{7}{2}i$

C) $\dfrac{1}{2} - \dfrac{7}{2}i$

D) $\dfrac{1}{2} + \dfrac{7}{2}i$

Answers and Explanations

Imaginary Numbers Practice Set

1.   A

Difficulty: Easy

Strategic Advice: Combine like terms.

Getting to the Answer: Combine the integers: $-4 + (-5) = -9$. Combine the terms with i: $3i + 9i = 12i$. Choice **(A)** is correct.

2.   C

Difficulty: Easy

Strategic Advice: Combine like terms.

Getting to the Answer: Combine the integers: $-3 - (-9) = 6$. Combine the terms with i: $-5i - 2i = -7i$. Choice **(C)** is correct.

3.   B

Difficulty: Medium

Strategic Advice: Distribute the factors outside the parentheses, then add the real and imaginary parts separately.

Getting to the Answer: Expand the expression to $-3i + 12 + 10i - 15$. Combine like terms to get $7i - 3$. Choice **(B)** is correct.

4.   3

Difficulty: Medium

Strategic Advice: Substitute $\sqrt{-1}$ for i and evaluate the expression.

Getting to the Answer: Substituting $\sqrt{-1}$ for i results in $9 + \sqrt{-1}\left(6\sqrt{-1}\right) = 9 + 6(-1) = 9 - 6 = \mathbf{3}$.

5.   B

Difficulty: Hard

Strategic Advice: Simplify the exponents, and then use $\sqrt{-1}$ for i and evaluate the expression.

Getting to the Answer: The given expression can be simplified by dividing all terms by i^2 to get $\frac{6i^2 - i}{3}$. Substitute -1 for i^2: $\frac{-6 - i}{3}$. In standard $a + bi$ form, this is $-2 - \frac{1}{3}i$. Choice **(B)** is correct.

6.   A

Difficulty: Hard

Strategic Advice: The choices have numerical denominators, so multiply the top and bottom of the fraction by the conjugate of the denominator in order to obtain a numerical denominator.

Getting to the Answer: Start with $\left(\frac{4 + 3i}{4 + 3i}\right)\frac{3 + i}{4 - 3i} = \frac{12 + 13i + 3i^2}{16 - 9i^2}$. Substitute -1 for i^2 to get $\frac{12 + 13i + 3(-1)}{16 - 9(-1)} = \frac{9 + 13i}{25} = \frac{9}{25} + \frac{13i}{25}$. Choice **(A)** is correct.

7.   B

Difficulty: Hard

Strategic Advice: Multiply the numerator and denominator by the conjugate of the denominator in order to get rid of i in the denominator. When converted to the form $a + bi$, b will be the coefficient of i.

Getting to the Answer: Start with $\left(\frac{2 - 3i}{2 - 3i}\right)\frac{-3 - 2i}{2 + 3i} = \frac{-6 - 4i + 9i + 6i^2}{4 - 9i^2}$. Since the only value needed is the coefficient of i, just evaluate the relevant part of the expression: $\frac{-4i + 9i}{4 - 9(-1)} = \frac{5i}{13}$. Choice **(B)** is correct.

8.   D

Difficulty: Hard

Strategic Advice: Multiply the numerator and denominator by i in order to get rid of i in the denominator, then evaluate the expression.

Getting to the Answer: Start by expanding the numerator using FOIL: $\frac{(i - 2)(i + 3)}{2i} = \frac{i^2 + i - 6}{2i} = \frac{-1 + i - 6}{2i} = \frac{-7 + i}{2i}$. Next, multiply the numerator and denominator by i to get $\frac{-7i + i^2}{2i^2} = \frac{-7i + (-1)}{2(-1)} = \frac{-1 - 7i}{-2} = \frac{1}{2} + \frac{7}{2}i$. Choice **(D)** is correct.

PART TWO

Math Practice Test

CHAPTER 16

Math Practice Test

How to Score Your Practice Test

For this Practice Test, convert your raw score, or the number of questions you answered correctly, to a scaled score using the table below. To get your raw score for Math, add the number of questions you answered correctly for the Math (No-Calculator) and Math (Calculator) sections.

Math			
Raw Score	Scaled Score	Raw Score	Scaled Score
0	200	30	530
1	200	31	540
2	210	32	550
3	230	33	560
4	240	34	560
5	260	35	570
6	280	36	580
7	290	37	590
8	310	38	600
9	320	39	600
10	330	40	610
11	340	41	620
12	360	42	630
13	370	43	640
14	380	44	650
15	390	45	660
16	410	46	670
17	420	47	670
18	430	48	680
19	440	49	690
20	450	50	700
21	460	51	710
22	470	52	730
23	480	53	740
24	480	54	750
25	490	55	760
26	500	56	780
27	510	57	790
28	520	58	800
29	520		

SAT Practice Test Answer Sheet (Math—Sections 3 and 4 Only)

Remove (or photocopy) this answer sheet and use it to complete the test. See the answer key following the test when finished.

Start with number 1 for each section. If a section has fewer questions than answer spaces, leave the extra spaces blank.

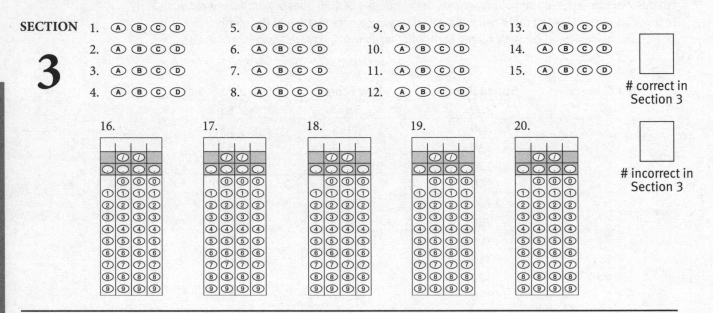

SECTION **3**

1. Ⓐ Ⓑ Ⓒ Ⓓ
2. Ⓐ Ⓑ Ⓒ Ⓓ
3. Ⓐ Ⓑ Ⓒ Ⓓ
4. Ⓐ Ⓑ Ⓒ Ⓓ

5. Ⓐ Ⓑ Ⓒ Ⓓ
6. Ⓐ Ⓑ Ⓒ Ⓓ
7. Ⓐ Ⓑ Ⓒ Ⓓ
8. Ⓐ Ⓑ Ⓒ Ⓓ

9. Ⓐ Ⓑ Ⓒ Ⓓ
10. Ⓐ Ⓑ Ⓒ Ⓓ
11. Ⓐ Ⓑ Ⓒ Ⓓ
12. Ⓐ Ⓑ Ⓒ Ⓓ

13. Ⓐ Ⓑ Ⓒ Ⓓ
14. Ⓐ Ⓑ Ⓒ Ⓓ
15. Ⓐ Ⓑ Ⓒ Ⓓ

correct in Section 3

incorrect in Section 3

16. 17. 18. 19. 20.

GO ON TO THE NEXT PAGE

SECTION

4

1. Ⓐ Ⓑ Ⓒ Ⓓ
2. Ⓐ Ⓑ Ⓒ Ⓓ
3. Ⓐ Ⓑ Ⓒ Ⓓ
4. Ⓐ Ⓑ Ⓒ Ⓓ
5. Ⓐ Ⓑ Ⓒ Ⓓ
6. Ⓐ Ⓑ Ⓒ Ⓓ
7. Ⓐ Ⓑ Ⓒ Ⓓ
8. Ⓐ Ⓑ Ⓒ Ⓓ

9. Ⓐ Ⓑ Ⓒ Ⓓ
10. Ⓐ Ⓑ Ⓒ Ⓓ
11. Ⓐ Ⓑ Ⓒ Ⓓ
12. Ⓐ Ⓑ Ⓒ Ⓓ
13. Ⓐ Ⓑ Ⓒ Ⓓ
14. Ⓐ Ⓑ Ⓒ Ⓓ
15. Ⓐ Ⓑ Ⓒ Ⓓ
16. Ⓐ Ⓑ Ⓒ Ⓓ

17. Ⓐ Ⓑ Ⓒ Ⓓ
18. Ⓐ Ⓑ Ⓒ Ⓓ
19. Ⓐ Ⓑ Ⓒ Ⓓ
20. Ⓐ Ⓑ Ⓒ Ⓓ
21. Ⓐ Ⓑ Ⓒ Ⓓ
22. Ⓐ Ⓑ Ⓒ Ⓓ
23. Ⓐ Ⓑ Ⓒ Ⓓ
24. Ⓐ Ⓑ Ⓒ Ⓓ

25. Ⓐ Ⓑ Ⓒ Ⓓ
26. Ⓐ Ⓑ Ⓒ Ⓓ
27. Ⓐ Ⓑ Ⓒ Ⓓ
28. Ⓐ Ⓑ Ⓒ Ⓓ
29. Ⓐ Ⓑ Ⓒ Ⓓ
30. Ⓐ Ⓑ Ⓒ Ⓓ

correct in
Section 4

incorrect in
Section 4

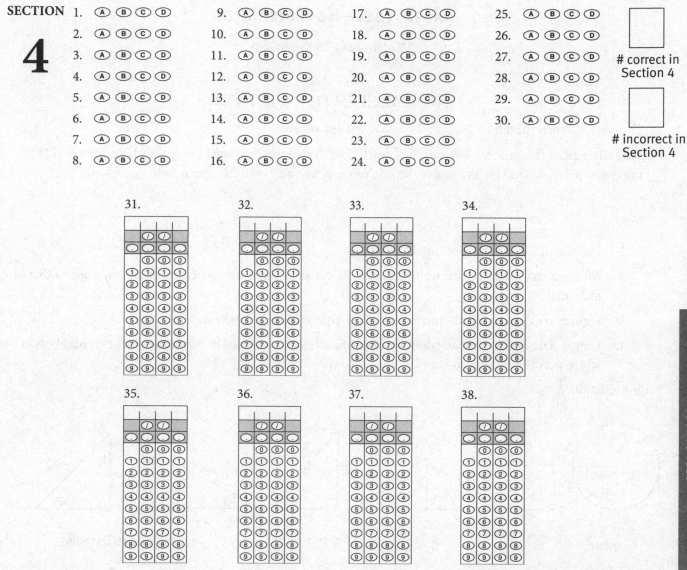

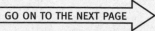
Practice Test

Math Test—No-Calculator

25 Minutes—20 Questions

NO-CALCULATOR SECTION

This section corresponds to Section 3 of your answer sheet.

Directions: For this section, solve each problem and decide which is the best of the choices given. Fill in the corresponding oval on the answer sheet. You may use any available space for scratchwork.

Notes:

1. Calculator use is NOT permitted.

2. All numbers used are real numbers, and all variables used represent real numbers, unless otherwise indicated.

3. Figures are drawn to scale and lie in a plane unless otherwise indicated.

4. Unless stated otherwise, the domain of any function f is assumed to be the set of all real numbers x, for which $f(x)$ is a real number.

Information:

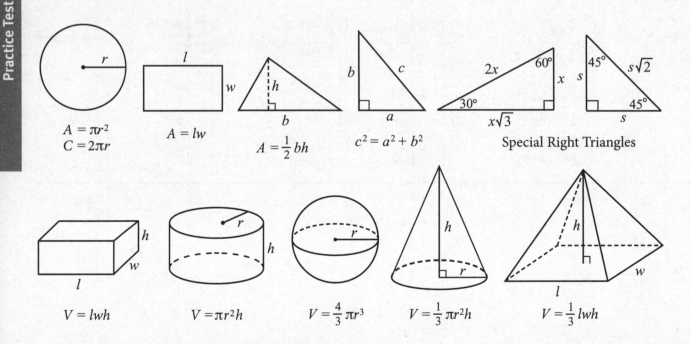

The sum of the degree measures of the angles in a triangle is 180.
The number of degrees of arc in a circle is 360.
The number of radians of arc in a circle is 2π.

GO ON TO THE NEXT PAGE

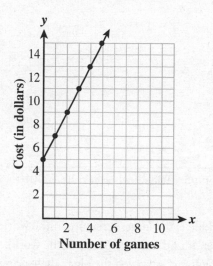

Number of games

1. The graph above shows the amount that a new high-tech video arcade charges its customers. What could the y-intercept of this graph represent?

   A) The cost of playing 5 games

   B) The cost per game, which is $5

   C) The entrance fee to enter the arcade

   D) The number of games that are played

$$\frac{3x}{x+5} \div \frac{6}{4x+20}$$

2. Which of the following is equivalent to the expression above, given that $x \neq -5$?

   A) $2x$

   B) $\dfrac{x}{2}$

   C) $\dfrac{9x}{2}$

   D) $2x + 4$

$$(x+3)^2 + (y+1)^2 = 25$$

3. The graph of the equation above is a circle. What is the area, in square units, of the circle?

   A) 4π

   B) 5π

   C) 16π

   D) 25π

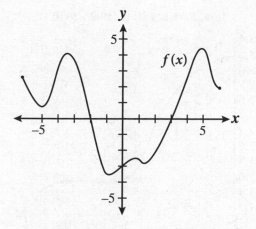

4. The figure above shows the graph of $f(x)$. For which value(s) of x does $f(x)$ equal 0 ?

   A) 3 only

   B) -3 only

   C) -2 and 3

   D) -3, -2, and 3

$$\frac{4(d+3)-9}{8} = \frac{10-(2-d)}{6}$$

5. In the equation above, what is the value of d ?

   A) $\dfrac{23}{16}$

   B) $\dfrac{23}{8}$

   C) $\dfrac{25}{8}$

   D) $\dfrac{25}{4}$

GO ON TO THE NEXT PAGE

Total Fertility Rate, 1960–2010

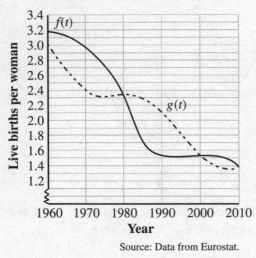

Source: Data from Eurostat.

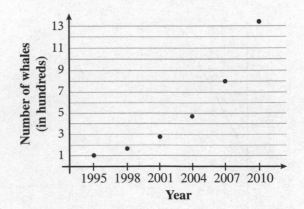

6. One indicator of a declining economy is a continued decline in birth rates. In 2010, birth rates in Europe were at an all-time low, with the average number of children that a woman has in her lifetime at well below two. In the figure above, $f(t)$ represents birth rates for Portugal between 1960 and 2010, and $g(t)$ represents birth rates in Slovakia for the same time period. For which value(s) of t is $f(t) > g(t)$?

A) $1960 < t < 1980$ only

B) $1980 < t < 2000$ only

C) $1960 < t < 1980$ and $1990 < t < 2000$

D) $1960 < t < 1980$ and $2000 < t < 2010$

7. The blue whale is the largest creature in the world and has been found in every ocean in the world. A marine biologist surveyed the blue whale population in Monterey Bay, off the coast of California, every three years between 1995 and 2010. The figure above shows her results. If w is the number of blue whales present in Monterey Bay and t is the number of years since the study began in 1995, which of the following equations best represents the blue whale population of Monterey Bay?

A) $w = 100 + 2t$

B) $w = 100 + \dfrac{t^2}{4}$

C) $w = 100 \times 2^t$

D) $w = 100 \times 2^{\frac{t}{4}}$

GO ON TO THE NEXT PAGE

Practice Test

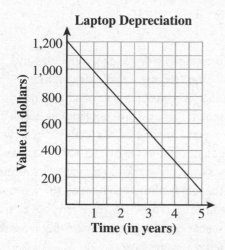

Laptop Depreciation

8. The figure above shows the straight-line depreciation of a laptop computer over the first five years of its use. According to the figure, what is the average rate of change in dollars per year of the value of the computer over the five-year period?

    A) −1,100

    B) −220

    C) −100

    D) 100

9. What is the coefficient of x^2 when $6x^2 - \frac{2}{5}x + 1$ is multiplied by $10x + \frac{1}{3}$?

    A) −4

    B) −2

    C) 2

    D) 4

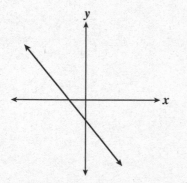

10. The graph above could represent which of the following equations?

    A) $-6x - 4y = 5$

    B) $-6x - 4y = -5$

    C) $-6x + 4y = 5$

    D) $-6x + 4y = -5$

$$\begin{cases} \frac{3}{4}x - \frac{1}{2}y = 12 \\ kx - 2y = 22 \end{cases}$$

11. If the system of linear equations above has no solution, and k is a constant, what is the value of k?

    A) $-\frac{4}{3}$

    B) $-\frac{3}{4}$

    C) 3

    D) 4

12. In Delray Beach, Florida, you can take a luxury golf cart ride around downtown. The driver charges \$4 for the first $\frac{1}{4}$ mile, plus \$1.50 for each additional $\frac{1}{2}$ mile. Which inequality represents the number of miles, m, that you could ride and pay no more than \$10?

    A) $3.25 + 1.5m \le 10$

    B) $3.25 + 3m \le 10$

    C) $4 + 1.5m \le 10$

    D) $4 + 3m \le 10$

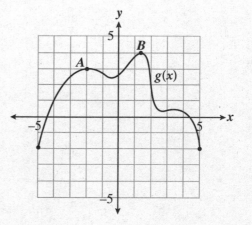

13. The graph of $g(x)$ is shown in the figure above. If $h(x) = -g(x) + 1$, which of the following statements is true?

    A) The range of $h(x)$ is $-3 \le y \le 3$.

    B) The minimum value of $h(x)$ is −4.

    C) The coordinates of the point equivalent to point A on the function $h(x)$ are $(2, 4)$.

    D) The graph of $h(x)$ is increasing between $x = -5$ and $x = -2$.

GO ON TO THE NEXT PAGE

14. If $a + bi$ represents the complex number that results from multiplying $3 + 2i$ by $5 - i$, what is the value of a ?

    A) 2

    B) 13

    C) 15

    D) 17

$$\frac{1}{x} + \frac{4}{x} = \frac{1}{72}$$

15. In order to create safe drinking water, cities and towns use water treatment facilities to remove contaminants from surface water and groundwater. Suppose a town has a treatment plant but decides to build a second, more efficient facility. The new treatment plant can filter the water in the reservoir four times as quickly as the older facility. Working together, the two facilities can filter all the water in the reservoir in 72 hours. The equation above represents the scenario. Which of the following describes what the term $\frac{1}{x}$ represents?

    A) The portion of the water the older treatment plant can filter in 1 hour

    B) The time it takes the older treatment plant to filter the water in the reservoir

    C) The time it takes the older treatment plant to filter $\frac{1}{72}$ of the water in the reservoir

    D) The portion of the water the new treatment plant can filter in 4 hours

GO ON TO THE NEXT PAGE

Directions: For questions 16–20, enter your responses into the appropriate grid on your answer sheet, in accordance with the following:

1. You will receive credit only if the circles are filled in correctly, but you may write your answers in the boxes above each grid to help you fill in the circles accurately.

2. Don't mark more than one circle per column.

3. None of the questions with Grid-in responses will have a negative solution.

4. Only grid in a single answer, even if there is more than one correct answer to a given question.

5. A **mixed number** must be gridded as a decimal or an improper fraction. For example, you would grid $7\frac{1}{2}$ as 7.5 or 15/2.

(Were you to grid it as ⎡7⎪1⎪/⎪2⎤, this response would be read as $\frac{71}{2}$.)

6. A **decimal** that has more digits than there are places on the grid may be either rounded or truncated, but every column in the grid must be filled in order to receive credit.

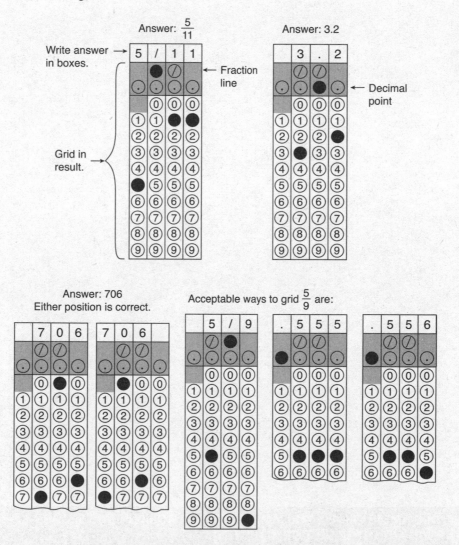

16. If $\frac{1}{4}x = 5 - \frac{1}{2}y$, what is the value of $x + 2y$?

$$\begin{cases} x + 3y \leq 18 \\ 2x - 3y \leq 9 \end{cases}$$

17. If (a, b) is a point in the solution region for the system of inequalities shown above and $a = 6$, what is the minimum possible value for b?

$$\frac{\sqrt{x} \cdot x^{\frac{5}{6}} \cdot x}{\sqrt[3]{x}}$$

18. If x^n is the simplified form of the expression above, what is the value of n?

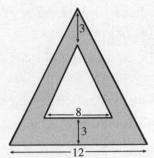

Note: Figure not drawn to scale.

19. In the figure above, the area of the shaded region is 52 square units. What is the height of the larger triangle?

20. If $y = ax^2 + bx + c$ passes through the points $(-3, 10)$, $(0, 1)$, and $(2, 15)$, what is the value of $a + b + c$?

IF YOU FINISH BEFORE TIME IS CALLED, YOU MAY CHECK YOUR WORK ON THIS SECTION ONLY. DO NOT TURN TO ANY OTHER SECTION IN THE TEST.

STOP

174 K

Math Test—Calculator

55 Minutes—38 Questions

CALCULATOR SECTION

This section corresponds to Section 4 of your answer sheet.

Directions: For this section, solve each problem and decide which is the best of the choices given. Fill in the corresponding oval on the answer sheet. You may use any available space for scratchwork.

Notes:

1. Calculator use is permitted.

2. All numbers used are real numbers, and all variables used represent real numbers, unless otherwise indicated.

3. Figures are drawn to scale and lie in a plane unless otherwise indicated.

4. Unless stated otherwise, the domain of any function f is assumed to be the set of all real numbers x, for which $f(x)$ is a real number.

Information:

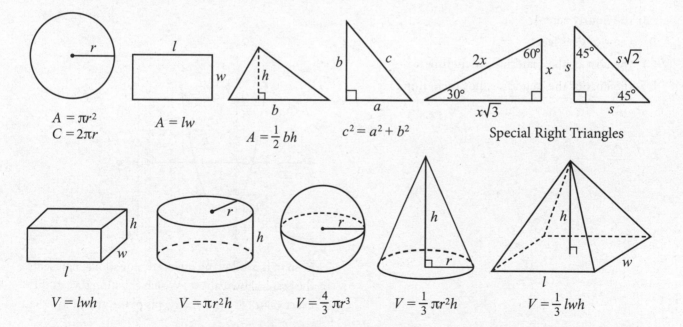

$A = \pi r^2$
$C = 2\pi r$

$A = lw$

$A = \frac{1}{2} bh$

$c^2 = a^2 + b^2$

Special Right Triangles

$V = lwh$

$V = \pi r^2 h$

$V = \frac{4}{3}\pi r^3$

$V = \frac{1}{3}\pi r^2 h$

$V = \frac{1}{3} lwh$

The sum of the degree measures of the angles in a triangle is 180.
The number of degrees of arc in a circle is 360.
The number of radians of arc in a circle is 2π.

Practice Test

1. Oceans, seas, and bays represent about 96.5 percent of Earth's water, including the water found in our atmosphere. If the volume of the water contained in oceans, seas, and bays is about 321,000,000 cubic miles, which of the following best represents the approximate volume, in cubic miles, of all the world's water?

   A) 308,160,000

   B) 309,765,000

   C) 332,642,000

   D) 334,375,000

2. An electrician charges a one-time site visit fee to evaluate a potential job. If the electrician accepts the job, he charges an hourly rate plus the cost of any materials needed to complete the job. The electrician also charges for tax, but only on the cost of the materials. If the total cost of completing a job that takes h hours is given by the function $C(h) = 45h + 1.06(82.5) + 75$, then the term $1.06(82.5)$ represents

   A) the hourly rate.

   B) the site visit fee.

   C) the cost of the materials, including tax.

   D) the cost of the materials, not including tax.

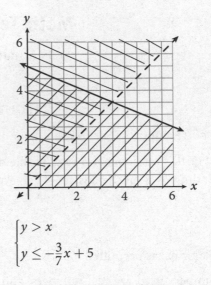

$$\begin{cases} y > x \\ y \le -\frac{3}{7}x + 5 \end{cases}$$

3. The figure above shows the solution set for the system of inequalities. Which of the following is not a solution to the system?

   A) (0, 3)

   B) (1, 2)

   C) (2, 4)

   D) (3, 3)

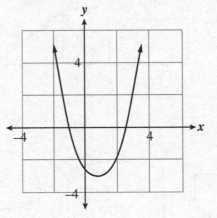

4. Each of the following quadratic equations represents the graph shown above. Which equation reveals the exact values of the x-intercepts of the graph?

   A) $y = \frac{1}{2}(2x - 5)(x + 1)$

   B) $y = x^2 - \frac{3}{2}x - \frac{5}{2}$

   C) $y + \frac{49}{16} = \left(x - \frac{3}{4}\right)^2$

   D) $y = \left(x - \frac{3}{4}\right)^2 - \frac{49}{16}$

GO ON TO THE NEXT PAGE

National Government Concerns

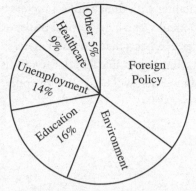

5. Margo surveyed all the students in the government classes at her school to see what they thought should be the most important concern of a national government. The results of the survey are shown in the figure above. If the ratio of students who answered "Foreign Policy" to those who answered "Environment" was 5:3, what percentage of the students answered "Environment"?

A) 16%

B) 21%

C) 24%

D) 35%

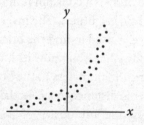

6. Which of the following best describes the type of association shown in the scatterplot above?

A) Linear, positive

B) Linear, negative

C) Exponential, positive

D) Exponential, negative

Average Annual Gas Prices

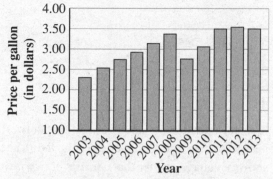

Source: Data from U.S. Energy Information Administration.

7. The figure above shows the average annual gas prices in the United States from 2003 to 2013. Based on the information shown, which of the following conclusions is valid?

A) A gallon of gas cost more in 2008 than in 2013.

B) The price more than doubled between 2003 and 2013.

C) The drop in price from 2008 to 2009 was more than $1.00 per gallon.

D) The overall change in price was greater between 2003 and 2008 than it was between 2008 and 2013.

$$\begin{cases} -2x + 5y = 1 \\ 7x - 10y = -11 \end{cases}$$

8. If (x, y) is a solution to the system of equations above, what is the sum of x and y ?

A) $-\dfrac{137}{30}$

B) -4

C) $-\dfrac{10}{3}$

D) -3

 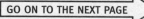

Practice Test

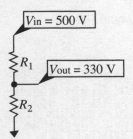

9. A voltage divider is a simple circuit that converts a large voltage into a smaller one. The figure above shows a voltage divider that consists of two resistors that together have a total resistance of 294 ohms. To produce the desired voltage of 330 volts, R_2 must be 6 ohms less than twice R_1. Solving which of the following systems of equations gives the individual resistances for R_1 and R_2?

A) $\begin{cases} R_2 = 2R_1 - 6 \\ R_1 + R_2 = 294 \end{cases}$

B) $\begin{cases} R_1 = 2R_2 + 6 \\ R_1 + R_2 = 294 \end{cases}$

C) $\begin{cases} R_2 = 2R_1 - 6 \\ R_1 + R_2 = \frac{294}{330} \end{cases}$

D) $\begin{cases} R_1 = 2R_2 + 6 \\ R_1 + R_2 = 330(294) \end{cases}$

10. If $\frac{2}{5}(5x) + 2(x-1) = 4(x+1) - 2$, what is the value of x?

A) $x = -2$

B) $x = 2$

C) There is no value of x for which the equation is true.

D) There are infinitely many values of x for which the equation is true.

11. Crude oil is being transferred from a full rectangular storage container with dimensions 4 meters by 9 meters by 10 meters into a cylindrical transportation container that has a diameter of 6 meters. What is the minimum possible length for a transportation container that will hold all of the oil?

A) 40π

B) $\dfrac{40}{\pi}$

C) 60π

D) $\dfrac{120}{\pi}$

12. The percent increase from 5 to 12 is equal to the percent increase from 12 to what number?

A) 16.8

B) 19.0

C) 26.6

D) 28.8

$$b = \frac{L}{4\pi d^2}$$

13. The brightness of a celestial body, like a star, decreases as you move away from it. In contrast, the luminosity of a celestial body is a constant number that represents its intrinsic brightness. The inverse square law, shown above, is used to find the brightness, b, of a celestial body when you know its luminosity, L, and the distance, d, in meters to the body. Which equation shows the distance to a celestial body, given its brightness and luminosity?

A) $d = \frac{1}{2}\sqrt{\frac{L}{\pi b}}$

B) $d = \sqrt{\frac{L}{2\pi b}}$

C) $d = \frac{\sqrt{L}}{2\pi b}$

D) $d = \frac{L}{2\sqrt{\pi b}}$

GO ON TO THE NEXT PAGE

> **Questions 14 and 15** refer to the following information.

Each month, the Bureau of Labor Statistics conducts a survey called the Current Population Survey (CPS) to measure unemployment in the United States. Across the country, about 60,000 households are included in the survey sample. These households are grouped by geographic region. A summary of the January 2014 survey results in one geographic region is shown in the table below.

Age Group	Employed	Unemployed	Not in the Labor Force	Total
16–19	8	5	10	23
20–24	26	7	23	56
25–34	142	11	28	157
35–44	144	8	32	164
45–54	66	6	26	98
Over 54	65	7	36	152
Total	451	44	155	650

14. According to the data in the table, for which age group did the smallest percentage of respondents report that they were unemployed in January 2014?

    A) 20 to 24 years

    B) 35 to 44 years

    C) 45 to 54 years

    D) Over 54 years

15. If one unemployed person from this sample is chosen at random for a follow-up survey, what is the probability that person will be between the ages of 45 and 54 ?

    A) 6.0%

    B) 13.6%

    C) 15.1%

    D) 44.9%

16. Which of the following are solutions to the quadratic equation $(x-1)^2 = \frac{4}{9}$?

    A) $x = -\frac{5}{3}, x = \frac{5}{3}$

    B) $x = \frac{1}{3}, x = \frac{5}{3}$

    C) $x = \frac{5}{9}, x = \frac{13}{9}$

    D) $x = 1 \pm \sqrt{\frac{2}{3}}$

17. Damien is throwing darts. He has a total of 6 darts to throw. He gets 5 points for each dart that lands in a blue ring and 10 points for each dart that lands in a red ring. If x of his darts land in a blue ring and the rest land in a red ring, which expression represents his total score?

    A) $10x$

    B) $10x + 5$

    C) $5x + 30$

    D) $60 - 5x$

18. Red tide is a form of harmful algae that releases toxins as it breaks down in the environment. A marine biologist is testing a new spray, composed of clay and water, hoping to kill the red tide that almost completely covers a beach in southern Florida. She applies the spray to a representative sample of 200 square feet of the beach. By the end of the week, 184 square feet of the beach is free of the red tide. Based on these results, and assuming the same general conditions, how many square feet of the 10,000-square-foot beach would still be covered by red tide if the spray had been used on the entire area?

A)   800

B)   920

C) 8,000

D) 9,200

$$\begin{cases} y = \frac{1}{2}x - 2 \\ y = -x^2 + 1 \end{cases}$$

19. If (a, b) is a solution to the system of equations above, which of the following could be the value of b?

A) −3

B) −2

C)   1

D)   2

20. Given the function $g(x) = \frac{2}{3}x + 7$, what domain value corresponds to a range value of 3 ?

A) −6

B) −2

C)   6

D)   9

21. A landscaper buys a new commercial-grade lawn mower that costs $2,800. Based on past experience, he expects it to last about 8 years, and then he can sell it for scrap metal with a salvage value of about $240. Assuming the value of the lawn mower depreciates at a constant rate, which equation could be used to find its approximate value after x years, given that $x < 8$?

A) $y = -8x + 2,560$

B) $y = -240x + 2,800$

C) $y = -320x + 2,800$

D) $y = 240x - 2,560$

22. A microbiologist is studying the effects of a new antibiotic on a culture of 20,000 bacteria. When the antibiotic is added to the culture, the number of bacteria is reduced by half every hour. What kind of function best models the number of bacteria remaining in the culture after the antibiotic is added?

A) A linear function

B) A quadratic function

C) A polynomial function

D) An exponential function

23. An airline company purchased two new airplanes. One can travel at speeds of up to 600 miles per hour and the other at speeds of up to 720 miles per hour. How many more miles can the faster airplane travel in 12 seconds than the slower airplane?

A) $\dfrac{1}{30}$

B) $\dfrac{2}{5}$

C) 2

D) 30

GO ON TO THE NEXT PAGE

State	Minimum Wage per Hour
Idaho	$7.25
Montana	$7.90
Oregon	$9.10
Washington	$9.32

24. The table above shows the 2014 minimum wages for several states that share a border. Assuming an average workweek of between 35 and 40 hours, which inequality represents how much more a worker who earned minimum wage could earn per week in Oregon than in Idaho?

    A) $x \geq 1.85$

    B) $7.25 \leq x \leq 9.10$

    C) $64.75 \leq x \leq 74$

    D) $253.75 \leq x \leq 364$

25. In the United States, the maintenance and construction of airports, transit systems, and major roads is largely funded through a federal excise tax on gasoline. Based on the 2011 statistics given below, how much did the average household pay per year in federal gasoline taxes?

    - The federal gasoline tax rate was 18.4 cents per gallon.
    - The average motor vehicle was driven approximately 11,340 miles per year.
    - The national average fuel economy for noncommercial vehicles was 21.4 miles per gallon.
    - The average American household owned 1.75 vehicles.

    A) $55.73

    B) $68.91

    C) $97.52

    D) $170.63

Rescued Dolphin Recovery

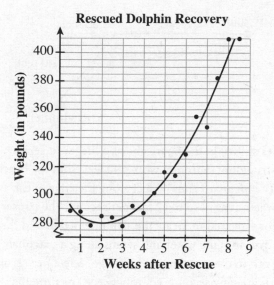

26. Following the catastrophic oil spill in the Gulf of Mexico in April of 2010, more than 900 bottlenose dolphins were found dead or stranded in the oil spill area. The figure above shows the weight of a rescued dolphin during its recovery. Based on the quadratic model fit to the data shown, which of the following is the closest to the average rate of change in the dolphin's weight between week 2 and week 8 of its recovery?

    A) 4 pounds per week

    B) 16 pounds per week

    C) 20 pounds per week

    D) 40 pounds per week

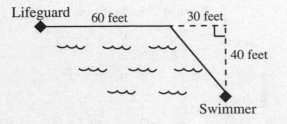

27. As shown in the figure above, a lifeguard sees a struggling swimmer who is 40 feet from the beach. The lifeguard runs 60 feet along the edge of the water at a speed of 12 feet per second. She pauses for 1 second to locate the swimmer again and then dives into the water and swims along a diagonal path to the swimmer at a speed of 5 feet per second. How many seconds go by between the time the lifeguard sees the struggling swimmer and the time she reaches the swimmer?

A) 16

B) 22

C) 50

D) 56

28. What was the initial amount of gasoline in a fuel trailer, in gallons, if there are now x gallons, y gallons were pumped into a storage tank, and then 50 gallons were added to the trailer?

A) $x + y + 50$

B) $x + y - 50$

C) $y - x + 50$

D) $x - y - 50$

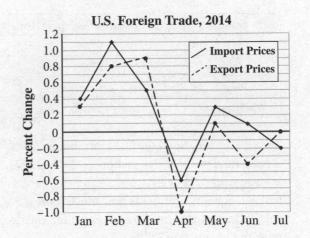

29. The figure above shows the net change, as a percentage, for U.S. import and export prices from January to July 2014 as reported by the Bureau of Labor Statistics. For example, U.S. import prices declined 0.2 percent in July while export prices remained unchanged for that month. Based on this information, which of the following statements is true for the time period shown in the figure?

A) On average, export prices increased more than import prices.

B) Import prices showed an increase more often than export prices.

C) Import prices showed the greatest change between two consecutive months.

D) From January to July, import prices showed a greater overall decrease than export prices.

$$\frac{3.86}{x} + \frac{180.2}{10x} + \frac{42.2}{5x}$$

30. The Ironman Triathlon originated in Hawaii in 1978. The format of the Ironman has not changed since then: it consists of a 3.86-kilometer swim, a 180.2-kilometer bicycle ride, and a 42.2-kilometer run, all raced in that order and without a break. Suppose an athlete bikes 10 times as fast as he swims and runs 5 times as fast as he swims. The variable x in the expression above represents the rate at which the athlete swims, and the whole expression represents the number of hours that it takes him to complete the race. If it takes him 16.2 hours to complete the race, how many kilometers did he swim in 1 hour?

A) 0.85

B) 1.01

C) 1.17

D) 1.87

Practice Test

Directions: For questions 31–38, enter your responses into the appropriate grid on your answer sheet, in accordance with the following:

1. You will receive credit only if the circles are filled in correctly, but you may write your answers in the boxes above each grid to help you fill in the circles accurately.

2. Don't mark more than one circle per column.

3. None of the questions with Grid-in responses will have a negative solution.

4. Only grid in a single answer, even if there is more than one correct answer to a given question.

5. A **mixed number** must be gridded as a decimal or an improper fraction. For example, you would grid $7\frac{1}{2}$ as 7.5 or 15/2.

   (Were you to grid it as 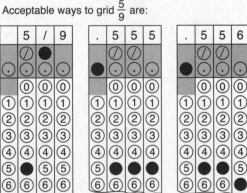, this response would be read as $\frac{71}{2}$.)

6. A **decimal** that has more digits than there are places on the grid may be either rounded or truncated, but every column in the grid must be filled in order to receive credit.

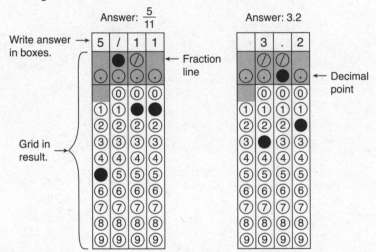

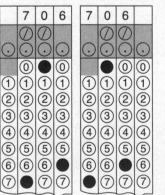

Answer: 706
Either position is correct.

Acceptable ways to grid $\frac{5}{9}$ are:

GO ON TO THE NEXT PAGE ⇨

31. What value of x satisfies the equation $\frac{2}{3}(5x + 7) = 8x$?

32. Some doctors base the dosage of a drug to be given to a patient on the patient's body surface area (BSA). The most commonly used formula for calculating BSA is BSA = $\sqrt{\frac{wh}{3,600}}$, where w is the patient's weight (in kilograms), h is the patient's height (in centimeters), and BSA is measured in square meters. How tall (in centimeters) is a patient who weighs 150 kilograms and has a BSA of $2\sqrt{2}$ square meters?

33. A college math professor informs her students that rather than grading the final exam on a curve, she will replace each student's lowest test score with the next-to-lowest test score and then re-average the test grades. If Leeza has test scores of 86, 92, 81, 64, and 83, by how many points does her final test average change based on the professor's policy?

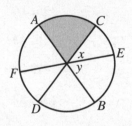

34. In the figure above, $\overline{AB}$, $\overline{CD}$, and $\overline{EF}$ are diameters of the circle. If $y = 2x - 12$, and the shaded area is $\frac{1}{5}$ of the area of the circle, what is the value of x ?

35. If the slope of a line is $-\frac{7}{4}$ and a point on the line is $(4, 7)$, what is the y-intercept of the line?

36. Rory left home and drove straight to the airport at an average speed of 45 miles per hour. He returned home along the same route, but traffic slowed him down and he only averaged 30 miles per hour on the return trip. If his total travel time was 2 hours and 30 minutes, how far is it, in miles, from Rory's house to the airport?

Questions 37 and 38 refer to the following information.

Chemical Makeup of One Mole of Chloroform

Element	Number of Moles	Mass per Mole (grams)
Carbon	1	12.011
Hydrogen	1	1.008
Chlorine	3	35.453

A chemical solvent is a substance that dissolves another to form a solution. For example, water is a solvent for sugar. Unfortunately, many chemical solvents are hazardous to the environment. One eco-friendly chemical solvent is chloroform, also known as trichloromethane ($CHCl_3$). The table above shows the chemical makeup of 1 mole of chloroform.

37. Carbon makes up what percent of the mass of 1 mole of chloroform? Round your answer to the nearest whole percent and ignore the percent sign when entering your answer.

38. If a chemist starts with 1,000 grams of chloroform and uses 522.5 grams, how many moles of chlorine are left? Round your answer to the nearest integer.

IF YOU FINISH BEFORE TIME IS CALLED, YOU MAY CHECK YOUR WORK ON THIS SECTION ONLY. DO NOT TURN TO ANY OTHER SECTION IN THE TEST.

STOP

K 185

Answer Key

Math Test—No-Calculator

1. C	6. D	11. C	16. 20
2. A	7. D	12. B	17. 1
3. D	8. B	13. A	18. 2
4. C	9. B	14. D	19. 14
5. B	10. A	15. A	20. 6

Math Test—Calculator

1. C	11. B	21. C	31. 1
2. C	12. D	22. D	32. 192
3. D	13. A	23. B	33. 3.4
4. A	14. D	24. C	34. 40
5. B	15. B	25. D	35. 14
6. C	16. B	26. C	36. 45
7. D	17. D	27. A	37. 10
8. B	18. A	28. B	38. 12
9. A	19. A	29. B	
10. C	20. A	30. D	

Answers and Explanations

Math Test—No-Calculator

1. C

Difficulty: Easy

Category: Heart of Algebra / Linear Equations

Getting to the Answer: To determine what the *y*-intercept could mean in the context of a word problem, examine the labels on the graph and note what each axis represents. According to the labels, the *y*-axis represents cost and the *x*-axis represents the number of games played. The *y*-intercept, (0, 5), has an *x*-value of 0, which means 0 games were played, yet there is still a cost of $5. The cost must represent a flat fee that is charged before any games are played, such as an entrance fee to enter the arcade. Choice **(C)** is correct.

2. A

Difficulty: Easy

Category: Passport to Advanced Math / Exponents

Getting to the Answer: To divide one rational expression by another, multiply the first expression by the reciprocal (the flip) of the second expression. Rewrite the division as multiplication, factor any factorable expressions, and then simplify if possible:

$$\frac{3x}{x+5} \div \frac{6}{4x+20} = \frac{3x}{x+5} \cdot \frac{4x+20}{6}$$

$$= \frac{3x}{x+5} \cdot \frac{4(x+5)}{6}$$

$$= \frac{12x}{6}$$

$$= 2x$$

Note that the question also states that $x \neq -5$. This doesn't affect your answer—it is simply stated because the denominators of rational expressions cannot equal 0. Choice **(A)** is correct.

3. D

Difficulty: Easy

Category: Additional Topics in Math / Geometry

Getting to the Answer: When the equation of a circle is written in the form $(x-h)^2 + (y-k)^2 = r^2$, the point (h, k) represents the center of the circle on a coordinate plane and r represents the length of the radius. To find the area of a circle, use the formula $A = \pi r^2$. In the equation given in the question, r^2 is the constant on the right-hand side (25)—you don't even need to solve for r because the area formula involves r^2, not r. Therefore, the area is $\pi(25)$, or 25π, which matches **(D)**.

4. C

Difficulty: Easy

Category: Passport to Advanced Math / Functions

Getting to the Answer: When using function notation, $f(x)$ is simply another way of saying y, so this question is asking you to find the values of x for which $y = 0$, or in other words, where the graph crosses the *x*-axis. The graph crosses the *x*-axis at the points $(-2, 0)$ and $(3, 0)$, so the values of x for which $f(x) = 0$ are -2 and 3, which matches choice **(C)**.

5. B

Difficulty: Medium

Category: Heart of Algebra / Linear Equations

Getting to the Answer: Choose the best strategy to answer the question. You could start by cross-multiplying to get rid of the denominators, but simplifying the numerators first will make the calculations easier:

$$\frac{4(d+3)-9}{8} = \frac{10-(2-d)}{6}$$

$$\frac{4d+12-9}{8} = \frac{10-2+d}{6}$$

$$\frac{4d+3}{8} = \frac{8+d}{6}$$

$$6(4d+3) = 8(8+d)$$

$$24d+18 = 64+8d$$

$$16d = 46$$

$$d = \frac{46}{16} = \frac{23}{8}$$

Choice **(B)** is correct.

6. D

Difficulty: Medium

Category: Passport to Advanced Math / Functions

Getting to the Answer: This is a crossover question, so quickly skim the first couple of sentences. Then, look for the relevant information in the last couple of sentences. It may also help to circle the portions of the graph that meet the given requirement.

Because *greater* means *higher* on a graph, the statement $f(t) > g(t)$ translates to "Where is $f(t)$ above $g(t)$?" The solid curve represents f and the dashed curve represents g, so $f > g$ between the years 1960 and 1980 and again between the years 2000 and 2010. Look for these time intervals in the answer choices: $1960 < t < 1980$ and $2000 < t < 2010$. This matches **(D)**.

7. D

Difficulty: Medium

Category: Passport to Advanced Math / Scatterplots

Getting to the Answer: Use the shape of the data to predict the type of equation that might be used as a model. Then, use specific values from the graph to choose the correct equation. According to the graph, the population of the whales grew slowly at first and then more quickly. This means that an exponential model is probably the best fit, so you can eliminate (A) (linear) and (B) (quadratic).

The remaining equations are both exponential, so choose a data point and see which equation is the closest fit. Be careful—the vertical axis represents *hundreds* of whales, and the question states that t represents the number of years since the study began, so $t = 0$ for 1995, $t = 3$ for 1998, and so on. If you use the data for 1995, which is the point (0, 100), the results are the same for both equations, so choose a different point. Using the data for 2007, $t = 2007 - 1995 = 12$, and the number of whales was 800. Substitute these values into (C) and (D) to see which one is true. Choice (C) is not true because $800 \neq 100 \times 2^{12}$. Choice **(D)** is correct because:

$$800 = 100 \times 2^{\frac{12}{4}} = 100 \times 2^3 = 100 \times 8$$

8. B

Difficulty: Medium

Category: Heart of Algebra / Linear Equations

Getting to the Answer: To find the average rate of change over the five-year period, find the slope between the starting point (0, 1,200) and the ending point (5, 100):

$$m = \frac{y_2 - y_1}{x_2 - x_1} = \frac{100 - 1,200}{5 - 0} = \frac{-1,100}{5} = -220$$

Choice **(B)** is correct. (The average rate of change is negative because the laptop decreases in value over time.)

Note: Because the question involves *straight-line* depreciation, you could have used any two points on the graph to find the slope. As a general rule, however, you should use the endpoints of the given time interval.

9. B

Difficulty: Medium

Category: Passport to Advanced Math/Exponents

Getting to the Answer: When multiplying polynomials, carefully multiply each term in the first factor by each term in the second factor. This question doesn't ask for the entire product, so check to make sure you answered the correct question (the coefficient of x^2). Set up an equation and solve:

$$\left(6x^2 - \frac{2}{5}x + 1\right)\left(10x + \frac{1}{3}\right)$$
$$= 6x^2\left(10x + \frac{1}{3}\right) - \frac{2}{5}x\left(10x + \frac{1}{3}\right) + 1\left(10x + \frac{1}{3}\right)$$
$$= 60x^3 + 2x^2 - 4x^2 - \frac{2}{15}x + 10x + \frac{1}{3}$$

The coefficient of x^2 is $2 + (-4) = -2$, which is **(B)**.

10. A

Difficulty: Medium

Category: Heart of Algebra / Linear Equations

Getting to the Answer: The line is decreasing, so the slope (m) is negative. The line crosses the y-axis below 0, so the y-intercept (b) is also negative. Put each answer choice in slope-intercept form, one at a time, and examine the signs of m and b. Begin with (A):

$$-6x - 4y = 5$$
$$-4y = 6x + 5$$
$$y = \frac{6x}{-4} + \frac{5}{-4}$$
$$y = -\frac{3}{2}x - \frac{5}{4}$$

You don't need to check any of the other equations. Choice **(A)** has a negative slope and a negative y-intercept, so it is the correct equation.

11. C

Difficulty: Hard

Category: Heart of Algebra / Systems of Linear Equations

Getting to the Answer: Graphically, a system of linear equations that has no solution indicates two parallel lines or, in other words, two lines that have the same slope. So write each of the equations in slope-intercept form ($y = mx + b$), and set their slopes (m) equal to each other to solve for k. Before finding the slopes, multiply the top equation by 4 to make it easier to manipulate:

$$4\left(\frac{3}{4}x - \frac{1}{2}y = 12\right) \rightarrow 3x - 2y = 48 \rightarrow y = \frac{3}{2}x - 24$$

$$kx - 2y = 22 \rightarrow -2y = -kx + 22 \rightarrow y = \frac{k}{2}x - 11$$

The slope of the first line is $\frac{3}{2}$, and the slope of the second line is $\frac{k}{2}$. Set them equal and solve for k:

$$\frac{3}{2} = \frac{k}{2}$$
$$2(3) = 2(k)$$
$$6 = 2k$$
$$3 = k$$

Choice **(C)** is correct.

12. B

Difficulty: Hard

Category: Heart of Algebra / Inequalities

Getting to the Answer: Before you write the inequality, you need to find the per-mile rate for the remaining miles. The driver charges \$4.00 for the first $\frac{1}{4}$ mile, which is a flat fee, so write 4. The additional charge is \$1.50 per $\frac{1}{2}$ mile, or $1.50 \times 2 = \$3.00$ per mile. The number of miles after the first $\frac{1}{4}$ mile is $m - \frac{1}{4}$, so the cost of the trip, not including the first $\frac{1}{4}$ mile, is $3\left(m - \frac{1}{4}\right)$.

This means the cost of the whole trip is $4 + 3\left(m - \frac{1}{4}\right)$. The clue "no more than \$10" means that much or less, so use the symbol $\leq$. The inequality is $4 + 3\left(m - \frac{1}{4}\right) \leq 10$, which simplifies to $3.25 + 3m \leq 10$. This matches **(B)**.

13. A

Difficulty: Hard

Category: Passport to Advanced Math / Functions

Getting to the Answer: Based on the equation, the graph of $h(x) = -g(x) + 1$ is a vertical reflection of $g(x)$, over the *x*-axis, that is then shifted up 1 unit. The graph looks like the dashed line in the following graph:

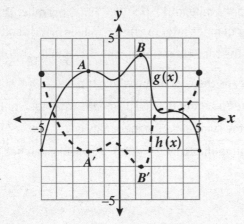

Now, compare the dashed line to each of the answer choices: the range of $h(x)$ is the set of *y*-values from lowest to highest (based on the dashed line). The lowest point occurs at point *B'* and has a *y*-value of -3; the highest value occurs at both ends of the graph and is 3, so the range is $-3 \leq y \leq 3$. This means **(A)** is correct, and you can move on to the next question. Don't waste valuable time checking the other answer choices unless you are not sure about the range. (Choice (B): the minimum value of $h(x)$ is -3, not -4. Choice (C): the coordinates of point *A* on $h(x)$ are $(-2, -2)$, not $(2, 4)$. Choice (D): the graph of $h(x)$ is decreasing, not increasing, between $x = -5$ and $x = -2$.)

14. D

Difficulty: Medium

Category: Additional Topics in Math / Imaginary Numbers

Getting to the Answer: Multiply the two complex numbers just as you would two binomials (using FOIL). Then, combine like terms and use the definition $i^2 = -1$ to simplify the result:

$$
\begin{aligned}
(3 + 2i)(5 - i) &= 3(5 - i) + 2i(5 - i) \\
&= 15 - 3i + 10i - 2i^2 \\
&= 15 + 7i - 2(-1) \\
&= 15 + 7i + 2 \\
&= 17 + 7i
\end{aligned}
$$

The question asks for *a* in $a + bi$, so the correct answer is 17, **(D)**.

15. A

Difficulty: Hard

Category: Exponents

Getting to the Answer: Think of the rate given in the question in terms of the constant term you see on the right-hand side of the equation. Working together, the two treatment plants can filter the water in 72 hours. This is equivalent to saying that they can filter $\frac{1}{72}$ of the water in 1 hour. If $\frac{1}{72}$ is the portion of the water the two treatment plants can filter *together*, then each term on the left side of the equation represents the portion that each plant can filter *individually* in 1 hour. Because the new facility is 4 times as fast as the older facility, $\frac{4}{x}$ represents the portion of the water the new plant can filter in 1 hour, and $\frac{1}{x}$ represents the portion of the water the older plant can filter in 1 hour. This matches **(A)**.

16. 20

Difficulty: Medium

Category: Heart of Algebra / Linear Equations

Getting to the Answer: Only one equation is given, and it has two variables. This means that you don't have enough information to solve for either variable. Instead, look for the relationship between the variable terms in the equation and those in the expression that you are trying to find, $x + 2y$. First, move the y term to the left side of the equation to make it look more like the expression you are trying to find. The expression doesn't have fractions, so clear the fractions in the equation by multiplying both sides by 4. This yields the expression that you are looking for, $x + 2y$, so no further work is required—just read the value on the right-hand side of the equation:

$$\frac{1}{4}x = 5 - \frac{1}{2}y$$

$$\frac{1}{4}x + \frac{1}{2}y = 5$$

$$4\left(\frac{1}{4}x + \frac{1}{2}y\right) = 4(5)$$

$$x + 2y = 20$$

The answer is **20**.

17. 1

Difficulty: Medium

Category: Heart of Algebra / Inequalities

Getting to the Answer: This question is extremely difficult to answer unless you draw a sketch. It doesn't have to be perfect—you just need to get an idea of where the solution region is. Don't forget to flip the inequality symbol when you graph the second equation.

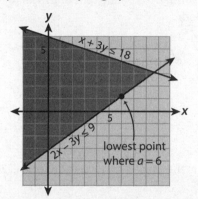

If (a, b) is a solution to the system, then a is the x-coordinate of any point in the darkest shaded region and b is the corresponding y-coordinate. When $a = 6$, the minimum possible value for b lies on the lower boundary line, $2x - 3y \leq 9$. It looks like the y-coordinate is 1, but to be sure, substitute $x = 6$ into the equation and solve for y. You can use $=$ in the equation, instead of the inequality symbol, because you are finding a point on the boundary line:

$$2x - 3y = 9$$

$$2(6) - 3y = 9$$

$$12 - 3y = 9$$

$$-3y = -3$$

$$y = \mathbf{1}$$

18. 2

Difficulty: Hard

Category: Passport to Advanced Math / Exponents

Getting to the Answer: Write each factor in the expression in exponential form: $\sqrt{x} = x^{\frac{1}{2}}$ and $\sqrt[3]{x} = x^{\frac{1}{3}}$. Then, use the rules of exponents to simplify the expression. Add the exponents of the factors that are being multiplied, and subtract the exponent of the factor that is being divided:

$$\frac{\sqrt{x} \cdot x^{\frac{5}{6}} \cdot x}{\sqrt[3]{x}} = \frac{x^{\frac{1}{2}} \cdot x^{\frac{5}{6}} \cdot x^{1}}{x^{\frac{1}{3}}}$$

$$= x^{\frac{1}{2}+\frac{5}{6}+1-\frac{1}{3}} = x^{\frac{3}{6}+\frac{5}{6}+\frac{6}{6}-\frac{2}{6}}$$

$$= x^{\frac{12}{6}} = x^{2}$$

Because n is the power of x, the value of n is **2**.

19. 14

Difficulty: Hard

Category: Additional Topics in Math / Geometry

Getting to the Answer: The shaded region is the area of the larger triangle minus the area of the smaller triangle. Set up and solve an equation using the information from the figure. You don't know the height of the smaller triangle, so call it h. You do know the area of the shaded region—it's 52 square units.

Larger triangle: base $= 12$; height $= h + 3 + 3$

Smaller triangle: base $= 8$; height $= h$

Shaded area $=$ large area $-$ small area

The area of the larger triangle is $\frac{1}{2}(12)(h+6) = 6(h+6)$.

The area of the smaller triangle is $\frac{1}{2}(8)(h) = 4h$.

So, $52 = 6(h+6) - 4h$. Solve for h:

$$6(h+6) - (4h) = 52$$
$$6h + 36 - 4h = 52$$
$$2h + 36 = 52$$
$$2h = 16$$
$$h = 8$$

Now h is the height of the smaller triangle.

The question asks for the height of the *larger* triangle, so the correct answer is $8 + 3 + 3 = $ **14**.

20. 6

Difficulty: Hard

Category: Passport to Advanced Math / Quadratics

Getting to the Answer: The highest power of x in the equation is 2, so the equation is quadratic. Writing quadratic equations can be tricky and time-consuming. If you know the roots, you can use factors to write the equation. If you don't know the roots, you need to create a system of equations to find the coefficients of the variable terms. You don't know the roots of this equation, so start with the point that has the easiest values to work with, $(0, 1)$, and substitute them into the equation $y = ax^2 + bx + c$:

$$1 = a(0)^2 + b(0) + c$$
$$1 = c$$

Now your equation looks like $y = ax^2 + bx + 1$. Next, use the other two points to create a system of two equations in two variables:

$$(-3, 10) \to 10 = a(-3)^2 + b(-3) + 1 \to 9 = 9a - 3b$$
$$(2, 15) \to 15 = a(2)^2 + b(2) + 1 \to 14 = 4a + 2b$$

You now have a system of equations to solve. None of the variables has a coefficient of 1, so use elimination to solve the system. If you multiply the top equation by 2 and the bottom equation by 3, the b terms will eliminate each other:

$$2[9a - 3b = 9] \to 18a - 6b = 18$$
$$3[4a + 2b = 14] \to \underline{12a + 6b = 42}$$
$$30a = 60$$
$$a = 2$$

Now, find b by substituting $a = 2$ into either of the original equations. Using the top equation, you get:

$$9(2) - 3b = 9$$
$$18 - 3b = 9$$
$$-3b = -9$$
$$b = 3$$

The value of $a + b + c$ is $2 + 3 + 1 = $ **6**.

Math Test—Calculator

1. C

Difficulty: Easy

Category: Problem Solving and Data Analysis / Rates, Ratios, Proportions, and Percentages

Getting to the Answer: You can use the formula Percent $= \frac{\text{part}}{\text{whole}} \times 100\%$ whenever you know two out of the three quantities. The clue "all" tells you that the "whole" is what you don't know. The percent is 96.5, and the part is 321,000,000:

$$96.5 = \frac{321,000,000}{w} \times 100\%$$
$$96.5w = 32,100,000,000$$
$$w = \frac{32,100,000,000}{96.5}$$
$$w = 332,642,487$$

The answer choices are rounded to the nearest thousand, so the answer is 332,642,000, **(C)**.

2. C

Difficulty: Easy

Category: Heart of Algebra / Linear Equations

Getting to the Answer: The total cost consists of the one-time site visit fee (a constant), an hourly cost (which depends on the number of hours), and the cost of the materials (which are taxed). The constant in the equation is 75 and is therefore the site visit fee; 45 is being multiplied by h (the number of hours), so $45 must be the hourly rate. That leaves the remaining term, 1.06(82.5), which must be the cost of the materials ($82.50) plus a 6% tax. This matches **(C)**.

3. D

Difficulty: Easy

Category: Heart of Algebra / Inequalities

Getting to the Answer: The intersection (overlap) of the two shaded regions is the solution to the system of inequalities. Check each point to see whether it lies in the region with the darkest shading. Don't forget to check that you answered the right question—you are looking for the point that is *not* a solution to the system. Each of the first three points clearly lies in the overlap. The point $(3, 3)$ looks like it lies on the dashed line, which means it is *not* included in the solution. To check this, plug $(3, 3)$ into the easier inequality: $3 \not> 3$ (3 is equal to itself, not greater than itself), so **(D)** is correct.

4. A

Difficulty: Easy

Category: Passport to Advanced Math / Quadratics

Getting to the Answer: Quadratic equations can be written in several forms, each of which reveals something special about the graph. The factored form of a quadratic equation reveals the solutions to the equation, which graphically represent the x-intercepts. Choice **(A)** is the only equation written in this form and therefore must be correct. You can set each factor equal to 0 and solve to find that the x-intercepts of the graph are $x = \frac{5}{2}$ and $x = -1$.

5. B

Difficulty: Easy

Category: Problem Solving and Data Analysis / Rates, Ratios, Proportions, and Percentages

Getting to the Answer: Break the question into steps. Before you can use the ratio, you need to find the percent of the students who answered either "Foreign Policy" or "Environment." The ratio given in the question is 5:3, so write this as 5 parts "Foreign Policy" and 3 parts "Environment." You don't know how big a *part* is, so call it x. This means that $5x + 3x$ equals the percent of the students who answered either "Foreign Policy" or "Environment," which is 100% minus all the other answers:

$$100 - (16 + 14 + 9 + 5) = 100 - 44 = 56$$
$$5x + 3x = 56$$
$$8x = 56$$
$$x = 7$$

Each part has a value of 7, and 3 parts answered "Environment," so the correct percentage is $3(7) = 21\%$. Choice **(B)** is the correct answer.

6. C

Difficulty: Easy

Category: Problem Solving and Data Analysis / Scatterplots

Getting to the Answer: A data set that has a linear association follows the path of a straight line; a data set that is exponential follows a path that is similar to linear data but with a curve to it because the rate of increase (or decrease) changes over time. This data set has a curve to it, so "exponential" describes the association better than "linear." This means you can eliminate (A) and (B). A positive association between two variables is one in which higher values of one variable correspond to higher values of the other variable, and vice versa. In other words, as the *x*-values of the data points go up, so do the *y*-values. This is indeed the case for this data set, so **(C)** is correct.

7. D

Difficulty: Easy

Category: Problem Solving and Data Analysis / Statistics and Probability

Getting to the Answer: Your only choice for this question is to compare each statement to the figure. Don't waste time trying to figure out the exact value for each bar—an estimate is good enough to determine whether each statement is true. Choice (A) is incorrect because the price in 2008 was slightly less (not more) than $3.50, while the price in 2013 was right around $3.50. Choice (B) is incorrect because the price in 2003 was more than $2.00, and the price in 2013 was not more than twice that ($4.00). Choice (C) is incorrect because the price in 2008 was about $3.40 and the price in 2009 was about $2.75—this is not a difference of more than $1.00. This means **(D)** must be correct. You don't have to check it—just move on. (Between 2003 and 2008, the change in price was about $3.40 − $2.30 = $1.10; between 2008 and 2013, the change in price was only about $3.50 − $3.40 = $0.10; the change in price was greater between 2003 and 2008.)

8.   B

Difficulty: Medium

Category: Heart of Algebra / Systems of Linear Equations

Getting to the Answer: Because none of the variable terms has a coefficient of 1, solve the system of equations using elimination (combining the equations). Before you choose an answer, check that you answered the right question (the sum of x and y). Multiply the top equation by 2 to eliminate the terms that have y's in them:

$$2[-2x + 5y = 1] \rightarrow -4x + 10y = 2$$
$$\underline{7x - 10y = -11 \rightarrow 7x - 10y = -11}$$
$$3x = -9$$
$$x = -3$$

Now, substitute the result into either of the original equations and simplify to find y:

$$-2x + 5y = 1$$
$$-2(-3) + 5y = 1$$
$$6 + 5y = 1$$
$$5y = -5$$
$$y = -1$$

The question asks for the *sum*, so add x and y to get $-3 + (-1) = -4$, which is **(B)**.

9.   A

Difficulty: Medium

Category: Heart of Algebra / Systems of Linear Equations

Getting to the Answer: Take a quick peek at the answers just to see what variables are being used, but don't study the equations. Instead, write your own system using the same variables as given in the answer choices. One of the equations in the system needs to represent the sum of the two resistors $(R_1 + R_2)$, which is equal to 294. This means you can eliminate (C) and (D). The second equation needs to satisfy the condition that R_2 is 6 less than twice R_1, or $R_2 = 2R_1 - 6$. This means **(A)** is correct.

10.   C

Difficulty: Medium

Category: Heart of Algebra / Linear Equations

Getting to the Answer: Use the distributive property to simplify each of the terms that contains parentheses. Then, use inverse operations to solve for x:

$$\frac{2}{3}\left(\cancel{3}x\right) + 2(x - 1) = 4(x + 1) - 2$$
$$2x + 2x - 2 = 4x + 4 - 2$$
$$4x - 2 = 4x + 2$$
$$-2 \neq 2$$

All of the variable terms cancel out, and the resulting numerical statement is false (because negative 2 does not equal positive 2), so there is no solution to the equation. Put another way, there is no value of x for which the equation is true. Choice **(C)** is correct.

11.   B

Difficulty: Medium

Category: Additional Topics in Math / Geometry

Getting to the Answer: Think about this question logically before you start writing things down—after it's transferred, the volume of the oil in the cylindrical container will be the same volume as the rectangular container, so you need to set the two volumes equal and solve for h. The volume of the rectangular container is $4 \times 9 \times 10$, or 360 cubic meters. The volume of a cylinder equals the area of its base times its height, or $\pi r^2 h$. Because the diameter is 6 meters, the radius, r, is half that, or 3 meters. Now, you're ready to set up an equation and solve for h (which is the height of the cylinder or, in this case, the length of the transportation container):

$$\text{Volume of oil} = \text{Volume of rectangular container}$$
$$\pi(3)^2 h = 360$$
$$9\pi h = 360$$
$$h = \frac{360}{9\pi} = \frac{40}{\pi}$$

Choice **(B)** is correct.

12. D

Difficulty: Medium

Category: Problem Solving and Data Analysis / Rates, Ratios, Proportions, and Percentages

Getting to the Answer: Even though this question uses the word *percent*, you are never asked to find the actual percent itself. Set this question up as a proportion to get the answer more quickly. Remember, percent change equals amount of change divided by the original amount:

$$\frac{12-5}{5} = \frac{x-12}{12}$$
$$\frac{7}{5} = \frac{x-12}{12}$$
$$12(7) = 5(x-12)$$
$$84 = 5x - 60$$
$$144 = 5x$$
$$28.8 = x$$

Choice **(D)** is correct.

13. A

Difficulty: Medium

Category: Passport to Advanced Math / Exponents

Getting to the Answer: Focus on the question at the very end—it's just asking you to solve the equation for d. First, multiply both sides of the equation by $4d^2$ to get rid of the denominator. Then, divide both sides of the equation by $4\pi b$ to isolate d^2. Finally, take the square root of both sides to find d:

$$b\left(4\pi d^2\right) = L$$
$$\frac{(4\pi b)d^2}{4\pi b} = \frac{L}{4\pi b}$$
$$d^2 = \frac{L}{4\pi b}$$
$$\sqrt{d^2} = \sqrt{\frac{L}{4\pi b}}$$
$$d = \sqrt{\frac{L}{4\pi b}}$$

Unfortunately, this is not one of the answer choices, so you'll need to simplify further. You can take the square root of 4 (it's 2), but be careful—it's in the denominator of the fraction, so it comes out of the square root as $\frac{1}{2}$. The simplified equation is $d = \frac{1}{2}\sqrt{\frac{L}{\pi b}}$. This matches **(A)**.

14. D

Difficulty: Easy

Category: Problem Solving and Data Analysis / Statistics and Probability

Getting to the Answer: To calculate the percentage of men in each age group who reported being unemployed in January 2014, divide the number in *that* age group who were unemployed by the total number in *that* age group. There are six age groups but only four answer choices, so don't waste time on the age groups that aren't represented. Choice **(D)** is correct because $7 \div 152 \approx 0.046 = 4.6\%$, which is a lower percentage than that of any other age group (20 to 24 = 12.5%; 35 to 44 $\approx$ 4.9%; 45 to 54 $\approx$ 6.1%).

15. B

Difficulty: Medium

Category: Problem Solving and Data Analysis / Statistics and Probability

Getting to the Answer: The follow-up survey targets only those respondents who said they were unemployed, so focus on that column in the table. There were 6 respondents out of 44 unemployed people who were between the ages of 45 and 54, so the probability is $\frac{6}{44} = 0.13\overline{6}$, or about 13.6%, **(B)**.

16. B

Difficulty: Medium

Category: Passport to Advanced Math / Quadratics

Getting to the Answer: Taking the square root is the inverse operation of squaring, and both sides of the equation are already perfect squares, so take their square roots. Then, solve the resulting equations. Remember, there will be two equations to solve. Set up and solve:

$$(x-1)^2 = \frac{4}{9}$$
$$\sqrt{(x-1)^2} = \sqrt{\frac{4}{9}}$$
$$x - 1 = \pm\frac{\sqrt{4}}{\sqrt{9}}$$
$$x = 1 \pm \frac{2}{3}$$

Now, simplify each equation: $x = 1 + \frac{2}{3} = \frac{3}{3} + \frac{2}{3} = \frac{5}{3}$ and $x = 1 - \frac{2}{3} = \frac{3}{3} - \frac{2}{3} = \frac{1}{3}$. Choice **(B)** is correct.

17. D

Difficulty: Medium

Category: Heart of Algebra / Linear Equations

Getting to the Answer: Write the expression in words first: points per blue ring (5) times number of darts in blue ring (x), plus points per red ring (10) times number of darts in red ring ($6 - x$). Now, translate the words into numbers, variables, and operations: $5x + 10(6 - x)$. This is not one of the answer choices, so simplify the expression by distributing the 10 and then combining like terms: $5x + 10(6 - x) = 5x + 60 - 10x = 60 - 5x$. This matches **(D)**.

18. A

Difficulty: Medium

Category: Problem Solving and Data Analysis / Statistics and Probability

Getting to the Answer: This is a science crossover question. Read the first two sentences quickly—they are simply describing the context of the question. The last two sentences pose the question, so read those more carefully. In the sample, 184 out of 200 square feet were free of red tide after applying the spray. This is $\frac{184}{200} = 0.92 = 92\%$ of the area. For the whole beach, $0.92(10,000) = 9,200$ square feet should be free of the red tide. Be careful—this is *not* the answer. The question asks how much of the beach would still be covered by red tide, so subtract to get $10,000 - 9,200 = 800$ square feet, **(A)**.

19. A

Difficulty: Medium

Category: Passport to Advanced Math / Quadratics

Getting to the Answer: The solution to a system of equations is the point(s) where its graphs intersect. You can solve the system algebraically by setting the equations equal to each other, or you can solve it graphically using your calculator. Both equations are given in calculator-friendly format ($y = \ldots$), so graphing them is probably the more efficient approach. The graph looks like the following:

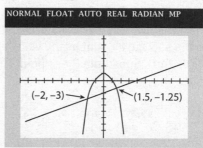

The solution point in the question is given as (a, b), so b represents the y-coordinate of the solution. The y-coordinates of the points of intersection are -3 and -1.25, so choice **(A)** is correct.

20. A

Difficulty: Medium

Category: Passport to Advanced Math / Functions

Getting to the Answer: The given range value is an output value, so substitute 3 for $g(x)$ and use inverse operations to solve for x, which is the corresponding domain value:

$$g(x) = \frac{2}{3}x + 7$$
$$3 = \frac{2}{3}x + 7$$
$$-4 = \frac{2}{3}x$$
$$-12 = 2x$$
$$-6 = x$$

Choice **(A)** is correct. Note that you could also graph the function and find the value of x (the domain value) for which the value of y (the range value) is 3. The point on the graph is $(-6, 3)$.

21. C

Difficulty: Medium

Category: Heart of Algebra / Linear Equations

Getting to the Answer: Write your own equation using the initial cost and the rate of change in the value of the lawn mower. Remember: when something changes at a constant rate, it can be represented by a linear equation. When a linear equation in the form $y = mx + b$ is used to model a real-world scenario, m represents the constant rate of change and b represents the starting amount. Here, the starting amount is easy—it's the purchase price, $2,800. To find the rate of change, think of the initial cost as the value at 0 years, or the point (0, 2,800), and the salvage amount as the value at 8 years, or the point (8, 240). Substitute these points into the slope formula:

$$m = \frac{y_2 - y_1}{x_2 - x_1} = \frac{240 - 2,800}{8 - 0} = \frac{-2,560}{8} = -320$$

The correct equation is $y = -320x + 2,800$. This matches **(C)**.

22. D

Difficulty: Medium

Category: Problem Solving and Data Analysis / Functions

Getting to the Answer: Determine whether the change in the number of bacteria is a common difference (linear function) or a common ratio (exponential function) or if the number of bacteria changes direction (quadratic or polynomial function). The question tells you that the number of bacteria is reduced by half every hour after the antibiotic is applied. The microbiologist started with 20,000, so after 1 hour, there are 10,000 left, or $20,000 \times \frac{1}{2}$. After 2 hours, there are 5,000 left, or $20,000 \times \frac{1}{2} \times \frac{1}{2}$, and so on. The change in the number of bacteria is a common ratio $\left(\frac{1}{2}\right)$, so the best model is an exponential function, **(D)**, of the form $y = a\left(\frac{1}{2}\right)^x$. In this scenario, a is 20,000.

23. B

Difficulty: Medium

Category: Problem Solving and Data Analysis / Rates, Ratios, Proportions, and Percentages

Getting to the Answer: Let the units in this question guide you to the solution. The speeds of the airplanes are given in miles per hour, but the question asks about the number of miles each airplane can travel in 12 seconds, so convert miles per hour to miles per second and multiply by 12 seconds:

Slower airplane:

$$\frac{600 \text{ miles}}{\text{hour}} \times \frac{1 \text{ hour}}{60 \text{ min}} \times \frac{1 \text{ min}}{60 \text{ sec}} \times 12 \text{ sec} = 2 \text{ miles}$$

Faster airplane:

$$\frac{720 \text{ miles}}{\text{hour}} \times \frac{1 \text{ hour}}{60 \text{ min}} \times \frac{1 \text{ min}}{60 \text{ sec}} \times 12 \text{ sec} = 2.4 \text{ miles}$$

The faster plane can travel $2.4 - 2 = 0.4$ miles farther, which is the same as $\frac{2}{5}$ miles. **(B)** is correct.

24. C

Difficulty: Medium

Category: Heart of Algebra / Inequalities

Getting to the Answer: Based on the data in the table, a worker earned $9.10 - $7.25 = $1.85 more for 1 hour of work in Oregon than in Idaho. A worker who logged 35 hours per week earned $35(1.85) = $64.75 more. An employee who worked 40 hours per week earned $40(1.85) = $74 more. So this worker would have earned somewhere between $64.75 and $74 more per week, which can be expressed as the compound inequality $64.75 \leq x \leq 74$. This matches **(C)**.

25. D

Difficulty: Medium

Category: Problem Solving and Data Analysis / Rates, Ratios, Proportions, and Percentages

Getting to the Answer: This is another question where the units can help you find the answer. Use the number of vehicles owned to find the total number of miles driven to find the total number of gallons of gas used to find the total tax paid:

$$1.75 \text{ vehicles} \times \frac{11{,}340 \text{ miles}}{\text{vehicle}} = 19{,}845 \text{ miles}$$

$$19{,}845 \text{ miles} \times \frac{1 \text{ gallon of gas}}{21.4 \text{ miles}} = 927.336 \text{ gallons}$$

$$927.336 \text{ gallons} \times \frac{\$0.184}{\text{gallon}} = \$170.63$$

Choice **(D)** is correct.

26. C

Difficulty: Medium

Category: Problem Solving and Data Analysis / Scatterplots

Getting to the Answer: The average rate of change of a function over a given interval, from a to b, compares the change in the outputs, $f(b) - f(a)$, to the change in the inputs, $b - a$. In other words, it is the slope of the line that connects the endpoints of the interval, so you can use the slope formula. Look at the quadratic model, not the data points, to find that the endpoints of the given interval, week 2 to week 8, are $(2, 280)$ and $(8, 400)$.

The average rate of change is $\frac{400 - 280}{8 - 2} = \frac{120}{6} = 20$, so the dolphin's weight increased by about 20 pounds per week, which matches **(C)**.

27. A

Difficulty: Hard

Category: Additional Topics in Math / Geometry

Getting to the Answer: In this question, information is given in both the diagram and the text. You need to relate the text to the diagram, one piece of information at a time, to calculate how long the lifeguard ran along the beach and how long she swam. Before you find the swim time, you need to know how *far* she swam. Whenever you see a right triangle symbol in a diagram, you should think Pythagorean theorem or, in this question, special right triangles. All multiples of 3-4-5 triangles are right triangles, so the length of the lifeguard's swim is the hypotenuse of a 30-40-50 triangle, or 50 feet. Add this number to the diagram. Now, calculate the times using the distances and the speeds given. Don't forget the 1 second that the lifeguard paused.

$$\text{Run time} = 60 \text{ feet} \times \frac{1 \text{ second}}{12 \text{ feet}} = \frac{60}{12} = 5 \text{ seconds}$$

$$\text{Pause time} = 1 \text{ second}$$

$$\text{Swim time} = 50 \text{ feet} \times \frac{1 \text{ second}}{5 \text{ feet}} = \frac{50}{5} = 10 \text{ seconds}$$

Total time $= 5 + 1 + 10 = 16$ seconds. Choice **(A)** is correct.

28. B

Difficulty: Hard

Category: Heart of Algebra / Linear Equations

Getting to the Answer: Call the initial amount A. After you've written your equation, solve for A.

Amount now $(x) =$ initial amount (A) minus y, plus 50:

$$x = A - y + 50$$
$$x + y - 50 = A$$

The initial amount was $x + y - 50$ gallons, **(B)**. Note that you could also use Picking Numbers to answer this question.

29. B

Difficulty: Hard

Category: Problem Solving and Data Analysis / Statistics and Probability

Getting to the Answer: When a question involves reading data from a graph, it is sometimes better to skip an answer choice if it involves long calculations. Skim the answer choices for this question—(A) involves finding two averages, each of which is composed of 7 data values. Skip this choice for now. Start with (B). Be careful—you are not looking for places where the line segments are increasing. The *y*-axis already represents the change in prices, so you are simply counting the number of positive values for the imports (5) and for the exports (4). There are more for the imports, so **(B)** is correct and you don't need to check any of the other statements. Move on to the next question.

30. D

Difficulty: Hard

Category: Passport to Advanced Math / Exponents

Getting to the Answer: The key to answering this question is deciding what you're trying to find. The question tells you that *x* represents the athlete's swim rate, and you are looking for the number of kilometers he swam in 1 hour—these are the same thing. If you find *x* (in kilometers per hour), you will know how many kilometers he swam in 1 hour. Set the equation equal to the total time, 16.2, and solve for *x*. To do this, write the variable terms over a common denominator, 10*x*, and combine them into a single term. Then, add the numerators and multiply both sides by 10*x* to get rid of the denominator, and go from there::

$$16.2 = \frac{10}{10}\left(\frac{3.86}{x}\right) + \frac{180.2}{10x} + \frac{2}{2}\left(\frac{42.2}{5x}\right)$$

$$16.2 = \frac{38.6}{10x} + \frac{180.2}{10x} + \frac{84.4}{10x}$$

$$16.2 = \frac{303.2}{10x}$$

$$10x(16.2) = 303.2$$

$$162x = 303.2$$

$$x = \frac{303.2}{162} \approx 1.87$$

Choice **(D)** is correct.

31. 1

Difficulty: Easy

Category: Heart of Algebra / Linear Equations

Getting to the Answer: Choose the best strategy to answer the question. If you distribute the $\frac{2}{3}$, it creates messy calculations. Instead, clear the fraction by multiplying both sides of the equation by 3. Then, use the distributive property and inverse operations to solve for *x*:

$$\frac{2}{3}(5x + 7) = 8x$$

$$3 \cdot \frac{2}{3}(5x + 7) = 3 \cdot 8x$$

$$2(5x + 7) = 24x$$

$$10x + 14 = 24x$$

$$14 = 14x$$

$$\mathbf{1} = x$$

32. 192

Difficulty: Medium

Category: Passport to Advanced Math / Exponents

Getting to the Answer: Before you start substituting values, quickly check that the units given match the units required to use the equation—they do, so proceed. The patient's weight (*w*) is 150 and the patient's BSA is $2\sqrt{2}$, so the equation becomes $2\sqrt{2} = \sqrt{\frac{150h}{3,600}}$. The only variable left in the equation is *h*, and you are trying to find the patient's height, so you're ready to solve the equation. To do this, square both sides of the equation and then continue using inverse operations. Be careful when you square the left side—you must square both the 2 and the root 2:

$$2\sqrt{2} = \sqrt{\frac{150h}{3,600}}$$

$$\left(2\sqrt{2}\right)^2 = \left(\sqrt{\frac{150h}{3,600}}\right)^2$$

$$2^2\left(\sqrt{2}\right)^2 = \frac{150h}{3,600}$$

$$4(2) = \frac{150h}{3,600}$$

$$28,800 = 150h$$

$$\mathbf{192} = h$$

33. 3.4

Difficulty: Medium

Category: Problem Solving and Data Analysis / Statistics and Probability

Getting to the Answer: The test average is the same as the mean of the data. The *mean* is the sum of all the values divided by the number of values. Break the question into short steps to keep your calculations organized. Before gridding in your answer, make sure you answered the correct question (how much the final test average changes).

Step 1: Find the original test average:

$$\frac{86 + 92 + 81 + 64 + 83}{5} = \frac{406}{5} = 81.2$$

Step 2: Find the average of the tests after replacing the lowest score (64) with the next to lowest score (81):

$$\frac{86 + 92 + 81 + 81 + 83}{5} = \frac{423}{5} = 84.6$$

Step 3: Subtract the original average from the new average: $84.6 - 81.2 = \textbf{3.4}$.

34. 40

Difficulty: Hard

Category: Additional Topics in Math / Geometry

Getting to the Answer: Because $\overline{AB}$, $\overline{CD}$, and $\overline{EF}$ are diameters, the sum of x, y, and the interior angle of the shaded region is 180°. The question tells you that the shaded region is $\frac{1}{5}$ of the circle, so the central angle must equal $\frac{1}{5}$ of the degrees in the whole circle, or $\frac{1}{5}$ of 360. Use what you know about y (that it is equal to $2x - 12$) and what you know about the shaded region (that it is $\frac{1}{5}$ of 360°) to write and solve an equation:

$$x + y + \frac{1}{5}(360) = 180$$
$$x + (2x - 12) + 72 = 180$$
$$3x + 60 = 180$$
$$3x = 120$$
$$x = \textbf{40}$$

35. 14

Difficulty: Hard

Category: Heart of Algebra / Linear Equations

Getting to the Answer: When you know the slope and one point on a line, you can use $y = mx + b$ to write the equation. The slope is given as $-\frac{7}{4}$, so substitute this for m. The point is given as $(4, 7)$, so $x = 4$ and $y = 7$. Now, find b:

$$y = mx + b$$
$$7 = -\frac{7}{\cancel{4}}(\cancel{4}) + b$$
$$7 = -7 + b$$
$$14 = b$$

The y-intercept of the line is **14**.

You could also very carefully graph the line using the given point and the slope. Start at $(4, 7)$ and move toward the y-axis by rising 7 and running *to the left* 4 (because the slope is negative). You should land at the point $(0, 14)$.

36. 45

Difficulty: Hard

Category: Problem Solving and Data Analysis / Rates, Ratios, Proportions, and Percentages

Getting to the Answer: Make a chart that represents rate, time, and distance and fill in what you know.

	Rate	Time	Distance
To airport	45 mph	t	d
Back to home	30 mph	$2.5 - t$	d

Now, use the formula $d = r \times t$ for both parts of the trip: $d = 45t$ and $d = 30(2.5 - t)$. Because both are equal to d, you can set them equal to each other and solve for t:

$$45t = 30(2.5 - t)$$
$$45t = 75 - 30t$$
$$75t = 75$$
$$t = 1$$

Now, plug the value of t back in to solve for d:

$$d = 45t$$
$$d = 45(1)$$
$$d = \mathbf{45}$$

37. 10

Difficulty: Medium

Category: Problem Solving and Data Analysis / Rates, Ratios, Proportions, and Percentages

Getting to the Answer: You don't need to know chemistry to answer this question. All the information you need is in the table. Use the formula $\text{Percent} = \frac{\text{part}}{\text{whole}} \times 100\%$. To use the formula, find the part of the mass represented by the carbon; there is 1 mole of carbon and it has a mass of 12.011 grams. Next, find the whole mass of the mole of chloroform: 1 mole carbon (12.011 g) + 1 mole hydrogen (1.008 g) + 3 moles chlorine (3×35.453 g = 106.359 g) = 12.011 g + 1.008 g + 106.359 g = 119.378 g. Now, use the formula:

$$\text{Percent} = \frac{12.011}{119.378} \times 100\%$$
$$= 0.10061 \times 100\%$$
$$= 10.061\%$$

Before you grid in your answer, make sure you follow the directions—round to the nearest whole percent, which is **10**.

38. 12

Difficulty: Hard

Category: Problem Solving and Data Analysis / Rates, Ratios, Proportions, and Percentages

Getting to the Answer: Think about the units given in the question and how you can use what you know to find what you need. Start with grams of chloroform; the chemist starts with 1,000 and uses 522.5, so there are $1,000 - 522.5 = 477.5$ grams left. From the previous question, you know that 1 mole of chloroform has a mass of 119.378 grams, so there are $477.5 \div 119.378 = 3.999$, or about 4 moles of chloroform left. Be careful—you're not finished yet. The question asks for the number of moles of *chlorine*, not chloroform. According to the table, each mole of chloroform contains 3 moles of chlorine, so there are $4 \times 3 = \mathbf{12}$ moles of chlorine left.